PENGUIN BOOKS

ETHNIC CUISINE

Elisabeth Rozin grew up in Brooklyn, NY, and has a Bachelor's Degree from Hunter College and a Master's Degree from Brandeis University. Her first book was *The Flavor-Principle Cookbook*, published in 1973. *Ethnic Cuisine*, here reissued, takes the "Flavor Principle" to the four corners of the globe by including a more comprehensive cuisine selection. Her third cookbook is *Blue Corn and Chocolate*, an account of new world food and its impact on old world and American cuisine. Elisabeth Rozin is a lecturer and consultant to the food industry. She currently lives in Havertown, Pennsylvania.

Seth Rozin is a graduate of University of Pennsylvania. He is an artist, illustrator, photographer, and theater director. He lives in Philadelphia.

ETHNIC CUISINE:

HOW TO CREATE THE AUTHENTIC FLAVORS OF 30 INTERNATIONAL CUISINES

BY
ELISABETH
ROZIN

ILLUSTRATED BY
SETH ROZIN

PENGUIN BOOKS

PENGUIN BOOKS
Published by the Penguin Group
Viking Penguin, a division of Penguin Books USA Inc.,
375 Hudson Street, New York, New York 10014, U.S.A.
Penguin Books Ltd, 27 Wrights Lane,
London W8 5TZ, England
Penguin Books Australia Ltd, Ringwood,
Victoria, Australia
Penguin Books Canada Ltd, 10 Alcorn Avenue, Suite 300,
Toronto, Ontario, Canada M4V 3B2
Penguin Books (N.Z.) Ltd, 182–190 Wairau Road,
Auckland 10, New Zealand

Penguin Books Ltd, Registered Offices:
Harmondsworth, Middlesex, England

First published in the United States of America by
The Stephen Greene Press, Inc., 1983
This edition published in Penguin Books 1992

10 9 8 7 6 5 4 3 2

Some of the material in this book was previously published as
The Flavor-Principle Cookbook by Hawthorn Books, Inc., copy-
right © Elisabeth Rozin, 1973

LIBRARY OF CONGRESS CATALOGING IN PUBLICATION DATA
Rozin, Elisabeth.
Ethnic cuisine: the flavor-principle cookbook/by Elisabeth
Rozin.
p.   cm.
Originally published: Lexington, Mass.: S. Greene Press,
c1983.
Includes indexes.
ISBN 0 14 046.931 1
1. Cookery, International.   I. Title.
[TX725.A1R689   1992]
641.59—dc20   91–41570

Printed in the United States of America
Set in Baskerville
Typography by Cheryl L. Cipriani
Illustrations by Seth Rozin

CONTENTS

PREFACE

The Flavor-Principle Cookbook was first published ten years ago to the loud acclaim of my family and friends. That seemed reward enough. But through the years I have received, and continue to receive, letters from people all over the country and, indeed, all over the world. They express tremendous enthusiasm about the idea on which the book was based: that almost all ethnic cuisines can be replicated by understanding the characteristic combinations of flavoring ingredients used to season the food. It is a simple idea that does not pretend to account for the inevitable complexity of any cuisine, but it is a useful idea because it permits a certain kind of authenticity in ethnic cooking without the necessity of adhering to all the rules of each culinary system.

It is to these supportive fellow cooks that *Ethnic Cuisine: The Flavor-Principle Cookbook* is dedicated. The book is new in that it is largely elaborated and completely reorganized. New flavor principles and new recipes have been added, while the best (hopefully) of the old have been retained. The premise of the book, however, remains the same: the rules that underlie the structure of any cuisine can be described and used not only to replicate already existing traditions but also to create dishes that are wholly new and unique.

To friends old and new, I offer this personal odyssey through a world of ethnic cuisines, with the sure knowledge that cooking styles not only differentiate us from one another but, more important, bring us together in the universal pleasure of good food.

ACKNOWLEDGMENTS

With warmest thanks to those who tested recipes and made valuable comments and suggestions:

Claire Dudley, Fifi Epstein, Bill Friedman, Rochel Gallistel, Sandra Norman, Marcia Pelchat, Patricia Pliner, Lillian Rozin, Paul Rozin, Ruth Sachs.

And with love to my family, who ate the whole thing.

INTRODUCTION

Of the myriad creatures who inhabit this earth, human beings are the only ones to cook their food. The implications of this simple fact are enormous, for throughout our history we have spent more time and energy in the preparation of food than we have in its consumption. Cooking—the deliberate and systematic manipulation of food—is as uniquely human a behavior as is art, or religion, or language. And just as each culture speaks, worships, and builds in different ways, culinary traditions also vary greatly. The differences in these traditions are the basis of what we call *cuisine*.

Why we cook our food is a complicated historical and sociological question. But *how* we cook our food is a matter that we can begin to describe and to analyze. Each ethnic group fashions its foodstuffs somewhat differently from the next, yet the general behavior of cooking always seems to form certain patterns, to follow rules that can be demonstrated. Just as any people have a system for producing language or art, so too do they have a system for producing cooked food. The system may not be codified or written down, but it exists in daily practice and is handed down from one generation to the next.

All people manipulate their food in some way, and this general behavior we call cooking. Every culture has its own set of rules or traditions about how to cook, and these individualized systems of food preparation we call *cuisines*. If we can find a way to describe the structure of any given cuisine, we then can begin to reproduce it. That is what this book is all about. For the curious and the gluttonous—and I am unashamedly both—the discovery of different ethnic cuisines is an intellectual as well as a gastronomic adventure. Let us try to describe, then, the critical factors in the structure of any culinary system.

Basic Foods

What makes one cuisine different from the next? We know that people in different parts of the world eat different kinds of food. Eskimos eat a lot of seal and caribou and very little rice or peaches; Laotians dine frequently on freshwater fish and rice but not very often on potatoes and beefsteak. These are the basic foodstuffs that are selected for culinary preparation and consumption. All cultures make such selections, whether in the dark recesses of the tropical jungle or in the spacious aisles of the suburban supermarket. The basis for the selection of food is dependent upon a wide variety of factors: availability, environmental variables such as climate, soil, and precipitation, ease of production or importation, nutritional benefit, palatability, custom, and religious or social sanction. These different basic foods produce varying flavors, aromas, textures, and appearances, qualities that are critical aspects of the human eating experience.

Cooking Techniques

With a description of a culture's basic foods we can begin to understand that particular cuisine. But we still don't have enough information. Let's say that a given group eats chicken and rice; this does not tell us enough to distinguish this cuisine from that of another group who also may eat chicken and rice. We need to know, for example, if the chicken is cut in large pieces or chopped into bite-sized morsels. Is it baked, fried, stewed, or smoked? Is it cooked with the rice or separately? The cooking techniques selected by any group are an important part of what makes that cuisine distinctive and unique.

It may seem as though there are many, many cooking techniques that have been developed in the course of culinary history, far too many to enumerate. If, however, we classify these techniques into several broad categories, there is a surprisingly small number of general cooking methods.

1. The first category includes those processes that change the *physical* size, shape, or mass of the food—in this category would be included techniques to reduce food substances to smaller and smaller elements, such as cutting, chopping, slicing, grinding, milling, grating, sifting, pulverizing, etc. When you cut up a chicken, chop vegetables, or grind grain into flour, you are using techniques in this category. Techniques of *separation* or *extraction* also are a part of this category. Examples are separating the white of an egg from the yolk, squeezing juice from an orange, or rendering fat from a piece of meat.

The third class of techniques is that of *incorporation,* whereby a food is altered by mixing or incorporating another substance into it. Such techniques include mixing, stirring, beating, or whipping. A raw egg white becomes a white fluffy mass when beaten; its volume increases as air is incorporated into it. This same fluffy mass, when folded into another substance, makes a dense texture less compact, as in a mousse or a soufflé.

2. The second broad category of cooking techniques involves *altering the water content* of a food substance either by adding or removing liquids. Soaking, as with dried beans, and marinating or flavoring with wine, vinegar, soy sauce, etc. are two ways of adding liquids to change the flavor or texture of a food.

Extended periods of marination can be used to cure or preserve foods; in this process, the natural water content of a food is replaced by the curing liquid. The curing liquid is usually either acidic or salty and, thus, retards the growth of microorganisms that cause food spoilage. Foods such as pickles (acid cure) or corned beef (salt cure) are the result of extended marination.

Drying and salting are two ways to reduce the water content of a food. Salt dehydrates organic substances, causing them to exude their natural water content. This technique is used frequently in the preparation of eggplant; salting the raw eggplant releases the bitter, natural juices. Exposing food to air or smoke causes dehydration by evaporation. These techniques are used in the production of dried vegetables and herbs, dried meats such as salami and jerky, and a variety of smoked products such as kippers and smoked bacon.

Last in this category is the technique of freezing. While used primarily as a preservative process, freezing is important in making a variety of desserts and confections, such as sherbets, ice creams, frozen mousses, etc.

3. In the third general category are those cooking techniques that change foods chemically. *Heat*, the most pervasive of all cooking techniques, is used in these distinct ways:

1. Dry heat (cooking without liquid)
   a. Direct: roast, barbecue, broil, grill
   b. Indirect: bake, parch, toast
2. Wet cooking (cooking with liquid)
   a. Direct: boil, simmer, stew, braise, poach
   b. Indirect: steam
3. Fat or oil cooking: deep fry, pan fry, sauté, stir-fry

Another way of chemically altering a food substance is by *fermentation*. Various yeasts, molds, and bacteria are introduced under controlled conditions of time and temperature, as in the culturing of dairy products (cheeses, yogurts, buttermilk, etc.), the fermentation of fruits and grains to produce wines and beers, the fermentation of various ingredients to produce condimental sauces (soy sauce, fish sauce), and the leavening of bread with yeast.

From these cooking techniques all cultures make a selection: to preserve fish, for example, the Kwakiutl Indians of the American Northwest smoke their salmon; the Portuguese salt their cod; and the Scandinavians pickle their herring.

As the sequence of the culinary techniques is determined, each culture makes critical judgments as to "how much" and "how long." Both the Chinese and the Jews cook chicken; the Chinese prefer their chicken slightly undercooked in firm nuggets, and the Jews prefer it cooked until it falls off the bone. This enormous difference in cooking technique probably arises from the vastly different traditions of these two cultures. From ancient times the Chinese suffered from a lack of cooking fuels and likely developed early in their history the means to cook food quickly and efficiently. The Jews, on the other hand, were forbidden by religious sanction to eat the blood of animals, which was considered sacred to God. A tradition of long, slow cooking developed in response to this belief. The selection of cooking techniques, then, as well as the interpretation of how those techniques are to be performed, are critical factors in determining what makes a cuisine distinctive and different from all others.

Flavor Principles

Now we come to what I regard as the most crucial element in ethnic cuisine: the flavorings. It is the taste that ultimately provides the ethnic definition of any given food. Flavoring a dish with soy sauce, for example, almost automatically identifies it as Oriental. That is because soy sauce is so ubiquitously used in Oriental cooking, imparting its own unique and characteristic flavor to food, that it acquires some sort of intense symbolic value as a culinary marker. Orientals use soy sauce in their foods and other ethnic groups do not; to put soy sauce into food is to say that the food *is* in some sense Oriental and is *not* Russian or French or Algerian.

Moreover, the somewhat general soy sauce–Oriental equation can be broken down into yet smaller and more discrete units that are markers of distinguishable cuisines that exist within the larger soy sauce family. If you add garlic, brown sugar, sesame seed, and chile to the basic soy sauce, you will obtain a seasoning compound that is definably Korean, because it is this very combination of flavoring ingredients that is used constantly in Korean cooking and in no other. Similarly, if you add garlic, molasses, ground peanuts, and chile to the basic soy sauce you will create a taste characteristically Indonesian; this combination of ingredients forms the unique flavor used on everything from rice to broiled meat to vegetable and salad preparations. Even though these two groups of flavor ingredients may be similar, they produce tastes that are clearly distinct from one another.

This is what is meant by the term *flavor principles*. If we look at almost any ethnic cuisine, be it Indian, Vietnamese, Hungarian, or Mexican, we will find within each culinary tradition the pervasive use of certain *combinations* of seasoning ingredients. Every culture tends to combine a small number of flavoring ingredients so frequently and so consistently that they become definitive of that particular cuisine.

Even within national or geographic boundaries, these flavor principles can be delineated further into smaller, regional principles. For example, the combination of soy sauce, rice wine, and gingerroot forms a classic and fundamental seasoning sauce widely used throughout China. But various regions have their own unique and characteristic ingredients which further individualize the flavor to produce a distinct "theme" for that cuisine. The cooking of Canton in southern China frequently is characterized by the additions of garlic and fermented black beans. The regional cooking of Peking in northern China often includes soy bean paste, garlic, and sesame oil. In the area of Szechuan in west central China the basic principle is varied by the characteristic addition of a hot seasoning, such as Szechuan (brown) pepper or chile pepper mixed with hot bean paste or oil.

Flavor principles characterize cooking styles or cuisines throughout the world; they differ from one another only in the choice of specific ingredients. In each example—the Chinese principle of soy sauce, rice wine, and gingerroot, the Vietnamese principle of fish sauce, lemon, and chile, and the Hungarian principle of paprika, lard, and onions—the seasoning combinations produce a unique and characteristic taste. As we go from one part of the world to another and from one flavor principle to another, we shall see that it is these characteristic combinations of seasonings that clearly define each ethnic cuisine.

Within any constellation of seasoning ingredients as defined by a given ethnic tradition, certain bonds of flavors seem to have a certain integrity. They resist combination with other flavoring ingredients. To give a concrete example: Greek cuisine offers a number of commonly used flavorings, among which are cinnamon, oregano, lemon, and tomato. The oregano forms a bond with the lemon, while the cinnamon forms a bond with the tomato. For reasons that are not apparent, the oregano does not combine with tomato in this cuisine, even though it does so quite successfully in other cuisines (Italian, for example). Why does oregano bond with tomato in Italian cuisine, but with lemon in Greek? There is no consistent way to account for the *formation* of flavor principles; we can only describe them as they exist, note how they are used, and marvel at the culinary and cultural value they seem to possess.

Themes and Variations

When we begin to look closely at any cuisine, we find rich and subtle variations in seasoning practices. The flavor principle, that characteristic bond of flavor ingredients, provides a culinary theme that is varied by the addition of other ingredients, by the use of different proportions, and by different cooking techniques. What results, then, is a set of variations on a general theme. We mentioned that Chinese cuisine is characterized by the use of soy sauce, rice wine, and gingerroot. But we cannot talk about soy sauce without indicating the incredible richness and variability of this basic seasoning ingredient. There is light (or thin) and dark (or heavy) soy sauce. It may be sweet or mushroom-flavored or shrimp-flavored. Each variety produces a slightly different and distinguishable flavor in the final preparation. Moreover, the basic theme of soy sauce, rice wine, and gingerroot can be varied by the use of other flavoring ingredients such as garlic, sesame oil, vinegar, etc., to provide a richness and a complexity to the cuisine. One might say that the skill with which variations on a flavor theme are manipulated is one index to how interesting a cuisine is. Sublety, complexity, and variation are the hallmarks of good eating everywhere, and as we go through the flavor principles we will see how most cuisines accomplish this.

About this Book
(or, the author confesses)

Cookbooks can serve many functions. The first and most basic is to present recipes. These can be organized as general collections or built around a specific theme. Secondly, cookbooks can provide interesting background information about the recipes they present so that we can learn, for example, how Apple Pan Dowdy got its name, or how my grandma's chopped liver differs from the accepted tradition. Thirdly, cookbooks can be a source of factual information about the food and the cultures from which the recipes are derived. In this sense, cookbooks can document an important area of human behavior, and thus can be of some value not only to the cook but to the student of comparative cuisine.

The primary purpose of this cookbook is to provide access to any ethnic cuisine by showing how that cuisine is shaped according to the three basic elements outlined above: basic foods, cooking techniques, and, most important, flavor principles. This leads to Confession One: not all cuisines are represented. Invariably, there will be those who want to know why I have not included recipes from Brazil or South Africa or Greenland. To those individuals I would reply first, that the recipes and cuisines in this book represent a personal selection of traditions that are familiar to me. Second, since no area of human behavior is ever completely consistent, there are some cuisines that do not illustrate as vividly as others the ideas on which this book is based, and so they have not been included. Their omission is not a judgment of any kind about how good or interesting they may be.

The second purpose of this book is to present good recipes for good food. Well prepared food that nourishes the body, pleases the palate, and uplifts the spirit is the ultimate goal of the serious cook. To that end

I have selected recipes I have found to be successful. Which leads to Confession Two: I occasionally cheat. Although I am fascinated by, and, indeed, am committed to the integrity of all ethnic culinary traditions, I find that it is not always possible to prepare a dish in an absolutely authentic manner. Sometimes it is difficult to obtain some of the more exotic ingredients, and in these instances reasonable substitutions have been made. Traditional cooking techniques are not always readily do-able in western kitchens, and again, substitute methods have to be used. I also have taken some liberties by departing from authentic tradition whenever necessary to produce a better recipe. Sometimes my version of an ethnic dish is better than any "authentic" version I have had and so, in the interest of good recipes for good food, I go with my own.

My third purpose is to encourage my fellow cooks everywhere to do their own thing. Use this book as a takeoff point for the creation of new and exciting foods. Confession Three: even though I have written a cookbook, and have composed hundreds and hundreds of recipes throughout the years, I don't often cook from recipes; rather, I cook from what I know about a particular dish or a particular cuisine, from what I have read in other cookbooks, and from what I have tasted and sampled of the world's fare.

The flavor principle idea is obviously a simplification of sorts, designed to abstract what is absolutely fundamental about a cuisine and, thus, to serve as a guide in cooking and developing new recipes. Many cultures have extracted elements from other cuisines throughout history as different ethnic traditions came together by way of trade, migration, war, and so on. The chapter on "Crossroads Cuisine" shows how the salient features of one ethnic cuisine can combine with the critical elements of another to form a new and unique culinary tradition. What one culture does quite naturally, any cook can do with conscious deliberation. The chapter called "Creative Cuisine" shows how the basic elements of any cuisine can be abstracted and reapplied in new ways to create a world of innovative cooking ideas.

Final confession: I am, unabashedly, an educator and proseletizer. This book has been designed deliberately to be read as well as to cook from. I would like to think that it provides some interesting and perhaps valuable information, good recipes for good eating, and above all, an incentive for you, the reader-cook, to explore the vast and exciting range of creative, ethnic cuisine.

FLAVOR PRINCIPLES

1. Soy Sauce–Rice Wine–Gingerroot (China)
   a. +Miso and/or Garlic and/or Sesame (Peking)
   b. +Sweet–Sour–Hot (Szechuan)
   c. +Black Bean–Garlic (Canton)
2. Soy Sauce–Sake–Sugar (Japan)
3. Soy Sauce–Brown Sugar–Sesame–Chile (Korea)
4. Soy Sauce–Brown Sugar–Peanut–Chile (Indonesia)
5. Fish Sauce–Lemon (Vietnam)
6. Fish Sauce–Coconut (Laos)
7. Fish Sauce–Curry–Chile (Thailand)
8. Onion–Gingerroot–Garlic–Turmeric–Chile (Burma)
9. Curry (India)
   a. Cumin–Ginger–Garlic + Variations (Northern India)
   b. Mustard Seed–Coconut–Tamarind–Chile + Variations (Southern India)
10. Cinnamon–Fruit–Nut (Central Asia)
11. Lemon–Parsley (Middle East)
12. Tomato–Cinnamon (Middle East)
13. Tomato–Peanut–Chile (West Africa)
14. Garlic–Cumin–Mint (Northeast Africa)
15. Cumin–Coriander–Cinnamon–Ginger + Onion and/or Tomato and/or Fruit (Morocco)
16. Tomato–Cinnamon (Greece)
17. Olive Oil–Lemon–Oregano (Greece)
18. Olive Oil–Garlic–Parsley and/or Anchovy (Southern Italy, Southern France)
    a. + Tomato
19. Olive Oil–Garlic –Basil (Italy, France)
    a. + Tomato
20. Olive Oil–Thyme–Rosemary–Marjoram–Sage (Provence)
    a. + Tomato
21. Olive Oil–Garlic–Nut (Spain)
22. Olive Oil–Onion–Pepper–Tomato (Spain)
23. Onion–Lard–Paprika (Hungary)
24. Onion–Chicken Fat (Eastern European Jewish Cuisine)
25. Sour Cream–Dill or Paprika or Allspice or Caraway (Northern and Eastern Europe)
26. Wine–Herb (France)

THE ORIENT

SOY SAUCE PRINCIPLES I

The Orient provides two great seasoning traditions, one based on soy sauce and one based on fish sauce. Into the soy sauce category fall the cultures of China, Japan, Korea, and Indonesia.

The soybean was probably indigenous to Southeast Asia and has been cultivated by the Chinese from very ancient times. It has one of the highest percentages of protein of any plant food known to man and so is extremely valuable in diets lacking in animal foods. Many elaborate ways of utilizing the soybean have developed in the Orient over thousands of years. Among the diverse products of this technology are soy bean flour, bean curd (*tofu*), bean cake (*tempeh*), various bean pastes and sauces, and, of course, soy sauce. Soy sauce is produced by mixing soy beans, roasted grain (wheat, barley), salt, sater, and a fermenting agent in wooden casks. Different lengths of time and different proportions determine the grade of soy sauce, all of which produce subtle variations in flavor.

Other seasoning ingredients commonly used throughout the Orient are various members of the onion family, garlic, gingerroot, sesame oil, sugar, rice wine and rice vinegar, star anise, and different forms of dried or fermented fish products. All of these ingredients seem to have existed in the Orient since antiquity, and appear to have been used along with soy sauce as part of an ancient and venerable tradition for seasoning food. The two popular seasoning ingredients that have been introduced to the Orient in comparatively recent times, following the discovery of the New World, are the peanut and the chile pepper. Though other kinds of nuts and peppers were known and are still used, these two products have been widely accepted as part of the flavoring traditions.

Although we will describe characteristic cooking techniques under the cuisines that typically use them, such as stir-frying in China, there is one technique that is common in many Oriental as well as in Indian cuisines. This technique consists of frying spices and foodstuffs in oil or fat, then adding liquid to the pot and allowing it to cook completely away. This is known as "letting the oil come out," because once the liquid has completely evaporated the food cooks further in the oil that remains. The technique is commonly used with larger pieces of meat or poultry that require a relatively longer cooking time than frying or stir–frying.

CHINA

The rich culture of China has always been central to the Orient, and the long fingers of her culinary traditions have reached out to touch almost every other cuisine in that vast area. In China cooking has always been regarded as a venerable art. Her people have long been accustomed to a tradition of good eating and have always considered it one of the great and important aspects of life. No wonder, then, that the cuisine is one of the world's most interesting and complex.

The most important basic food in China, as in all of the Orient, is rice. It is a fundamental part of almost every meal. There are many varieties—long grain, short grain, sweet, glutinous, etc.—each of which provides a distinct experience in flavor and texture. The wheat-based culture of northern China has also produced an ancient tradition of noodles and pastas of various kinds which have become extremely popular throughout the Orient. Unlike other areas of the world, milled wheat was never used in China for the production of breads (except for a kind of steamed bun) but, rather, for the manufacture of various noodles and dumplings. Rice flour and bean starch also are used in the making of an astounding variety of noodle products.

Other basic foods are chicken, duck, and pork, and a wide variety of freshwater fish and seafood. Beef is a comparatively recent addition to the diet and, though well-liked and accepted, is expensive and relatively scarce. An enormous variety of root and green leafy vegetables completes the basic food inventory. These vegetables play so important a part in the cuisine that small truck gardens are maintained throughout the year, even in winter.

The most characteristic Chinese cooking technique is stir-frying. With this technique, foods are cut into small bite-sized pieces and cooked very quickly by being stirred around in very hot oil. Typically, the non-liquid seasoning ingredients (garlic, gingerroot, chile pepper, etc.) are added at the beginning of the process, while the liquids (soy sauce, wine, stock, etc.) are added at the very end and usually in relatively small amounts. Pre-mixed with a thickening agent such as cornstarch, the liquid quickly comes to a boil, thickens, and coats the pieces of food with a sauce; due to the short cooking time, the food retains its natural flavor and texture (crispness, crunchiness, chewiness, etc.). Texture seems to be a crucial factor in the Chinese eating experience.

Because stir-frying cooks foods so quickly, it is possible that the technique developed historically at least in part as a response to a shortage of cooking fuel. The use of stir-frying and the characteristic cooking vessel, the wok, has spread from China to other parts of the

Orient, even though they may be used somewhat differently in other culinary traditions. It should be compared with the classic French technique of sautéeing and deglazing (see page 140).

Other characteristic Chinese cooking techniques are: steaming, a method that enhances the natural texture and flavor of foods; deep-frying; and, somewhat less common, braising.

The basic flavor principle of all Chinese cooking is the combination of soy sauce, rice wine, and gingerroot. This theme remains constant regardless of the many different seasoning ingredients that may be used. The regional variations on this basic theme are as follows:

1. Peking (northern China): soy sauce, rice wine, gingerroot + soybean paste (miso), and/or garlic and/or sesame oil.
2. Szechuan (west central China): soy sauce, rice wine, gingerroot + hot pepper and/or sweet-sour.
3. Canton (southern China): soy sauce, rice wine, gingerroot + garlic, and/or stock, and/or fermented black beans.

Other seasoning variations are achieved with the use of such ingredients as vinegar, sugar, various condimental bean pastes and sauces (such as hoisin), star anise, dried shrimp, and peanuts.

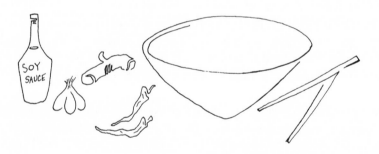

CHINESE RECIPES

CHINESE DUCK SOUP

CHINESE ROAST PORK

FRIED WON TONS

DIM SUN MUSHROOMS

CHINESE MUSHROOM-STUFFED EGGS

MU SHU PORK

SZECHUAN TWICE-COOKED PORK

SPICY PORK SLICES

CHINESE ORANGE BEEF

ROAST CAPON WITH BROWN SAUCE

CHICKEN AND SNOW PEAS IN BLACK BEAN SAUCE

CHINESE FISH FILLETS WITH PORK

POACHED FISH IN BROWN SAUCE

SHRIMP LO MEIN

SZECHUAN SHRIMP

SPICED BEAN CURD

FISH-FRAGRANT EGGPLANT

CHINESE SALAD

CHINESE DUCK SOUP

1 roasted duck carcass with any leftover meat and skin; giblets and liver from duck, if possible
3 quarts water
¼ cup soy sauce
¼ cup dry sherry
2 slices gingerroot, about size and thickness of a quarter
2 pieces star anise
2 scallions, chopped
1 teaspoon salt
½ teaspoon sugar
½ teaspoon five-spice powder

1. Chop carcass into small pieces and place in a large pot with giblets and liver, water, soy sauce, sherry, gingerroot, star anise, scallions, and salt. Bring to boil, then simmer uncovered over low to moderate heat for 2½–3 hours.
2. Strain stock, then return to pot. Add sugar and five-spice powder and simmer another 20 minutes. Chill, then skim off any congealed fat. Reheat to serve.

Serves 6

CHINESE ROAST PORK

3 tablespoons soy sauce
3 tablespoons dry sherry
2 tablespoons hoisin sauce
2 tablespoons honey
2 cloves garlic, finely minced
1 teaspoon gingerroot, finely minced
1–1½ pounds lean boneless loin of pork

1. Combine soy sauce, sherry, hoisin, honey, garlic, and gingerroot. Mix well. Pour over pork and marinate for 2 hours, turning meat frequently in marinade.
2. Preheat oven to 350°. Roast pork on a rack over a pan of hot water for 50 minutes. Let stand 15 minutes before slicing.
3. Cut into thin slices and serve with duck sauce if desired.

Serves 3–4 as main course
6–8 as appetizer

FRIED WON TONS

In old China, a mother-in-law judged her daughter-in-law's domestic competence by the way she folded won tons. The technique is a little tricky, so practice on a few wrappers without the filling in order to get the hang of it. Keep extra wrappers covered with a damp cloth while you work, as they dry out quickly.

½ pound ground raw pork
½ pound raw chicken or shrimp, finely chopped
1 cup celery, finely chopped
3 scallions, finely minced
3 tablespoons soy sauce
1 tablespoon dry sherry
2 teaspoons gingerroot, finely minced
2 cloves garlic, finely minced
½ teaspoon salt
15 egg roll wrappers, cut in quarters, or 60 won ton wrappers
3 cups peanut oil

1. Combine all ingredients except wrappers and oil, mix well and let stand ½ hour.
2. Placing a wrapper in a diamond position in front of you, put one teaspoon filling on wrapper. Bring bottom corner up to top and moisten with a little cold water to seal. Bring left corner into center, then top corner down, and right corner over to center. Moisten corners with a little cold water, then pinch to seal.
3. Heat oil in a deep 3–4 quart pot to 350–360°. Drop in won tons, no more than 4 or 5 at a time, and fry until they rise to the surface and are a deep golden brown.
4. Remove fried won tons from oil with a slotted spoon and drain in a colander or large strainer set over absorbent paper to catch the drips. Do not pile won tons on top of each other or they will get soggy. (After frying oil has cooled, it can be strained, bottled, and used again.)
5. Serve won tons hot with duck sauce or Chinese mustard. They may be frozen and reheated in a 400° oven for 30–40 minutes.

Makes 50–60 won tons

DIM SUN MUSHROOMS

Dim sun are a class of Chinese hors d'oeuvres, hot savories to eat with tea. Here a traditional meat filling is used to stuff fresh mushroom caps. They then are steamed and eaten hot.

3 medium dried Chinese mushrooms
½ cup ground raw pork (about ¼ pound)
½ cup raw shrimp, finely chopped (about ¼ pound)
3 scallions, minced
⅔ cup cabbage, finely chopped
⅔ cup mushrooms stems, finely chopped
2 tablespoons soy sauce
1 tablespoon dry sherry
1 teaspoon gingerroot, finely minced
¼ teaspoon sugar
¼ teaspoon salt
2 tablespoons sesame oil
30–35 medium to large fresh mushroom caps

1. Soak dried mushrooms in warm water to cover for 20–30 minutes. Drain and squeeze out excess moisture. Remove tough center cores and discard. Chop fine.
2. Combine chopped, dried mushrooms with all other ingredients except mushroom caps and mix well. Stuff the mushroom caps with filling, mounding the mixture generously. Any leftover filling can be shaped into little balls. (This part can be completed early in the day and the mushrooms refrigerated until cooking time.)
3. Place a dishcloth over a perforated steamer rack or colander in a large pot containing several inches of boiling water. The steamer should be over, not touching, the water. Place the stuffed mushrooms on the dishcloth, cover the pot, and steam for 15–20 minutes. Serve hot, with duck sauce, if desired.

Makes 30–35 stuffed mushrooms

CHINESE MUSHROOM–STUFFED EGGS

6 large eggs
1 tablespoon peanut oil
½ teaspoon gingerroot, finely minced
2 cloves garlic, finely minced
1½ teaspoons Chinese fermented black beans, mashed
1 cup fresh mushrooms, finely chopped
1 tablespoon soy sauce
1 tablespoon dry sherry
⅛ teaspoon sugar
1 tablespoon sesame oil

1. Place eggs in a medium saucepan with enough cold water to cover. Bring to boil, turn heat low, and simmer uncovered for 5 minutes. Cover pot, turn off heat, and let stand 15 minutes. Run cold water into pot. Shell eggs and set aside.
2. In a medium frying pan or wok, heat oil over high heat. Add gingerroot and garlic, and stir-fry just until it starts to smell good. Add mashed black beans and stir-fry another few seconds. Add mushrooms and cook, stirring, about 1 minute.
3. Add soy sauce, sherry, and sugar and cook over moderate heat, stirring, about 2 minutes or until mushrooms are dark and liquid is almost but not completely reduced. Remove from heat.
4. Cut eggs in half lengthwise. Carefully scoop out yolks, place in a bowl and mash well.
5. Add mushroom mixture and sesame oil to egg yolks and mix well. Heap yolk mixture into egg-white shells, mounding and shaping with fingers. Chill.

Makes 12 stuffed egg halves

MU SHU PORK

The success of this dish depends on the very fine shredding of the pork, allowing it to cook quickly without losing its succulence, and on the generous use of sesame oil, a primary flavoring ingredient in northern Chinese cuisine. This recipe was developed by Paul Rozin.

4 medium dried Chinese mushrooms
20 tiger lily buds (golden needles)
2 tablespoons dried tree ears
½ cup sesame oil
4 eggs, lightly beaten
¼ cup soy sauce
2 tablespoons dry sherry
2 teaspoons sugar
2 teaspoons cornstarch
1½ cups lean pork, finely shredded (about ⅔ pounds)—meat is easier to shred if partially frozen
4 scallions, slivered
1 cup fresh beansprouts, rinsed in cold water and thoroughly drained

1. Place mushrooms, lily buds, and tree ears in a bowl and cover them with warm water. Let stand ½ hour. Drain, then blot thoroughly with paper towels. Cut out and discard tough center core from mushrooms. Cut mushrooms and tree ears into slivers about ⅛-inch thick.
2. In a large frying pan or wok, heat 2 tablespoons sesame oil over high heat. Add eggs and cook until set. Remove from pan, cut into slivers, and set aside.
3. In a small bowl combine soy sauce, sherry, sugar, and cornstarch. Mix well and set aside.
4. In same frying pan or wok heat 6 more tablespoons sesame oil over high heat. Add pork shreds and scallions and stir-fry until pork loses its pink color. Add mushrooms, lily buds, and tree ears and stir briefly.
5. Add sauce mixture and stir thoroughly. When sauce begins to boil and thicken, add egg slivers and bean sprouts. Mix well, just long enough to heat through.
6. Serve immediately, with Peking doilies if desired (see below).

Serves 3–4

Peking Doilies:

3 cups all-purpose flour
1 cup boiling water
sesame oil

1. Place flour in a large bowl, add boiling water, and mix well with a wooden spoon. Dough will be very dry. Knead the dough with the hands or a dough hook until it is smooth, elastic, and nonsticky. Cover with a towel and let rest for 15–20 minutes.
2. Divide dough into 2 equal parts and form each part into a long roll about 2 inches in diameter. Cut each roll into 9 or 10 parts.
3. On a floured board place one circle of dough. Pat down lightly with fingers. Brush upper surface of dough lightly but completely with sesame oil. Place another circle of dough on top of it, and pat the two pancakes down with the fingers.
4. With a floured rolling pin, roll out the 2 circles into thin rounds about 6–7 inches in diameter, making sure dough is evenly rolled.
5. Heat an ungreased griddle or frying pan over moderate heat. Place the double pancake on the griddle and cook until bubbles begin to rise on the upper surface (about ½ minute). Turn the pancake over and cook on the other side until very lightly browned.
6. Remove pancakes to a plate and carefully pull apart the 2 layers. Fold each layer into quarters and cover with a towel. Continue making pancakes with rest of dough.
7. To serve the Mu Shu pork, lightly spread a doily with hoisin sauce, and fill with a few spoonfuls of pork mixture and a scallion. Roll up the doily and eat with your fingers.

Makes 18–20 doilies

NOTE: Peking doilies can be made early in the day, refrigerated, and then reheated at serving time in a cloth-lined steamer.

SZECHUAN TWICE-COOKED PORK

A famous dish of Szechuan province, this dish is so named because the meat is first braised and then stir-fried.

1–1½ pounds lean boneless loin of pork
2 cups water
1 tablespoon dark soy sauce
1 slice gingerroot
2 pieces star anise
3 tablespoons miso
3 tablespoons bottled chili sauce
2 tablespoons dry sherry
1 tablespoon white vinegar
1 teaspoon sugar
3 tablespoons sesame oil
4 cloves garlic, finely minced
1 tablespoon gingerroot, finely minced
¼ teaspoon crushed dried red peppers
1 large onion, cut in sixths, then separated into layers
1 cup snow peas, sliced broccoli, or green or red sliced peppers

1. Place pork, water, soy sauce, gingerroot slice, and star anise in a saucepan and cook, uncovered, over moderate heat for one hour. Remove pork from pot and cool thoroughly. Cut into thin slices.
2. Combine miso, chili sauce, sherry, vinegar, and sugar; mix well and set aside.
3. In a large frying pan or wok, heat oil over high heat. Add garlic, minced gingerrroot, and red peppers, and stir-fry for a few seconds.
4. Add onion and stir-fry for 30 seconds. Add pork slices, then vegetables and stir-fry for about one minute.
5. Add sauce mixture and cook, stirring constantly, until food is hot and well coated with sauce.

Serves 4–5

SPICY PORK SLICES

1½ pounds lean boneless loin of pork or pork tenderloin
2–3 tablespoons miso
2 tablespoons soy sauce
1 tablespoon dry sherry
2 cloves garlic, finely minced
1 teaspoon gingerroot, finely minced
1 piece star anise
2–3 tablespoons sugar
2 cups hot water
Garnish: chopped scallions or chopped, fresh coriander

1. Rub the miso all over the pork and allow to stand 3 hours.
2. In a medium saucepan combine all other ingredients and bring to a boil. Add pork, and simmer, uncovered, over low heat for 1½ hours. Turn pork frequently.
3. Remove pork from pot and allow to cool slightly. Meanwhile, continue to simmer sauce until it is reduced by about half and is quite thick.
4. Cut pork in thin slices. Return slices to sauce and heat through. Let cool.
5. Arrange pork slices on serving plate and serve at room temperature. Garnish with chopped scallions or chopped fresh coriander if desired.

Makes about 20–25 slices

CHINESE ORANGE BEEF

1½ pounds lean boneless beef (top round or sirloin)
1 tablespoon dark soy sauce
1 tablespoon cornstarch
½ teaspoon baking soda
1 tablespoon sesame oil
2 tablespoons orange juice concentrate
1 tablespoon dark soy sauce
1 tablespoon rice vinegar
1 teaspoon brown sugar
1 teaspoon cornstarch
3 tablespoons peanut oil
3 large cloves garlic, finely minced
1 tablespoon gingerroot, finely minced
1 tablespoon orange peel, shredded
¼ teaspoon (more or less to taste) crushed dried red peppers
1–2 tablespoons sesame oil

1. With a sharp knife cut beef into fine shreds. This is much easier to do if meat is partially frozen. Combine beef shreds with next four ingredients, mix thoroughly, and let stand 1–3 hours.
2. In a small bowl or cup combine next five ingredients and set aside.
3. Heat peanut oil in a wok over high heat. Add garlic, gingerroot, orange peel, and hot peppers, and stir-fry for a few minutes until mixture smells good and starts to brown.
4. Add beef shreds and stir fry over high heat until thoroughly browned and just beginning to crisp.
5. Add sauce ingredients and mix well; cook just until mixture comes to a boil and thickens. Splash on sesame oil and serve with rice.

Serves 4

ROAST CAPON WITH BROWN SAUCE

1 capon, about 7 pounds (or chicken or duck)
1 tablespoon peanut oil
4 cloves garlic, finely minced
5–6 cloves whole garlic, peeled
1 teaspoon gingerroot, finely minced
2 tablespoons miso
1 tablespoon soy sauce
¼ cup dry sherry
1 teaspoon sugar

1. Wash capon and dry thoroughly inside and out with paper towels.
2. In a small saucepan, heat oil over high heat. Add minced garlic and gingerroot and stir-fry about ½ minute. Add miso, soy sauce, sherry, and sugar. Simmer over low heat for 5 minutes. Cool.
3. Place capon in roasting pan and rub some of the cooled sauce all over the outside. Let stand 2 hours.
4. Place whole garlic cloves inside capon. Roast in a preheated 350° oven 1¾–2 hours, basting frequently with sauce and with drippings in pan. If capon starts to brown too much, cover it lightly with a tent of aluminum foil. Let stand 5–10 minutes before carving.

Serves 6–8

NOTE: The amount of sauce given here is enough to glaze the skin of the bird and impart a delicate garlic flavor to the meat. If you want additional sauce to serve with the bird, double the amount as given in the recipe.

CHICKEN AND SNOW PEAS IN BLACK BEAN SAUCE

1½–2 pounds boneless chicken breasts, skinned and cut in 1-inch cubes
1 egg white
4 tablespoons dry sherry
½ teaspoon salt
1 tablespoon plus 1 teaspoon cornstarch
2 tablespoons soy sauce
1 teaspoon sugar
6 tablespoons peanut oil
5 cloves garlic, finely minced
2 teaspoons gingerroot, finely minced
1½ tablespoons fermented black beans, mashed
2 small onions, quartered and separated into layers
1 cup fresh snow peas (or green pepper strips or fresh mushrooms)

1. Mix chicken cubes, egg white, 2 tablespoons sherry, salt, and one tablespoon cornstarch and marinate in refrigerator from ½–3 hours.
2. In a small bowl combine soy sauce, 2 tablespoons sherry, one teaspoon cornstarch, and sugar; mix well and set aside.
3. In a large frying pan or wok, heat 4 tablespoons oil over high heat. Add chicken cubes and stir-fry for about 2 minutes or just until chicken loses its pink color. Remove from pan and set aside.
4. Add 2 tablespoons oil to pan. Add garlic, gingerroot, and mashed beans, and stir-fry over high heat for 20–30 seconds. Add onions and snow peas and stir-fry another 30 seconds. Return chicken to pan, add sauce mixture, and stir rapidly until well mixed and hot.

Serves 4–6

CHINESE FISH FILLETS WITH PORK

⅓ pound lean ground pork
2 tablespoons soy sauce
½ teaspoon sugar
½ teaspoon gingerroot, finely minced
2 tablespoons peanut oil
¼ cup celery, finely minced
1 tablespoon cornstarch
¼ teaspoon five-spice powder (or ¼ teaspoon anise seed)
½ cup water
1 tablespoon dry sherry
1 scallion, minced
½ pound fish fillets (flounder, sole, perch, etc.)

1. Combine ground pork with one tablespoon soy sauce, sugar, and gingerroot. Mix well and let stand ½ hour.
2. Heat oil in frying pan or wok over moderately high heat. Add pork mixture and stir-fry until meat loses its pink color. Add celery and stir-fry another few seconds. Remove mixture to a bowl, stir in cornstarch and five-spice powder. Set aside.
3. In same pan or wok place water, one tablespoon soy sauce, sherry, and scallion. When liquid begins to simmer, place fish fillets in liquid and poach gently. Turn fillets once and cook until just tender; for small fillets this will be no more than 7–8 minutes. Remove fish from pan and place on warm serving plate.
4. Return pork mixture to pan and cook quickly over high heat, just long enough to heat through and thicken slightly. Pour over fish and serve.

Serves 2–3

POACHED FISH IN BROWN SAUCE

1½–2 pounds rockfish, rock cod, or sea bass (have fish split and
    eviscerated, and head and tail removed)
cornstarch
3 tablespoons peanut oil
2 tablespoons soy sauce
¼ cup dry sherry
2 tablespoons miso
1½ teaspoons sugar
2 teaspoons gingerroot, finely minced
3 cloves garlic, finely minced
2 scallions, finely minced

Garnish: chopped scallions

1. Dry fish thoroughly with paper towels, then dust lightly all over with
   cornstarch.
2. In a large frying pan or wok, heat peanut oil until very hot. Add fish
   and sear briefly on each side. Remove from pan and set aside.
3. Combine soy sauce, sherry, miso, and sugar and mix well.
4. To hot oil in pan, add gingerroot, garlic, and scallions. Stir-fry over
   high heat for about 30 seconds.
5. Return fish to pan, add soy sauce mixture, turn heat low, and cover.
   Simmer gently about 15–20 minutes, turning fish once. Serve
   immediately, garnished with chopped scallions if desired.

Serves 3–4

SHRIMP LO MEIN

This is a flavorful peasant dish sold by vendors in the streets of Peking.
Note that, just as with the rice in Chinese fried rice, the noodles are
boiled and chilled before being fried in oil. This is a good way to use
leftovers, as almost any kind of meat or vegetable can be substituted.

½ pound lo mein noodles (available fresh in Oriental groceries), or ½
    pound spaghettini or vermicelli
4 tablespoons sesame oil
3 tablespoons soy sauce
3 tablespoons dry sherry
2 tablespoons miso
1 teaspoon sugar
1 teaspoon cornstarch
2 tablespoons peanut oil
2 teaspoons gingerroot, finely minced

4 cloves garlic, finely minced
1 pound raw shrimp, peeled and deveined
1 cup fresh beansprouts, rinsed in cold water and drained
3 scallions, chopped
2 stalks celery, finely sliced

1. Cook lo mein noodles in boiling water for 3 minutes; if using spaghettini, cook *al dente* according to package instructions. Rinse in cold water, drain thoroughly, and place in a bowl. Mix in well 2 tablespoons sesame oil and place in refrigerator.
2. Combine soy sauce, sherry, miso, sugar, and cornstarch in a small bowl. Mix well and set aside.
3. In a large frying pan or wok, heat peanut oil and 2 tablespoons sesame oil over high heat. Add gingerroot and garlic and stir-fry for a few seconds. Add shrimp and stir-fry just until shrimp turn pink, about 2 minutes.
4. Add bean sprouts, scallions, and celery and stir-fry a few seconds.
5. Add chilled noodles and cook, stirring, until noodles are hot.
6. Add soy sauce mixture and cook, stirring, until all ingredients are well mixed and hot, and sauce is slightly thickened.

Serves 4

SZECHUAN SHRIMP

The hotness of this dish can be varied according to taste and to the type of hot bean paste used. This recipe was developed by Paul Rozin.

2 tablespoons soy sauce
7 tablespoons water
3 tablespoons white vinegar
¼ cup sugar
½–¾ teaspoons hot bean paste
3 tablespoons bottled chili sauce
3 tablespoons sesame oil
¼ cup gingerroot, finely minced
6 cloves garlic, finely minced
2 tablespoons chopped scallions
1 pound raw shrimp, peeled and deveined
1 tablespoon cornstarch

1. In a small bowl combine soy sauce, 5 tablespoons water, vinegar, sugar, bean paste, and chili sauce. Mix thoroughly until bean paste is smooth. Set aside.
2. In a large frying pan or wok, heat sesame oil over high heat. Add gingerroot, garlic, and scallions and stir-fry for a few seconds.

3. Add shrimp and stir-fry just until shrimp turns pink, about 2 minutes.
4. Add soy sauce mixture and bring quickly to a simmer, stirring constantly. Combine cornstarch and 2 tablespoons water. Gradually pour into pan, stirring, until sauce thickens. Use just enough cornstarch mixture to thicken slightly. Serve immediately with plain rice.

Serves 3

SPICED BEAN CURD

2 tablespoons dark soy sauce
1 tablespoon rice wine or dry sherry
2 tablespoons peanut butter
1 teaspoon brown sugar
1 teaspoon Chinese hot sauce
1 pound firm bean curd (tofu), cut in ½-inch cubes
3–4 tablespoons sesame oil
1 tablespoon gingerroot, finely minced
1 tablespoon garlic, finely minced
2 cups fresh beansprouts, washed and drained thoroughly
3 scallions, chopped

Garnish: 3 tablespoons peanuts, chopped

1. In a small bowl combine the first five ingredients, mix well and set aside.
2. In a wok or frying pan, heat sesame oil over high heat. Add cubes of bean curd and stir-fry until the cubes are a golden brown, about 5 minutes. Remove bean curd from wok with slotted spoon and set aside.
3. To oil in wok add gingerroot and garlic and stir-fry over high heat just until it starts to brown and smells good. Add sauce ingredients and mix well.
4. Return bean curd to wok and mix thoroughly. Add beansprouts and scallions and mix until everything is hot and well coated with sauce.
5. Garnish with peanuts and serve.

Serves 4

NOTE: This Chinese peanut sauce is very versatile and can be used with any number of foods. You can double the amount of sauce if necessary. It is excellent with stir-fried shrimp, stir-fried mushrooms (serve these at room temperature as an hors d'oeuvre), and with roast pork. For a marvelous buffet dish, roast lean pork fillets, chill, and slice thinly. Arrange pork slices on a serving dish, cover with peanut sauce, and garnish with chopped peanuts.

FISH-FRAGRANT EGGPLANT

This dish, characteristic of Szechuan cuisine, is called "fish-fragrant" because of the mock fish sauce; fish is a highly prized food in this landlocked province.

1 large eggplant
½ pound lean boneless pork, cut in small, thin slices
6 tablespoons soy sauce
1 tablespoon cornstarch
2 tablespoons dry sherry
5 tablespoons sugar
¼ cup distilled white vinegar
¼ cup water
6 tablespoons peanut oil
1 teaspoon crushed dried red peppers
6 slices gingerroot (about size and thickness of a quarter)
4 scallions, chopped (separate white and green parts)

1. Cut stem end off eggplant but do not peel. Slice eggplant and dice into small cubes. One handful at a time, place eggplant cubes in a clean dishtowel and squeeze out as much liquid as possible. When you are finished, eggplant should be about ½ original volume.
2. Combine pork slices with 2 tablespoons soy sauce, cornstarch, sherry, and one tablespoon sugar. Mix well and set aside.
3. In a small bowl combine 4 tablespoons soy sauce, the remaining 4 tablespoons sugar, vinegar, and water.
4. In a large frying pan or wok, heat 2 tablespoons oil over moderate heat. Add red peppers and stir-fry briefly. Add the squeezed eggplant and sauté approximately 8–10 minutes, stirring occasionally, until eggplant is thoroughly cooked.
5. Add soy sauce mixture and cook over high heat until liquid is almost completely evaporated and eggplant is thoroughly coated with reduced sauce (about 5 minutes). Remove eggplant from pan and set aside.
6. In same pan heat remaining 4 tablespoons peanut oil over high heat. Add sliced gingerroot and chopped white part of scallions and stir-fry ½ minute. Add pork slices with liquid and stir-fry 2 minutes.
7. Add eggplant to pork, mix well, and cook together about 2 minutes. Add chopped green part of scallions and stir to blend. Serve hot, with plain rice.

Serves 4

CHINESE SALAD

2 cups shredded cabbage
1 medium cucumber, peeled and shredded
2 carrots, shredded
1 medium green pepper, seeded and shredded
1 medium sweet red pepper, seeded and shredded
1 tablespoon salt
1 teaspoon gingerroot, finely minced
1 teaspoon sugar
1 teaspoon soy sauce
2 teaspoons distilled white vinegar
1 tablespoon dry sherry
2 teaspoons sesame oil

1. Thoroughly mix the shredded vegetables with the salt and let stand one hour.
2. In a small bowl mix together all the other ingredients, blending well with a fork.
3. Place the shredded vegetables in a large strainer or colander and wash thoroughly with running cold water. Drain thoroughly.
4. Pour dressing over vegetables and mix well. Chill before serving.

Serves 6

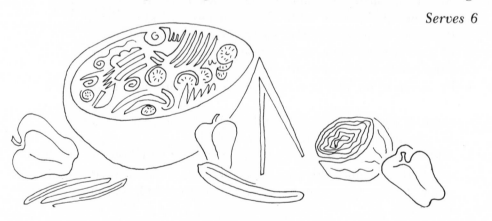

JAPAN

Japanese soy sauce is generally more refined and lighter in color and flavor than Chinese soy sauce. It is equivalent to what the Chinese call "thin" soy sauce. The basic Japanese flavor principle is the combination of soy sauce, rice wine (*sake*), and sugar. *Mirin*, a sweet rice wine used exclusively in cooking, frequently replaces the sugar and sake in this equation. This flavor principle is used most often with broiled foods such as *yakitori*. Variations in flavor are achieved with the use of gingerroot, sesame oil, and hot pepper. In the preparation of the very popular liquid-based chafing dish recipes such as Chicken and Oyster Casserole, the basic principle combines with *dashi*, a fish-flavored stock widely used in Japanese cuisine. *Dashi*, prepared from kelp and bonito, is one of the many foods derived from the sea. It is not difficult to prepare but is available in a convenient instant form in Japanese groceries.

Japanese cuisine generally tends to be more delicate and subtler in flavor than Chinese; it requires much less oil and fat and relies more heavily on the techniques of broiling and poaching. It is a highly visual cuisine, emphasizing the aesthetic appearance and arrangement of the food items to be cooked and eaten. Some of the great classic Japanese dishes are prepared more appropriately in restaurants than in the home kitchen and for that reason *tempura* (deep-fried foods), and *sashimi* and *sushi* (raw fish and rice preparations) are not represented here. The delicacy of many Japanese foods is enhanced by the frequent use of piquant condiments such as pickled gingerroot, hot radish (*daikon*), and various pickles.

JAPANESE RECIPES

JAPANESE CLAM AND MUSHROOM SOUP

JAPANESE CHICKEN LIVERS

BEEF TERIYAKI

YAKITORI

CHICKEN AND OYSTER CASSEROLE

JAPANESE BROILED FISH

JAPANESE EGGPLANT

JAPANESE CLAM AND MUSHROOM SOUP

Very easy, very good, and very low in calories.

5 cups *Dashi* (see p. 248)
1 tablespoon thin (regular) soy sauce
½ tablespoon *Mirin*
3 slices fresh gingerroot
1 cup fresh mushrooms, sliced
2 ounces fresh spinach, washed, drained, and coarsely chopped
8-ounce(s) can chopped clams, with juice
6 ounces fresh beansprouts

1. In a medium sized pot, combine *Dashi*, soy sauce, *Mirin*, and gingerroot. Simmer, uncovered, for about 20 minutes.
2. Add mushrooms, spinach, and clams and cook just until spinach is wilted and soup is very hot.
3. Divide beansprouts among individual soup bowls and ladle the hot soup over them.

Serves 6

JAPANESE CHICKEN LIVERS

¾–1 pound chicken livers, cut in half
¼ cup soy sauce
¼ cup sake
½ cup water
1 tablespoon sugar
1 clove garlic, finely minced
½ teaspoon gingerroot, finely minced
¼ teaspoon crushed dried red peppers
3–4 scallions, finely chopped
8-ounce can water chestnuts, drained and sliced
   sesame seeds (optional)

1. In a medium saucepan, combine chicken livers with all ingredients except water chestnuts and sesame seeds. Simmer over moderate heat, uncovered, for about 15 minutes. Cool, then cover and refrigerate several hours or overnight.
2. Remove livers from marinade, slice, and serve on toothpicks with sliced water chestnuts. If desired, dip livers into sesame seeds. (Livers may also be served hot in the sauce with plain rice.)

Makes about 30 slices

BEEF TERIYAKI

2-pound boneless round or sirloin steak
¾ cup soy sauce
¾ cup sake
¼ cup sugar
1 clove garlic, mashed

1. Cut the steak against the grain into very thin slices (easier to do if meat is partially frozen).
2. In a large shallow pan, combine the soy sauce, sake, sugar, and garlic and mix well. Add the beef slices, mix thoroughly, and marinate for 2 hours, stirring occasionally.
3. Soak bamboo skewers in water for a few minutes. Remove the beef slices from the marinade and thread on skewers. Broil over hot charcoal for 1–2 minutes. Serve immediately. If desired, the marinade may be simmered for 5 minutes and served as a sauce.

Serves 6

YAKITORI

The sauce for Yakitori is exactly the same as that for Teriyaki; the only difference between the preparation techniques is that the meat in Teriyaki is marinated for several hours, whereas Yakitori is simply basted with the sauce while cooking. Teriyaki traditionally uses beef or fish; Yakitori, chicken and chicken parts. Both are excellent summer outdoor dishes.

½ cup soy sauce
½ cup sake
¼ cup sugar
2 large chicken breasts, boned and cut in 1-inch cubes
½ pound chicken livers, cut in half
4–6 scallions, cut into 2-inch pieces

1. Combine soy sauce, sake, and sugar and mix well.
2. Thread chicken cubes and liver halves on skewers, ending with a piece of scallion on each skewer.
3. Brush skewered meat with sauce. Grill over hot charcoal about 5–6 minutes or until chicken is just tender, turning skewers frequently and basting continuously with sauce. Brush generously with sauce before serving.

Serves 4–6

CHICKEN AND OYSTER CASSEROLE

2 tablespoons peanut oil
2 teaspoons gingerroot, finely minced
1½ pounds boneless chicken, cut in small cubes
2 teaspoons sugar
2 tablespoons soy sauce
1 tablespoon sake (or dry sherry)
1 cup *Dashi*
4 scallions, cut into 1-inch pieces
2 cups shredded spinach leaves or watercress
1 cup fresh mushrooms, sliced
8–10 ounces fresh shucked oysters

1. In a wok, frying pan, or electric chafing dish, heat oil over high heat; add ginger and chicken cubes and stir-fry just until chicken loses its pink color.
2. Sprinkle chicken with sugar, then soy sauce and sake, then add the *Dashi*. Turn heat low and simmer for about 10 minutes until chicken is done. Add vegetables and oysters and cook just until vegetables are wilted and edges of oysters are curled. Serve with plain rice.

Serves 4–6

JAPANESE BROILED FISH

3 tablespoons soy sauce
3 tablespoons sake
1 teaspoon sugar
sesame oil
2 pounds any sea fish (mackerel, sea bass, trout, rockfish), split and eviscerated

Garnish: 2 scallions, sliced thinly lengthwise

1. In a large shallow pan, combine soy sauce, sake, and sugar and mix well. Lay fish in marinade and place in refrigerator 2–3 hours. Turn fish occasionally.
2. Brush both sides of fish lightly with sesame oil and broil about 3 minutes on each side. Garnish with sliced scallions.

Serves 4

JAPANESE EGGPLANT

1 medium eggplant
3 tablespoons soy sauce
3 tablespoons sake
2 teaspoons sugar
3 tablespoons peanut oil

1. Cut stem end off eggplant but do not peel. Cut eggplant into 1-inch cubes.
2. In a cup, combine soy sauce, sake, and sugar and mix well.
3. In a large frying pan or wok, heat oil over moderate heat. Add eggplant cubes and sauté slowly, stirring occasionally, until cubes are soft and lightly browned, about 5–7 minutes.
4. Add soy sauce mixture and continue to cook, stirring occasionally, until liquid is completely absorbed and eggplant is a deep glazed brown.

Serves 4

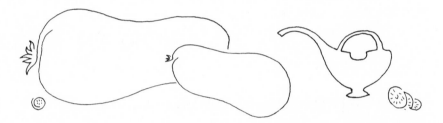

KOREA

Although Korean cuisine emphasizes rice and soy sauce as do the Chinese and Japanese cuisines, Korean food generally tends to be heartier and more heavily flavored. Korean soy sauce is darker and richer than Japanese; hot chile pepper is used more frequently and with a heavier hand. Most traditional cooking is done over small charcoal fires. The Chinese-style wok is frequently used, but the grilling of meats directly over charcoal is a more characteristic technique. Because the country suffers a harsh winter climate, many vegetables are preserved in order to add variety to winter menus. The most well known of these preserved vegetable products is *kim chee*, a shredded cabbage that is salted, fermented in earthenware containers, and liberally spiked with hot pepper.

The basic flavor principle of Korean cuisine is the combination of soy sauce, garlic, brown sugar, and sesame—either sesame seed or sesame oil. Chile pepper and gingerroot are used to provide variation.

KOREAN RECIPES

MARINATED MUSHROOMS KOREAN STYLE

KOREAN BEEFSTEAK

BUL GOKI

FAR EASTERN MEATBALLS

MARINATED MUSHROOMS KOREAN STYLE

1 pound small fresh mushrooms
¼ cup dark soy sauce
3 tablespoons distilled white vinegar
3 tablespoons brown sugar
3 cloves garlic, mashed
2 tablespoons toasted sesame seeds*

1. Wipe mushrooms with a damp cloth and cut off stem ends. Place mushrooms in a glass or ceramic bowl.
2. In a small saucepan, combine soy sauce, vinegar, sugar, and garlic. Simmer for a few minutes over moderate heat.
3. Pour sauce over mushrooms and refrigerate. Allow to marinate at least 6 hours or overnight, stirring occasionally to make sure that all the mushrooms are coated with the liquid.
4. To serve, drain mushrooms thoroughly, spear on toothpicks, and dip into toasted sesame seeds.

*To toast sesame seeds, place a heavy pan over high heat. Add sesame seeds and toss constantly for a few minutes until seeds are a light golden brown.

Makes 3–4 cups

KOREAN BEEFSTEAK

⅓ cup dark soy sauce
3 tablespoons brown sugar
4 cloves garlic, mashed
2 pound boneless round or sirloin steak
2 scallions, chopped
3 tablespoons toasted sesame seeds

1. In a large shallow pan, combine soy sauce, brown sugar, and garlic and mix well. Place steak in pan and marinate 4–6 hours, turning occasionally.
2. Remove steak from marinade and broil over hot charcoal. For 1-inch thick steak, broil 4 minutes on each side for rare; 6 minutes on each side for medium.
3. Cut steak in thin slices against the grain; serve topped with chopped scallions and sesame seeds.

Serves 4–6

BUL GOKI

⅓ cup dark soy sauce
4 cloves garlic, mashed
3 tablespoons brown sugar
2 tablespoons toasted sesame seeds
¼ teaspoon crushed dried red peppers
2 pounds boneless pork tenderloin or pork cutlets

1. Combine soy sauce, garlic, sugar, sesame seeds, and hot peppers in a blender and blend for a few seconds.
2. Pour mixture over the pork and marinate 4–6 hours, turning pork occasionally.
3. Remove pork from marinade and broil over hot charcoal until well done (about 5 minutes each side).
4. Slice pork thin; serve with additional toasted sesame seeds sprinkled on the top if desired.

Serves 4–6

FAR EASTERN MEATBALLS

1½ pounds lean ground beef, or combination of beef and pork
¼ cup dark soy sauce
⅓ cup brown sugar
4 cloves garlic, mashed
2 teaspoons gingerroot, finely minced, or 1 teaspoon ground ginger
1 egg, lightly beaten
20-ounce can litchi nuts, drained
½ cup toasted sesame seeds

1. Combine ground meat with all ingredients except litchi nuts and sesame seeds. Mix thoroughly and form into small balls.
2. Place meatballs on a baking sheet or rimmed pan and bake in a preheated 350° oven for ½ hour.
3. Mix meatballs with litchi nuts in a casserole or chafing dish. If serving as a main course, sprinkle sesame seeds over the top; if serving as an appetizer or buffet dish, let guests spear meatballs with toothpicks and dip into a dish of sesame seeds.

Makes about 50 meatballs
Serves 4–6 as main course

INDONESIA

Between the Indian Ocean and the Pacific Ocean lie the islands of Indonesia, and their cooking truly exhibits the features of a genuine "crossroads" cuisine. Here several distinct flavoring traditions merge into a unique culinary tradition. In the section on "Crossroads Cuisine" we will see how combinations of various flavor principles are used in specific recipes. A large part of Indonesia's cuisine, however, belongs to the soy sauce family from which it has developed a characteristic flavor principle using soy sauce, molasses or brown sugar, garlic, and ground peanuts.

Indonesian soy sauce, like the Korean, is darker and more viscous than the Japanese and is fuller in flavor. (It is interesting to note, incidentally, the similarity between the Indonesian word for soy sauce, *ketjap*, and the word for America's favorite seasoning sauce, ketchup.) Variations on the basic theme are achieved with the use of coconut, lemon grass, shrimp paste (*trasi*), and the frequent addition of chile pepper.

The basic foods of Indonesia are similar to those of the rest of Southeast Asia; chicken, fish, shellfish, rice, noodles, and vegetables. Less pork is used due to the significant Islamic influence on the culture. Cooking techniques are also similar; cooking with the wok, and grilling meats over charcoal. Sambals, condimental or mixed side dishes fiery with chile peppers, are served with most meals.

INDONESIAN RECIPES

INDONESIAN PEANUT SOUP

INDONESIAN LAMB SATE

NASI GORENG (INDONESIAN FRIED RICE)

SHRIMP SATE

INDONESIAN FRUIT AND VEGETABLE SALAD

For additional Indonesian Recipes See:
Indonesian Vegetable Scramble p. 196
Indonesian Peanut Chicken Salad p. 210

INDONESIAN PEANUT SOUP

4 cups chicken stock
2 tablespoons dark soy sauce
1½ tablespoons molasses
juice ½ lemon
2 cloves garlic, mashed
¼ cup peanut butter
⅓ cup roasted peanuts, chopped
⅔ cup cooked chicken or pork, shredded, or chopped shrimp (or mixture)
½ cup scallions, chopped

1. In a large pot, heat stock, soy sauce, molasses, lemon juice, and garlic. Simmer gently for 20 minutes.
2. Add peanut butter and stir until well blended. Just before serving add the chopped peanuts, meat, and scallions. Serve hot.

Serves 6–8

INDONESIAN LAMB SATE

1½ cups roasted peanuts, ground
2 large cloves garlic, mashed
½ cup dark soy sauce
2 tablespoons molasses
1 teaspoon crushed dried red peppers
½ cup water
2 pounds boneless leg of lamb or lamb sirloin, cut in 1-inch cubes
juice 1 lemon

1. In a small saucepan, combine ground peanuts, garlic, soy sauce, molasses, peppers, and water. Simmer over low heat for a few minutes. Cool slightly.
2. Pour sauce over lamb cubes, mix well, and marinate 2–4 hours.
3. Remove lamb from marinade, thread on skewers, and broil over hot charcoal, turning once, about 4 minutes each side.
4. Sprinkle with lemon juice before serving. Remaining marinade may be heated and served as a sauce.

Serves 4–6

NASI GORENG
(Indonesian Fried Rice)

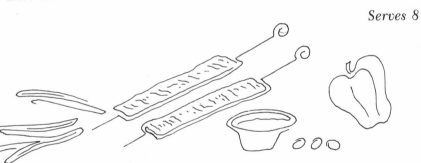

¼ cup peanut oil
1 medium onion, chopped
2 teaspoons curry powder
½ teaspoon turmeric
1 teaspoon gingerroot, finely minced, or ½ teaspoon ground ginger
½ teaspoon crushed dried red peppers
1½ cups long-grain rice
3 cups hot chicken stock
1½ tablespoons molasses
3 tablespoons dark soy sauce
½ cup roasted peanuts, finely chopped
1 cup cooked chicken, pork, or shrimp (or mixture), minced
2 scallions, chopped
⅓ cup cooked green peas

1. Heat oil in a large pot. Add onion, curry powder, turmeric, gingerroot, and red peppers and sauté for 5 minutes. Add rice and sauté another 5 minutes or until rice is golden and oil is absorbed.
2. Add stock, cover, and cook over low heat 15–20 minutes or until all liquid is absorbed and rice is tender.
3. Stir in all other ingredients and mix well. Let stand, covered, 5 minutes. (The rice may be refrigerated at this point and reheated later in a covered casserole for 20 minutes in a preheated 400° oven.)

Serves 8

SHRIMP SATE

2 pounds large raw shrimp, peeled and deveined
1 cup fresh or canned pineapple chunks, drained
vegetable oil
1 cup roasted peanuts, ground
¼ cup dark soy sauce
3 tablespoons molasses
2 cloves garlic, mashed
½ teaspoon crushed dried red peppers
½ cup water
2 lemons, cut in quarters

1. Thread shrimp on skewers alternately with pineapple chunks. Brush generously with oil.
2. In a small saucepan combine ground peanuts, soy sauce, molasses, garlic, peppers, and water. Simmer gently for 5 minutes.
3. Grill skewered shrimp over hot charcoal, turning once, a few minutes on each side. Serve hot, with lemon quarters. Dip shrimp in hot peanut sauce.

Serves 6

INDONESIAN FRUIT AND VEGETABLE SALAD

A good selection of any or all of the following: shredded green and red cabbage, cucumber strips, carrot strips, cooked green beans, tomato wedges or cherry tomatoes, green and red pepper strips, melon chunks, pineapple chunks, avocado slices dipped in lemon juice, hard-cooked egg wedges.

1. Arrange a selection of the fruits, vegetables, and egg wedges attractively on a large platter. Pass the following peanut sauce separately with the salad.

Peanut Sauce:

½ cup roasted peanuts, ground or finely chopped
2 tablespoons molasses
2 tablespoons soy sauce
3 cloves garlic, mashed
pinch crushed dried red peppers
juice ½ lemon
½ cup water
1 tablespoon peanut oil

1. In a small saucepan combine all ingredients except peanut oil. Simmer gently for 10 minutes. Remove from heat and beat in oil. Chill before serving.

Makes about ⅔ cup sauce

FISH SAUCE PRINCIPLES II

Fish sauce, the second great seasoning ingredient of the Orient, is equivalent to soy sauce both in the manner of its production and in its culinary use. Different varieties of fish—saltwater, fresh, or a mixture of both—are salted, mixed with water, and allowed to ferment in wooden casks. The resultant liquid is clear, light to dark brown in color, salty in taste, and fishy in aroma, although the fishiness tends to disappear in cooking. Fish sauce, like soy sauce, is used the way Westerners use salt, both in cooking and at the table.

The manufacture of fish sauces seems to be an ancient tradition. Fish, or the flavor of fish, originally may have been preserved to store for scarcer times. The fish sauce tradition now seems to belong almost exclusively to the Orient; but the cuisine of ancient Rome, as described in a cookbook written by Apicius more than two thousand years ago, heavily used a fish sauce called *garum* or *liquamen*. This Roman fish sauce was produced in much the same manner as are the Oriental sauces, and it was used in much the same way. With the Roman decline, this seasoning recipe was forgotten; but curiously, it survived in that far Roman outpost of Great Britain in the form of worcestershire, a popular seasoning sauce based on salted anchovies.

The primary fish sauce traditions in the Orient are to be found in the cuisines of Vietnam, Thailand, Cambodia, Laos, and to a lesser extent, in Burma and the Philippines. Each cuisine has its own distinctive variety, none of which should be confused with the many salted and/or fermented fish pastes and dried fish products. These are used widely throughout the Orient as varietal, rather than as primary, seasoning ingredients. Other products commonly added to the fish sauce seasoning are coconut, onion, garlic, lemon grass, gingerroot, lemon or lime juice, fresh coriander leaf, and two relatively recent introductions from the New World, peanuts and chile pepper.

33

VIETNAM

The cuisine of Vietnam is varied and subtle. Of all the cuisines of Southeast Asia, this probably is the most accessible to western palates. Although influenced in many ways by the Chinese, Vietnamese cooking is much lighter and more delicate because it does not rely heavily on oil and fat. In Vietnam, as in all Southeast Asia, the diet is based on rice, but there is a striking taste for noodles of every kind throughout the country. Pork, chicken, fish and shellfish, particularly shrimp and crab, also are common; and due to French influences, beef has become very popular. A wide variety of vegetables, particularly bean sprouts and leafy greens, completes their diet. Vegetables, such as lettuce, scallions and cucumber, often are eaten raw as salads to compliment the meal.

Vietnamese fish sauce, *nuoc mam*, is light brown, clear, and delicate in flavor. It is produced from saltwater fish, primarily anchovies, and is an extremely versatile seasoning ingredient. (Along with the salt and pepper, we keep a bottle of *nuoc mam* on the table for our Vietnamese son, who sprinkles it on everything from hamburgers to spaghetti.) The basic flavor principle of Vietnamese cuisine is the combination of *nuoc mam* and lemon, with the frequent addition of chile peppers. Seasoning variations are achieved with the use of garlic, gingerroot, lemon grass, sugar, and fresh coriander leaf.

VIETNAMESE RECIPES

PHO (BEEF NOODLE SOUP)

MIEN GA (CHICKEN NOODLE SOUP)

CHA GIO (VIETNAMESE EGG ROLLS)

VIETNAMESE CARAMEL PORK

see also
Vietnamese Hamburgers p. 210

PHO
(Vietnamese Beef Noodle Soup)

This is probably "the" national dish of Vietnam, and the first dish I learned to prepare for our Vietnamese son when he arrived seven years ago. I believe it is one of the great soups of the world: rich in flavor, but delicate in taste; hearty, but not overwhelming. Stock for Vietnamese soups is always clear, skimmed of all fat, and salted with *nuoc mam*. If you do not wish to make your own stock, use diluted beef bouillon so it can be flavored with *nuoc mam*.

8 cups undersalted beef stock
2–3 tablespoons *nuoc mam*
1 tablespoon lemon or lime juice
2 pieces star anise
1 large onion, thinly sliced
½ pound pho noodles (if not available, substitute vermicelli)
½–¾ pound boneless beef (top round or sirloin), cut in very thin slices
    against the grain
¼ cup scallions, chopped
¼ cup fresh coriander leaf, chopped
6–8 ounces fresh beansprouts, washed and drained

Garnish: lemon or lime wedges, *nuoc mam*, crushed hot chile pepper

1. In a medium sized pot, combine beef stock, *nuoc mam*, lemon juice, star anise, and onion; simmer, uncovered, for 20–30 minutes.
2. Meanwhile cook pho noodles in boiling water for 5 minutes. Drain. (If using vermicelli, cook according to package instructions.)
3. Combine chopped scallions and coriander. Set aside.
4. To assemble and serve: Place a small handful of beef strips in a strainer or large perforated spoon. Lower into simmering stock and cook just until beef loses its red color. Remove from stock and place in individual soup bowls. Cook the rest of the beef in a similar fashion and distribute among the soup bowls.
5. To each soup bowl add some noodles, beansprouts, and about one tablespoon chopped scallions and coriander. Fill soup bowls with simmering stock and serve immediately. Pass lemon or lime, *nuoc mam*, and chile pepper as individual garnishes.

Serves 8

MIEN GA
(Vietnamese Chicken Noodle Soup)

Ga in Vietnamese means chicken; *mien* means noodle, specifically, thin, translucent cellophane noodles. This is a very good soup and is easy to prepare. If you don't want to make your own stock, use diluted chicken bouillon so the addition of *nuoc mam* won't make the soup too salty.

8 cups undersalted chicken stock (see p. 142)
2 tablespoons (or more to taste) *nuoc mam*
1 tablespoon lemon or lime juice
6 scallions, chopped, white and green parts separated
1–1½ cups cooked chicken, shredded
6 ounces cellophane noodles
6–8 ounces fresh beansprouts, rinsed in cold water and drained
2–3 tablespoons fresh coriander, chopped (optional)

1. In a medium sized saucepan, combine stock, *nuoc mam*, lemon juice, and white parts of scallion. Simmer for 20–30 minutes. Taste for salt; if more is needed, add some *nuoc mam*.
2. Cover cellophane noodles with cold water for ½ hour. Drain.
3. To serve: divide chicken, noodles, beansprouts, and scallions among the soup bowls. Ladle simmering stock over them, garnish with coriander, and serve.

Serves 8

CHA GIO
(Vietnamese Egg Rolls)

This popular Vietnamese appetizer is much smaller than the Chinese egg roll. The wrappers are made of rice flour rather than wheat flour, and are quite brittle. It is necessary to brush them with egg and water until they are pliable enough to shape. These little eggrolls are always served with lettuce and fresh coriander (in fact, they are frequently wrapped in lettuce leaves as they are eaten), and with *nuoc cham*, a favorite dipping sauce (see below). *Cha gio* may be made early in the day and reheated in a 400° oven for 15–20 minutes until they are sizzling hot. They also may be frozen.

Filling:

6 ounces ground raw pork
6–6½ ounces flaked crabmeat (canned is okay)
2 ounces cellophane noodles
1 medium onion, finely chopped
3 tree ears
couple of grinds of black pepper
2 teaspoons *nuoc mam*

1. Soak tree ears in warm water for 1/2 hour. Drain and chop fine.
2. Soak cellophane noodles in cold water for 10–15 minutes. Drain and chop.
3. Combine all filling ingredients and mix well.

Wrapping:

1 package rice paper rounds
1 egg, lightly beaten with 1 tablespoon water
oil for frying

1. Brush one side of a rice paper round completely with egg mixture; let stand for a few minutes. With a sharp knife cut round into 3 equal parts. Place one part in front of you with the point facing down.
2. Place a heaping teaspoonful of the filling in a horizontal line along the middle of the triangle, but not all the way to the edges. Fold the bottom point of the triangle up over the filling, then fold in the sides, and continue rolling upward into a little cylinder. Squeeze lightly to close. Make all the *cha gio* in this way.
3. Put enough oil to generously cover the bottom of a large frying pan. Over moderate heat, fry the eggrolls until they are nicely browned, about 5–6 minutes on each side. Remove from pan. Serve with lettuce and dipping sauce.

Nuoc cham *(dipping sauce)*

1 clove garlic, mashed
2 tablespoons *nuoc mam*
1 tablespoon lemon or lime juice
1 teaspoon sugar
2 tablespoons water
¼ teaspoon (more or less to taste) crushed red pepper
a few shreds of carrot

1. Combine all ingredients in a small bowl and mix well.

VIETNAMESE CARAMEL PORK

Here is a fine example of the Oriental technique of cooking until "the oil comes out." The dish is done traditionally with a somewhat fatty cut of meat; as the meat simmers in water, the fat is rendered out and when the liquid has cooked away, the meat then browns in its own fat. The vegetables are added and stir-fried at the very end. If you use a lean cut of meat, add a few tablespoons of sesame oil when the liquid has cooked away; I have tried this several times and Vietnamese friends assure me that it not only works well but gives the dish added flavor.

2–2½ pounds boneless pork, cut in ½-inch cubes
water to cover
4 scallions, white parts chopped
1 tablespoon sugar
1 teaspoon ground lemon grass
2 tablespoons *nuoc mam*
⅔ cups assorted vegetables: sliced carrots, sliced green peppers, sliced mushrooms, broccoli, bean sprouts, etc.

Garnish: 4 scallions, green tops chopped

1. In a deep skillet or pot, place pork cubes, scallions, sugar, lemon grass, and enough water to cover. Bring to a simmer and cook uncovered for about 2 hours or until pork is tender. (If water cooks away before meat is tender, add some more.)
2. After meat is tender and water has cooked away, there should be some fat remaining in the pot. If not, add some sesame oil (see above). Add *nuoc mam* and vegetables and continue to cook, stirring, until meat is nicely browned and vegetables are tender but still crisp. Garnish with chopped scallions. Serve with plain rice.

Serves 4–6

LAOS

The culinary tradition of Laos is, in many ways, unique. Because it has no acccess to the South China Sea, Laos relies heavily on the freshwater fish found in the Mekong River and its tributaries, and on a wide variety of wild game. Rice again provides the basis of the cuisine, but the Laotians prefer glutinous rice to other varieties. Wok-cooking, steaming, and grilling are the typical cooking techniques used.

The Laotian fish sauce, *nam pa*, is ususally made from freshwater fish, or sometimes a combination of fresh and saltwater fish. It is stronger in odor and flavor than the Vietnamese or Thai varieties, and frequently contains large chunks of fermented fish *(nam padek)*. Laotian fish sauce is often made in the home but stored outside because the aroma is reputed to be both pungent and unforgettable.

The basic flavor principle of Laotian cuisine is the combination of fish sauce and coconut milk, with the frequent addition of garlic, fresh coriander, lemon grass, gingerroot, and chile pepper.

LAOTIAN RECIPES

LAOTIAN FISH BALLS
COCONUT MILK

LAOTIAN FISH BALLS

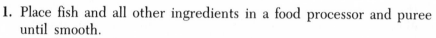

1 pound fillets of any white fish
2 cloves garlic
¼ cup coconut milk (see below)
2 eggs
2 tablespoons fish sauce (*nuoc mam*)
2 tablespoons fresh coriander, chopped
dash black pepper

1. Place fish and all other ingredients in a food processor and puree until smooth.
2. Shape with the hands into small walnut-sized balls. Drop a few balls at a time into simmering water and poach for about 3–4 minutes. Remove from water with slotted spoon. Serve as is or put in soup.

Traditionally these tasty little fish balls are wrapped in banana leaves and steamed. You can substitute small squares of aluminum foil, but I find the poaching works just as well. Serve them just as they are or, as I prefer, in a plain chicken stock seasoned with a little fish sauce, some chopped scallion, and perhaps a few fresh bean sprouts.

Makes about 30

To make coconut milk:

2 cups *unsweetened* dried coconut, shredded
2¼ cups very hot water

Combine coconut and water, mix well and let stand one hour. Place mixture in a blender, and blend at high speed for a few seconds. Squeeze mixture through cheesecloth into a jar, cover and refrigerate.

Makes about 2 cups

THAILAND

Thai cuisine shares many features of the neighboring cuisines of China, Vietnam, Laos, and Cambodia; it is based on rice and noodles, and on a similar selection of meat, fish, and vegetables.

Thai fish sauce, *nam bla*, is very similar to Vietnamese *nuoc mam* and the two may be used interchangeably. Although many of the same seasonings are used by both cuisines, Thai cookery liberally uses both garlic and chile pepper; indeed, the tiny, birdseye chile pepper, used commonly in Thai cooking, is unforgettably hot. Fresh coriander leaf and coriander root are used more frequently than in Vietnamese cuisine.

The most characteristic feature of Thai cuisine are the curries of which there are two basic types: the "Indian," in which *nam bla* is combined with spices frequently found in Indian curries—cumin, turmeric, coriander; and the Southeast Asian type, in which *nam bla* is combined with lemon grass, shrimp paste, and gingerroot. Almost all curries contain garlic and chile pepper. Chopped roasted peanuts are used as a main ingredient and as a garnish.

THAI RECIPES

THAI SHRIMP CURRY

THAI SHRIMP CURRY

2 ounces cellophane noodles
2–3 tablespoons peanut oil
1 medium onion, finely minced
4 cloves garlic, finely minced
1¼ pound raw shrimp, peeled and deveined
2 teaspoons lemon grass, ground
1 teaspoon cumin
1 teaspoon ground coriander
1 teaspoon turmeric
¼ teaspoon crushed, hot, dried red peppers*
1½ tablespoons fish sauce
2 tablespoons roasted peanuts, finely chopped

1. In a wok or frying pan, heat oil over high heat. Add cellophane noodles and cook just until beginning to brown on one side. Turn and let brown on other side. Remove from pan with slotted spoon, place on absorbant paper and set aside.
2. To oil in pan, add onion and garlic and stir-fry just until they begin to brown. Add raw shrimp, then sprinkle with spices, and stir-fry for a few minutes. Add fish sauce and continue to cook just until shrimp are done.
3. Remove shrimp to serving dish and garnish with crumbled fried noodles and chopped peanuts. Serve with plain rice, if desired.

Serves 4

* The Thais would make this dish quite hot, but I have made it without any hot pepper and it is quite good. Adjust the hot pepper to your own taste.

BURMA

The cuisine of Burma clearly shows the convergence of two separate flavoring traditions; the cuisines of Southeast Asia, and the cuisine of India. Burma is the northern-most country of the fish sauce seasoners; its fish sauce is called *ngan pya ye*, and although a common flavoring ingredient, it is not used nearly as frequently as in Vietnam or Laos.

Burma sits directly across the Bay of Bengal from India and the influence of Indian culinary traditions on Burmese cuisine is clear. The most characteristic dishes in Burmese cuisine are the curries. These are inevitably flavored with the combination of onion, gingerroot, garlic, turmeric, and chile pepper. Fish sauce or shrimp paste may or may not be added; if not, salt is used. The flavor of Burmese curries is reminiscent of, but not identical to, the flavor of many Indian curries; my family loves it provided I go easy on the chile peppers.

BURMESE CURRIED SPARERIBS

1 tablespoon peanut oil
1 tablespoon sesame oil
2 large onions, finely minced
6 cloves garlic, finely minced
1 tablespoon gingerroot, finely minced
3–4 pounds very lean country style spareribs, cut in individual pieces
(or 2 pounds lean boneless pork or beef, cut in 1-inch cubes)
2 tablespoons fish sauce
2 teaspoons turmeric
½ teaspoon crushed dried red peppers
2 large, ripe tomatoes, coarsely chopped

1. In a covered heavy pot or deep heavy skillet, heat oils over moderate heat. Add onion, garlic, and gingerroot and fry slowly, stirring, until mixture starts to brown and smell good.
2. Add meat and all other ingredients, cover, and cook over low to moderate heat for 1½–2 hours or until meat is very tender. Serve with plain rice.

Serves 4

INDIA

The cuisine of India is grand, complex, and infinitely varied. Nowhere is the idea of theme and variation so aptly illustrated as in this country where, from ancient times, many cultures have come together to form a unique and enduring culinary tradition.

From a culinary point of view, India historically has been both cursed and blessed. It has always been an overpopulated country with a capricious and difficult climate, with ill-managed natural resources that have not met the nutritional needs of its people. Traditional religions— Hinduism, Jainism, Buddhism—have emphasized vegetarianism by placing taboos on certain meats or by rejecting all animal foods; this may be, in part, a response to the fact that the land cannot support enough livestock for its population.

But India has been blessed with an amazing variety of native herbs and spices, and with a genius for using them. In India, as in so many other parts of the world, dependence on plant foods has fostered culinary inventiveness; skillful seasoning, particularly in grain and vegetable dishes, is the distinguishing feature of Indian cuisine.

Wheat and rice are the primary grains, wheat being more predominant in the north and rice in the south. Wheat is used chiefly in breads, of which chapattis, round, unleavened, griddle-cooked loaves are the most common form. Just as the Oriental cuisines use soybeans and other beans, India utilizes a wide variety of pulses—lentils and split peas—for its protein needs. A vast array of vegetables (peas, cauliflower, eggplant, potatoes, leafy greens, etc.) complete the basic diet.

Chicken and lamb are the most common meats, but in coastal regions fish and seafood also are popular. Eating pork is forbidden by the Moslems in the north; the cow is sacred to Hindus and cannot be killed or consumed. Cow's milk however, is acceptable, and is utilized in the form of clarified butter (*ghee*) for cooking, and in yogurt, which contributes valuable animal protein to the diet. Yogurt is indispensable for nutrition and for flavoring in Indian cuisine and consistently appears in sauces and marinades.

The flavor theme of Indian cookery is known to the outside world as "curry," while in India the term refers not to a taste but to a dish with a sauce. Curry powder, commercial blends of commonly used Indian spices, does not exist in India, where individual spice mixtures are prepared for each dish. A vast array of seasoning ingredients is available, the most common of which are gingerroot, garlic, cumin, coriander, cardamom, turmeric, fenugreek, cloves, cinnamon, mustard seed, and fresh coriander leaf.

These flavorings, among many others, are used throughout India, but their emphasis varies from region to region and from dish to dish. Northern cooking shows a more intense use of cumin, fenugreek, ginger, and garlic, while southern cooking relies more heavily on coconut milk, mustard seed, tamarind (a sour fruit), and asafoetida. Chile peppers are used throughout India, but much more heavily in the south. Mustard oil is characteristic of Bengali cooking, while in other regions *ghee* is favored for frying or sautéeing. It is fascinating to observe when cooking and eating Indian food, that with such an amazing number of seasoning ingredients used in different mixtures and varying proportions, the flavor produced in any dish is both unique and characteristic. There is a flavoring theme throughout all Indian cooking that allows for an almost unlimited number of individual and regional variations.

Regionally, differences in seasonings are frequently subtle: the primary distinction in Indian cooking, however, is between the north and the south. The south retains a classic tradition of curries (sauced dishes) based largely on rice, vegetables, and pulses. In terms of basic foods, cooking techniques, and certain primary seasonings (coconut, tamarind, fresh coriander), the south seems more closely affiliated with the whole Southeast Asian complex of culinary traditions. The north, on the other hand, has been heavily influenced by cooking traditions brought from central Asia by aryan nomads, largely Moslem, who have settled the country many times over in India's history. These pastoral herdsmen from the Asian steppes introduced the traditions of meat cookery, grilling kabobs on spits over an open fire, a heavy use of yogurt, and an elaborate bread tradition. This basic northern cuisine combined happily with the classical spice tradition of India, producing a style of cookery that is truly unique.

INDIAN RECIPES

EGGPLANT BHURTA

SAMOSAS

MULLIGATAWNY SOUP

LAMB AND LENTIL CURRY

SHAMI KEBABS

SPICED LAMB KABOBS

LAMB BIRYANI

CURRIED MEATBALLS

SPICED CHICKEN CUTLETS

TANDOORI CHICKEN

CODFISH IN COCONUT CURRY

SEEKH KEBABS

PILAU

FUL GOBI (CAULIFLOWER CURRY)

SPICED PURÉE OF GREENS AND POTATOES

DHAL (SPLIT PEA CURRY)

MIXED VEGETABLE CURRY

For additional Indian recipes see:
Sour Beef Curry p. 174
Stir-Fried Vegetable Curry p. 212
Raita p. 189
Chapattis p. 221
Nan p. 220
Chutneys pp. 178–180

EGGPLANT BHURTA
(Spiced Eggplant Purée)

1 medium to large eggplant
2 tablespoons mustard oil or vegetable oil
1 medium onion, finely chopped
2 cloves garlic, finely minced
1 teaspoon gingerroot, finely minced
1 teaspoon mustard seeds
½ teaspoon ground cumin
½ teaspoon ground coriander
¼ teaspoon turmeric
½ teaspoon salt
¼ teaspoon crushed dried red peppers
dash freshly ground black pepper
juice ½ lime
2 heaping tablespoons yogurt

Garnish: chopped fresh coriander

1. Place whole unpeeled eggplant in a shallow pan; make a few slashes in eggplant. Roast in hot 450° oven for 30–40 minutes until eggplant is soft all over. Remove from oven and cool.
2. Cut stem end off eggplant and peel off skin. Place eggplant pulp in blender or food processor.
3. In a small frying pan, heat oil over moderate heat. Add onion, garlic, gingerroot, and mustard seeds and sauté until seeds start to pop. Add all other ingredients except lime and yogurt and sauté a few more minutes, stirring.
4. Add spice mixture to eggplant pulp and purée until smooth. Stir in lime juice and yogurt. Serve at room temperature, garnished with chopped fresh coriander, if desired. May be used as a vegetable or as a dip with crackers or triangles of Arabic bread.

Serves 6

SAMOSAS
(Curried Meat Pastries)

1 pound lean ground beef or lamb
3 tablespoons butter
1 medium onion, finely chopped
1 tart green apple, cored and finely chopped
1 clove garlic, minced
2 teaspoons ground cumin
2 teaspoons gingerroot, finely minced or 1 teaspoon ground ginger
1 teaspoon turmeric
½ teaspoon ground coriander
1½ teaspoons salt
⅛ teaspoon freshly ground black pepper
¼ teaspoon crushed dried red peppers
2 tablespoons fruit chutney
¼ cup dark raisins
⅓ cup cashew nuts
3–4 tablespoons yogurt

1. In a frying pan, brown ground meat over high heat until it loses its pink color. Drain thoroughly and set aside.
2. In a large frying pan, melt butter over moderate heat. Add onion, apple, and garlic and sauté just until tender. Add the cumin, gingerroot, turmeric, coriander, salt, and peppers and sauté, stirring, for 5 minutes.
3. Add browned meat, chutney, raisins, and cashews. Remove from heat and add enough yogurt so that mixture just holds together but is not too mushy. Chill in refrigerator 1–2 hours.

Yogurt pastry:

3 cups all-purpose flour
½ teaspoon salt
4 tablespoons melted butter
½ cup yogurt
¼ cup water

1. Sift flour with salt into a large bowl. Stir in melted butter, then yogurt, then water. Stir together until blended. Dough will appear dry and lumpy.
2. Pinch off a piece of dough the size of a small walnut. Roll between the palms to form a ball. On a well-floured board roll out ball of dough to form a thin circle about 3–4 inches in diameter.

3. Place one tablespoon chilled filling on dough circle. Fold over to form a semicircle. Trim off any rough edges with a sharp knife. Moisten edges of semicircle with a little water and pinch to seal. Repeat rolling and filling, using up remaining dough and filling.
4. Place 2 cups vegetable oil in a large frying pan and heat over high heat. Fry pastries 4 or 5 at a time, turning once, until they turn a deep golden brown. Drain on paper towels. Serve hot. (These pastries can be frozen; to reheat, place in 400° oven for 20–30 minutes.)

Makes 25–30 pastries

MULLIGATAWNY SOUP

Soups are not a significant part of Indian culinary tradition, and Mulligatawny soup is very likely an English adaptation of the many spiced split pea and lentil dishes that form a cornerstone of Indian peasant cuisine (see recipe for Dhal p. 61).

1 cup lentils
2 tablespoons butter
1 medium onion, chopped
2 cloves garlic, mashed
1 teaspoon gingerroot, finely minced (or ½ teaspoon ground ginger)
2 teaspoons ground cumin
¼ teaspoon crushed dried red peppers
½ teaspoon ground coriander
½ teaspoon mustard seeds
½ teaspoon turmeric
⅛ teaspoon freshly ground black pepper
8 cups chicken stock
1½ teaspoons salt
juice 2 limes
1 cup cooked chicken or lamb, chopped (optional)

1. Soak lentils overnight in enough water to cover. Drain well.
2. In a large pot melt butter. Add onion, garlic, and all spices and sauté over low heat for about 5 minutes.
3. Add drained lentils and stock and simmer gently for about 2 hours. Taste for salt and add as much as necessary. Cool slightly, add lime juice and purée in food mill or blender. If soup is too thick it can be thinned with additional stock. Reheat before serving, adding chicken or lamb if desired.

Serves 8–10

LAMB AND LENTIL CURRY

1 cup lentils
4 tablespoons butter or *ghee*
1 large onion, chopped
3 cloves garlic, finely minced
2 teaspoons gingerroot, finely minced
¼ teaspoon freshly ground black pepper
¼–½ teaspoon crushed dried red peppers
1½ teaspoons ground cumin
1 teaspoon turmeric
½ teaspoon ground coriander
½ teaspoon ground fenugreek
½ teaspoon crushed cardamom seeds or ground cardamom
1 cup canned tomatoes, drained, or 2 medium fresh tomatoes, chopped
1 cup hot water
½ teaspoon ground cumin
½ teaspoon ground coriander
¼ teaspoon cinnamon
2¾ teaspoons salt
1½–2 pounds lean boneless lamb, cut in 1-inch cubes
1 cup yogurt
juice 1 lime

1. Soak lentils overnight in enough water to cover. Drain well.
2. In a large pot, heat 2 tablespoons butter or *ghee* over moderate heat. Add onion, garlic, and gingerroot and sauté, stirring, for a few minutes. Add peppers, cumin, turmeric, coriander, fenugreek, and cardamon and sauté for a few more minutes.
3. Add drained lentils, tomatoes, and hot water and bring to simmer. Continue to simmer while preparing meat.
4. In a large frying pan heat 2 tablespoons butter or *ghee* over moderate heat. Add cumin, coriander, cinnamon, and salt and stir for a few minutes. Add lamb cubes, turn heat high, and brown quickly on all sides. Stir in yogurt and mix well.
5. Add lamb mixture to the lentils and simmer, uncovered, 1½–2 hours or until lamb and lentils are tender. Taste for salt. Stir in lime juice. Serve curry with plain rice or chapattis.

Serves 6

SHAMI KEBABS

½ cup dried lentils
3 tablespoons butter
1 medium onion, finely chopped
2 cloves garlic, finely minced
½ teaspoon fennel seeds
1½ teaspoons salt
¼ teaspoon freshly ground black pepper
¼ teaspoon crushed dried red peppers
½ teaspoon turmeric
1 teaspoon ground cumin
½ teaspoon ground coriander
¼ teaspoon crushed cardamom seed or ground cardamom
grated rind 1 lemon
juice ½ lemon
½ cup yogurt
1½ pounds lean ground lamb
flour

Garnish: chopped fresh mint

1. Soak lentils overnight in enough water to cover. Drain thoroughly and grind through meat grinder.
2. In a large frying pan, heat 2 tablespoons butter over moderate heat. Add onion, garlic, and fennel seeds and fry for a few minutes, stirring. Add salt, peppers, cumin, turmeric, coriander, and cardamom and sauté a few more minutes.
3. Add spice mixture, ground lentils, lemon rind, lemon juice, and yogurt to lamb and mix thoroughly. Shape into 8 oval patties.
4. In same frying pan heat one tablespoon butter over moderate heat. Dredge lamb patties lightly in flour and sauté slowly on both sides until done, about 8 minutes altogether.
5. Place on serving plate and sprinkle with chopped mint. Serve with a good fruit chutney.

Serves 4

SPICED LAMB KEBABS

2 pounds boneless leg of lamb or lamb sirloin, cut in 1-inch cubes
2 cups yogurt
3 tablespoons butter or oil
1 medium onion, chopped
2 cloves garlic, finely minced
2 teaspoons gingerroot, finely minced
2 teaspoons ground cumin
¼ teaspoon crushed dried red peppers
¼ teaspoon freshly ground black peppers
1 teaspoon turmeric
½ teaspoon ground coriander
¼ teaspoon ground cloves
1 teaspoon salt
juice 2 limes

1. Combine lamb cubes and yogurt, mix well, and marinate overnight.
2. In a small pan, heat butter or oil over moderate heat. Add onion, garlic, and gingerroot and sauté for a few minutes, stirring. Add all other ingredients except lime juice and sauté, stirring, another few minutes. Cool slightly.
3. Remove lamb cubes from yogurt, wiping off most but not all of the yogurt from cubes. Pour spice mixture over lamb, mix thoroughly, and marinate 4–6 hours.
4. Thread lamb on skewers and broil over hot charcoal, turning once, about 4 minutes each side. Sprinkle kebabs with lime juice and serve with pilau (p. 58) or nan (p. 220).

Serves 4–6

LAMB BIRYANI

A *biryani* is a north Indian dish equivalent to our casserole, in which several foods are cooked together to make a one-dish meal. In this case a lamb curry is baked with a rice pilau and condiments. The preparation is somewhat complicated, but the dish can be assembled and baked ahead of time and reheated in the oven before serving. The *biryani* is traditionally a rich and elaborate preparation, as evidenced by the butter, saffron, raisins, and nuts.

⅓ cup fresh or dried unsweetened coconut, grated
1 cup milk
1 teaspoon saffron threads
1 cup hot chicken stock

10 tablespoons butter or *ghee*
3 medium onions, chopped
1 tablespoon gingerroot, finely minced
2½ teaspoons salt
2 teaspoons ground cumin
1 teaspoon turmeric
1 teaspoon ground coriander
¼ teaspoon ground cloves
½ teaspoon crushed cardamom seeds, or ground cardamom
1 teaspoon crushed dried red peppers
½ teaspoon freshly ground black pepper
2 cups long-grain rice
2 cups boiling water
2 cloves garlic, finely minced
2 pounds boneless lean lamb, cut in 1-inch cubes
2 cups yogurt
juice 1 lime
½ cup dark raisins
½ cup slivered blanched almonds or cashews

1. Soak coconut in milk for one hour. Strain milk through cheesecloth, squeezing all liquid from coconut. Set liquid aside; discard coconut.
2. Soak saffron threads in hot stock for one hour. Set aside.
3. In a large pot heat 6 tablespoons butter or *ghee*. Add gingerroot and 2 of the chopped onions and sauté over moderate heat for a few minutes. Add one teaspoon salt, cumin, turmeric, coriander, cloves, cardamom, and peppers. Sauté, stirring, about 5 minutes.
4. Add rice and sauté, stirring, another few minutes. Add water, stir, cover, and cook over low heat 5 minutes. Remove from heat and let stand, covered.
5. In a large frying pan heat 4 tablespoons butter or *ghee*. Add one chopped onion and garlic and sauté over moderate heat for a few minutes. Add 1½ teaspoons salt and lamb cubes. Turn heat high and brown lamb cubes quickly on all sides. Add yogurt and lime juice and stir to blend.
6. To assemble: spread ⅓ of the rice mixture on the bottom of a large buttered casserole. Spread ½ of the lamb mixture on top of the rice, then sprinkle with ½ the raisins and ½ of the nuts. Add another ⅓ of the rice, cover with remaining meat, then add remaining raisins and nuts. Top with remaining rice.
7. Pour coconut milk and saffron-stock mixture carefully into casserole. Cover and bake in a preheatd 375° oven for one hour.

Serves 8

CURRIED MEATBALLS

A wonderful hot dish for a buffet table, these can be prepared a day or two in advance and reheated, or frozen.

1½ pounds lean ground beef
½ cup dry bread crumbs
1½ teaspoons salt
⅛ teaspoons freshly ground black pepper
1 teaspoon ground ginger
1 egg
2 tablespoons oil

1. Combine meat with all ingredients except oil. Mix thoroughly and shape into small balls.
2. In a large frying pan heat oil over moderate heat. Brown meatballs on all sides, turning frequently. Remove browned balls from pan with slotted spoon and add to the following sauce:

¼ cup butter
1 large onion, chopped
1 tart green apple, cored and chopped
2 cloves garlic, finely minced
1 teaspoon gingerroot, finely minced, or 1 teaspoon ground ginger
1 teaspoon salt
⅛ teaspoon freshly ground black pepper
¼ teaspoon crushed dried red peppers
2 teaspoons ground cumin
1 teaspoon ground coriander
½ teaspoon turmeric
½ teaspoon crushed cardamom seeds or ground cardamom
1 teaspoon curry powder
2 tablespoons flour
2 cups boiling beef stock, or 2 cups boiling water and 2 beef bouillon cubes
½ teaspoon Gravy Master or Kitchen Bouquet
¼ cup dark raisins
¼ cup golden raisins
2 heaping tablespoons any fruit chutney

1. In a large pot, melt butter over moderate heat. Add onion, apple, garlic, and gingerroot and sauté for a few minutes. Add salt, peppers, cumin, coriander, turmeric, cardamom, and curry powder. Sauté another few minutes, stirring.
2. Add flour and cook 2 minutes longer, stirring.

3. Add boiling stock and bring to the simmer, whisking to smooth. Add Gravy Master, raisins, and chutney, and mix well.
4. Add browned meatballs and simmer uncovered over low heat for about ½ hour. Serve hot with plain rice, if desired.

Serves 6

SPICED CHICKEN CUTLETS

A fine example of Indian culinary art, this dish should please the most knowledgeable and fastidious eater.

3 pounds boned chicken breasts, skinned
flour for dredging
4–5 tablespoons clarified butter or *ghee*
salt and pepper
2 tablespoons butter or *ghee*
1 tablespoon gingerroot, finely minced
6 cloves garlic, minced
1 small onion, minced
2 teaspoons mustard seed
1½ cups yogurt
½ teaspoon cumin
½ teaspoon ground coriander
juice ½ lime
salt to taste
2–3 tablespoons fresh coriander leaf, chopped (optional)

1. Cut chicken breasts in half, then pound between sheets of waxed paper until the cutlets are of uniform thickness, about ¼-inch thick.
2. Heat butter or *ghee* in a large frying pan over moderate heat. Dredge cutlets lightly with flour, then sauté a few minutes on each side until golden brown. Remove cutlets from pan, salt and pepper lightly, set aside and keep warm while preparing sauce.
3. In the same pan, melt butter or *ghee*, add ginger, garlic, onion, and mustard seed and fry over moderate to high heat, stirring, until mustard seeds start to pop and mixture smells good.
4. Turn heat down a little, add yogurt, cumin, coriander, and lime juice and mix well. Heat until simmering. Taste for salt and add a dash or two if needed. Pour hot sauce over chicken cutlets (or return cutlets to pan and heat through) and garnish with chopped coriander, if desired. Serve with a rice pilaf cooked in chicken stock and lightly flavored with saffron and cinnamon.

Serves 6–8

TANDOORI CHICKEN

This famous dish of northern India is so named because it is cooked in the *tandoor*, a small clay oven heated to very high temperatures with charcoal at the bottom. The chicken is spitted and roasted in the oven over the charcoal, while loaves of *nan* (see p. 220) are baked directly on the hot clay walls of the oven. The spice mixture that flavors the chicken gets its charactersitic red color from the ground annatto seeds.

3 small broiling chickens
3–4 cups yogurt
1 tablespoon gingerroot, finely minced
6 cloves garlic, finely minced or mashed
3 bay leaves, crumbled
2 tablespoons ground annatto seeds (*achiote*)
1½ teaspoons ground cumin
1–2 teaspoons crushed dried red peppers
½ teaspoons ground cloves
2 teaspoons cinnamon
½ teaspoon freshly ground black pepper
½ teaspoon crushed cardamom seed or ground cardamom
1 teaspoon ground coriander
3 teaspoons salt
juice of 3 limes

1. Skin the chickens completely and coat them inside and out with yogurt. Marinate in the refrigerator overnight.
2. Mix all the other ingredients except the lime juice and add just enough yogurt to make a thick paste. Remove chickens from marinade and wipe most but not all yogurt off of them. Prick the chickens all over with a sharp fork, then thoroughly rub the spice mixture all over them. Marinate 4–6 hours.
3. Roast chickens in a pan in a hot preheated 450° oven for 40–45 minutes, or spit and roast over hot charcoal, turning frequently, until tender.
4. Cut chickens in half and sprinkle liberally with lime juice. Serve with *nan*.

Serves 6

CODFISH IN COCONUT CURRY

¼ cup dried unsweetened coconut, shredded
¾ cup milk
¼ cup butter or *ghee*
1 large onion, sliced
1 teaspoon gingerroot, finely minced
1 teaspoon ground cumin
½ teaspoon turmeric
½ teaspoon ground coriander
¼ teaspoon ground cloves
¼ teaspoon crushed dried red peppers
2 teaspoons salt
¼ teaspoon freshly ground black pepper
½ teaspoon saffron, crushed
2 pounds codfish steaks (halibut, haddock, or any thick, firm white fish
   may be substituted)
juice 1 lime

Garnish: chopped fresh coriander

1. Combine coconut and milk. Let stand one hour, then strain through
   cheesecloth, squeezing out all liquid and discarding coconut.
2. In a large heavy skillet melt butter over moderate heat. Add onion,
   gingerroot, cumin, turmeric, coriander, cloves, salt, peppers, and
   saffron. Sauté, stirring, about 5 minutes.
3. Add fish steaks and sauté briefly on both sides.
4. Add coconut milk and lime juice, bring to a simmer and cook over
   low heat for about 15 minutes, turning steaks once. Serve with plain
   rice. Garnish with chopped fresh coriander, if desired.

Serves 4–6

SEEKH KEBABS

1 pound lean ground beef or lamb
¼ cup chick pea flour or potato flour
1 medium onion, finely minced
1 clove garlic, finely minced
1 teaspoon gingerroot, finely minced
1½ teaspoons salt
⅛ teaspoon freshly ground black pepper
2 teaspoons ground cumin
½ teaspoon ground coriander
¼ teaspoon ground cloves
¼ teaspoon crushed dried red peppers
juice 1 lime
½ cup yogurt
2 tablespoons melted butter

1. Combine all ingredients and knead thoroughly with the hands. Chill for at least 2 hours.
2. Form mixture into eight 3–4 inch cylindrical kabobs and broil over hot charcoal about 5 minutes, turning once. Serve hot with *pilau* or *nan*.

Serves 4

PILAU

¼ teaspoon saffron threads or powdered saffron
¼ cup hot water
¼ cup butter or *ghee*
1 medium onion, finely chopped
2 teaspoons gingerroot, finely minced, or 1 teaspoon ground ginger
1 teaspoon ground cumin
½ teaspoon ground coriander
½ teaspoon turmeric
½ teaspoon cinnamon
¼ teaspoon ground cloves
¼ teaspoon crushed dried red peppers
⅛ teaspoon freshly ground black pepper
1 cup long-grain rice
1¾ cups hot chicken stock (or boiling water with bouillon cubes)
⅓ cup dark raisins
⅓ cup cooked or frozen green peas
¼ cup chopped or slivered almonds or cashews

1. Soak saffron in ¼ cup hot water for ½ hour.
2. In a medium pot heat butter over moderate heat. Add onion, gingerroot, and all spices and sauté, stirring, about 5 minutes. Add rice and cook another 5 minutes, stirring, until rice is golden and all butter is absorbed.
3. Add saffron water and stock. Cover and cook over low heat for 15–20 minutes until all liquid is absorbed and rice is tender.
4. Add raisins, peas, and nuts. Let stand, covered, 5 minutes.

Serves 6

FUL GOBI
(Cauliflower Curry)

1 medium head cauliflower
3 tablespoons butter or *ghee*
1 medium onion, finely chopped
2 cloves garlic, finely minced
1 teaspoon fennel seeds
2 teaspoons mustard seeds
1 teaspoon cumin seeds
1 teaspoon salt
⅛ teaspoon freshly ground black pepper
¼ cup water
½ teaspoon ground coriander
½ teaspoon ground cumin
½ cup fresh or frozen peas

1. Cut leaves and tough stem from cauliflower; separate head into medium sized flowerets.
2. In a large skillet or pot, heat butter or *ghee* over moderate heat. Add onion, garlic, fennel, mustard, and cumin seeds and sauté, stirring, until mustard seeds begin to pop. Add salt, pepper, and cauliflower to pot and mix well. Add water, cover, and cook over low heat for about 10 minutes.
3. Add ground coriander, cumin, and peas to pot and continue to cook, uncovered, until peas are just done. Shake pot frequently, Curry will be moderately dry.

Serves 4–6

SPICED PURÉE OF GREENS AND POTATO

This is an absolutely superb dish that can be served as part of an Indian meal or as an accompaniment to almost any roast meat or poultry. Any combination of greens can be used—spinach, kale, collard, mustard greens, etc.—but my personal preference is a mixture of spinach and collard.

1 pound fresh spinach, kale, collard greens, etc., or mixture
3 medium potatoes, peeled and cubed
2 heaping tablespoons yogurt
½ teaspoon salt
2 tablespoons oil
1 small onion, minced
3 cloves garlic, minced
½ tablespoon fresh gingerroot, minced
1 teaspoon mustard seed
½ teaspoon cumin
¼ teaspoon ground coriander
few drops of lime juice

Garnish: 2–3 tablespoons fresh coriander, chopped

1. Remove tough stems from greens, wash thoroughly, drain. Cook the greens in the water clinging to the leaves just until wilted. Drain again, then purée in a blender or food processor.
2. Cook the potatoes in boiling water until tender. Drain, then purée with the yogurt. Combine green and potato purées, add salt, and mix well.
3. In a medium sized skillet, heat oil over moderate to high heat. Add onion, garlic, gingerroot, and mustard seed and fry, stirring, until mustard seeds begin to pop and mixture smells good. Add mixed purée and continue to cook, stirring, until mixture is very hot.
4. Sprinkle cumin, ground coriander, and lime juice over purée and mix well. Garnish with fresh coriander and serve.

Serves 4

DHAL
(Split Pea Curry)

1 cup orange or yellow split peas
¼ cup butter or *ghee*
1 medium onion, chopped
2 cloves garlic, finely minced
1 teaspoon mustard seeds
1 teaspoon ground cumin
½ teaspoon ground fenugreek
½ teaspoon ground coriander
1 teaspoon turmeric
2 teaspoons salt
¼ teaspoon finely ground black pepper
¼ teaspoon crushed dried red peppers
1 cup fresh or canned tomatoes, coarsely chopped
2 medium potatoes, peeled and cubed (optional)
juice 1 lime

1. Rinse split peas and soak in water for several hours or overnight. Drain thoroughly.
2. In a large pot, melt butter or *ghee* over moderate heat. Add onion, garlic, and mustard seed and sauté for a few minutes until mustard seeds begin to pop. Add all other seasonings and continue to sauté, stirring, for a few more minutes.
3. Add tomatoes, drained split peas, and enough water to cover. Simmer uncovered for about one hour or until split peas are tender. Potatoes may be added for last 20 minutes of cooking. Stir in lime juice and serve hot with plain rice or chapattis.

Serves 6–8

MIXED VEGETABLE CURRY

2 tablespoons oil or butter
1 onion, chopped
3 cloves garlic, mashed
1 teaspoon cumin
1 teaspoon ground ginger
½ teaspoon turmeric
½ teaspoon ground fenugreek
1 teaspoon salt
¼ teaspoon freshly ground black pepper
4–6 small potatoes, peeled and cut in 1-inch cubes
1 cup string beans, cut in 1-inch pieces
1 large red or green pepper, sliced
½ small head cabbage, coarsely chopped
1 cup yogurt

Garnish: chopped fresh coriander

1. In a medium sized pot or deep skillet, heat oil or butter over low to moderate heat. Add onion, garlic, and other seasonings and sauté, stirring, until onion is soft and spices smell good.
2. Cook potatoes and string beans in boiling salted water for a few minutes. Drain.
3. Add potatoes, string beans, and other vegetables to spice mixture; stir in yogurt and mix well. Cook uncovered over low heat for about 30–40 minutes, stirring occasionally. Garnish with chopped fresh coriander if desired.

Serves 6

NOTE: Other vegetables can be added to or substituted: cauliflower, peas, chick peas, chopped tomatoes.

CENTRAL ASIA

For the purposes of this book, the area we are calling central Asia is quite a large one, ranging from Afghanistan in the east, westward through Iran, Iraq, and into Turkey, the westernmost part of Asia. It also includes certain regions of the Soviet Union traditionally known as Armenia, Georgia, and the Caucasus. This is an area of mountains, steppes, and grasslands, with hot summers and cold winters.

It is in this part of the world where the cereal grains wheat and barley first were cultivated some five to six thousand years ago. These two grains still dominate the diet, even though rice has been introduced and very widely accepted. Wheat is used in flour for breads and as bulgur, a cracked wheat cereal that is cooked in liquid and used as a basis for many dishes.

Central Asia is the region where sheep and goats originally were domesticated and it remains the enclave of herdsmen and pastoral nomads who guide their flocks from one grazing area to another. Lamb is by far the most common meat, and yogurt is used pervasively. This, too, is the area where many of the most familiar temperate fruits and nuts are thought to have originated: apples, apricots, pomegranates, plums, quince, almonds, walnuts, pistachios. Many of these fruits are dried for winter use, and such products as raisins and dried apricots may have had their beginnings here.

Spit-roasting meat over an open fire is the characteristic cooking technique of the nomad; wherever the kabob is found in the areas adjacent to central Asia, you may be fairly certain it was introduced by a highland group. Such dishes as *seekh kebab* in northern India, *shashlik* in Russia and eastern Europe, *shish kebab* in Turkey and the Middle East, and *souvlakia* in Greece all are likely to have had their origin in the steppes of central Asia. The Huns, Scythians, Tartars, and Mongols have earned their nomadic appellation; they managed throughout their history to get around a large part of the world, sharing their culinary traditions.

As is the case in most temperate regions where there is a greater reliance on meats and animal products (yogurt, milk, and cheese), there is less emphasis on the seasonings and sauces that characterize southern and tropical cuisines. The complex spice mixtures of India gradually diminish in use from Afghanistan westward, and the prevalent garnish, fresh coriander leaf, is replaced by dill. Cinnamon is the spice most commonly used throughout central Asia, frequently combined with a variety of fruits and nuts.

The tremendous importance of yogurt in another flavor principle of central Asia is discussed in the chapter on General Principles   II cultured milk products, pp. 182.

CENTRAL ASIAN RECIPES

CHICKEN IN POMEGRANATE AND WALNUT SAUCE
MIDDLE EASTERN STUFFED CHICKEN
MEATBALLS WITH FRUIT
AFGHANI PILAU

CHICKEN IN POMEGRANATE AND WALNUT SAUCE

3 chicken breasts, cut in half
1 tablespoon butter
1 tablespoon oil
1 large onion, chopped
½ cup pomegranate syrup (see below)
½ cup chicken stock
½ cup walnuts, freshly ground
1 teaspoon cinnamon
⅛ teaspoon freshly ground black pepper
juice 1 lemon

1. In a large skillet, melt butter and oil over moderate heat. Brown chicken breasts on both sides; remove from pan and salt and pepper lightly.
2. To oil in pan add onion and sauté just until onion starts to brown. Add all other ingredients, mix well, and bring to a simmer. Return chicken breasts to pan, cover, and cook over low heat for about ½ hour.
3. Uncover pan and allow sauce to thicken. When chicken is done, remove from pan, set aside and keep warm. Cook sauce rapidly until it is fairly thick. Taste for salt; pour over chicken and serve with rice or bulgur pilaf.

Serves 4–6

To make pomegranate syrup: With a hand or electric juicer, squeeze the juice from 8–10 pomegranates. Strain the juice of any seeds and combine in a small pot with ½ cup sugar and a few drops of lemon juice. Cook over moderate heat for about 20 minutes until juice is clear and slightly syrupy. Store in a covered jar in the refrigerator. Pomegranates are readily available usually in the fall and early winter. Take advantage of them and make enough syrup to last for a while. It is wonderful in fruit salad or in mixed drinks. Grenadine syrup used to be made from real pomegranate juice but now is made with red food coloring, and is a bartender's standby.

MIDDLE EASTERN STUFFED CHICKEN

¼ cup butter
1 small onion, minced
½ cup bulgur
1 teaspoon cinnamon
1 cup chicken stock
⅓ cup tomato sauce
¼ cup dried apricots, finely chopped
¼ cup raisins
¾ teaspoon salt
dash freshly ground black pepper
1 tablespoon lemon juice
4–4½-pound roasting chicken
¼ cup honey
3–4 tablespoons sesame seeds

1. In a medium saucepan, heat 2 tablespoons butter over moderate heat. Add the onion and sauté, stirring, about 5 minutes. Add bulgur and sauté, stirring, another 5 minutes.
2. Add cinnamon, stock, tomato sauce, apricots, raisins, ¼ teaspoon salt, pepper, and lemon juice. Cook, covered, over low heat about 5 minutes. Remove from heat and let stand, covered, one hour.
3. Wash chicken, then dry inside and out with paper towels.
4. In a small saucepan, heat honey, 2 tablespoons butter, and ½ teaspoon salt over low heat until butter melts.
5. Stuff chicken with bulgur mixture. Place in roasting pan, then brush thoroughly with honey-butter mixture. Roast in a preheated 350° oven 1¼ hours. Brush frequently with reserved honey-butter mixture while roasting.
6. After one hour, baste chicken for the last time with honey-butter and drippings from pan. Carefully sprinkle sesame seeds all over the surface of the chicken. Return to oven for 15 more minutes. Let stand 5 minutes before carving.

Serves 6

MEATBALLS WITH FRUIT

⅔ cups bulgur
½ cup very hot water
2 pounds lean ground beef
1 small onion, finely minced
2 teaspoons salt
¼ teaspoon pepper
2 teaspoons cinnamon
2–3 tablespoons oil
1 medium onion, chopped
½ cup pomegranate syrup (see p. 65)
½ cup beef stock
⅛ teaspoon pepper
1 teaspoon lemon juice
1 teaspoon cinnamon
½ cup walnuts, freshly ground
½ cup mixed dried fruits, diced (peaches, apricots, apples, raisins, etc.)

1. Soak bulgur in hot water for about 45 minutes until water is completely absorbed. Combine bulgur, ground beef, onion, salt, pepper, and 2 teaspoons cinnamon and mix well. Shape into small walnut-sized balls.
2. Heat oil in large frying pan and brown meatballs over moderate heat, turning frequently. When balls are completely browned, remove from pan with slotted spoon and set aside.
3. Discard all but about one tablespoon oil from the pan. Sauté the onion until golden, then add all other ingredients and bring to a simmer. Return meatballs to the sauce and cook, uncovered, over low heat for about 20 minutes. Serve with rice pilaf.

Makes about 50–60 meatballs
Serves 6–8

AFGHANI PILAU

¼ cup pine nuts
¼ cup almonds, sliced or slivered
¼ cup butter
1 cup barley
1 cup bulgur
1 large onion, chopped
5 cups chicken stock
¼ teaspoon pepper
2 teaspoons cinnamon
¾ cup raisins
rind of 1 large orange, finely slivered (about 2 tablespoons) plus juice
1½–2 cups cooked lamb, shredded

1. In a small skillet, sauté the nuts in butter until lightly browned. Set aside.
2. In a large pot, combine all other ingredients except orange rind, lamb, and nuts. Cover and cook over low heat until all liquid is absorbed, about 50–60 minutes.
3. Stir in nuts and butter, orange rind and juice, and lamb. Mix well, place in a buttered casserole, cover, and bake at 300° for 30–40 minutes.

Serves 8

THE MIDDLE EAST

The Middle East, as its name suggests, lies in the heart of the Mediterranean, with easy access to Europe, Africa, and Asia through numerous land and sea routes. Traditionally this area has served as a middleman, conveying goods and ideas from East to West and back again. Although its unique geographic position and its mercantile history have made it open to many influences, it has retained its own character and individuality, particularly in terms of culinary traditions, some of which are many of thousands of years old.

The Middle East is the ancient cradle of wheat and barley cultivation, of chick peas and fava beans, of lamb and goat, and these foods still predominate in the basic diet. It is also the ancestral home of the olive oil industry; this oil is an important cooking and flavoring ingredient, whose use intensifies in southern Europe and the Mediterranean.

Sesame seed is used, not in the form of a flavoring oil as in the Orient, but as a thick paste called *tahini*, an important basic food. The yogurt tradition of central Asia remains strong as does the tradition of spit-roasted meats. But it is here that true ovens make their first appearance; baking and slow cooking in liquid are important techniques.

The Middle East uses a wide variety of flavorings. Fresh parsley, dill, and mint are herbs of paramount importance, and cinnamon remains the single most widely used spice. Lemon juice is used liberally, taking over the same flavoring function that vinegar or tamarind play in the Orient. The tomato, a relatively new import from the New World via the Mediterranean, is used with great frequency, both in salads and in seasoning sauces.

Two basic flavor principles are evident in the Middle East: the first is a combination of tomato sauce and cinnamon. Flavor variations are achieved with the use of lemon and dill. The second flavor principle is the combination of lemon and parsley, varied with the use of garlic and mint. It should be noted that some of the recipes illustrating these flavor principles do not come from countries technically belonging to the Middle or Near East. This simply testifies to the fact that culinary traditions do not restrict themselves necessarily to geographic or political boundaries. The cuisines of Greece and the Balkans, for example, have been heavily influenced by traditions from the Middle East and from central Asia.

MIDDLE EASTERN RECIPES

LEMON-PARSLEY PRINCIPLE

PURÉED CHICK PEA SOUP

HUMMUS BI TAHINI

BABA GHANOUJ

LEBANESE MEATBALLS

TABBOULEH

LEBANESE BEAN SALAD

KAFTA KEBABS

TOMATO-CINNAMON PRINCIPLE

LEBANESE MEAT PASTRIES

YAKNE

KIBBEH

MIDDLE EASTERN STUFFED EGGPLANT

PURÉED CHICK PEA SOUP

3–4 cups cooked or canned chick peas, drained
½ cup parsley, chopped
juice 1½ lemons
⅛ teaspoon freshly ground black pepper
3 cups beef or veal stock

Garnish: ¼ cup parsley, chopped

1. Purée chick peas and parsley in a blender or food processor.
2. Add chick pea mixture, lemon juice, and pepper to stock and simmer gently for 20 minutes. Add salt if necessary. Serve hot, with additional parsley sprinkled on top. (This soup can also be served chilled.)

Serves 6–8

HUMMUS BI TAHINI

Used as a sauce for fish or vegetables, but more importantly as an appetizer dip with Arabic bread.

2–2½ cups cooked chick peas (with cooking liquid), or 20-ounce can chick peas (with liquid)
⅓ cup fresh lemon juice
5 cloves garlic
½ cup parsley, chopped
¼ cup tahini (sesame paste)
¼ teaspoon salt
dash freshly ground black pepper
1 tablespoon olive oil

1. Drain chick peas, reserving liquid. Purée in blender or food processor with lemon juice, garlic, and parsley. If more liquid is needed to blend properly, use some of the reserved chick pea liquid.
2. Place puréed mixture in a serving bowl and stir in tahini, salt and pepper. Mix to blend thoroughly.
3. Just before serving, pour olive oil on top of the hummus. Serve at room temperature as a dip with small triangles of Arabic bread. (This can be prepared a day ahead and refrigerated, but bring to room temperature before serving.)

Makes about 3 cups

BABA GHANOUJ

A spread or dip similar to hummus, but one that uses eggplant instead of chick peas.

2 medium eggplants
⅓ cup fresh lemon juice
5 cloves garlic
⅓ cup parsley, chopped
½ teaspoon salt
2 tablespoons olive oil
⅓ cup tahini

1. Broil whole unpeeled eggplants over charcoal, turning frequently, until outsides are charred and insides are soft; or, make several slashes in eggplants and bake in a hot 450° oven for about 40 minutes or until insides are soft. Cool eggplants, then carefully remove the skin and discard.
2. Purée eggplant pulp in blender or food processor with lemon juice, garlic, parsley, salt, and olive oil.
3. Place purée in serving bowl and stir in tahini, blending well. Serve at room temperature with triangles of Arabic bread. (This can be prepared a day ahead and refrigerated, but bring to room temperature before serving.)

Makes about 2 cups

LEBANESE MEATBALLS

⅓ cup bulgur
¼ cup hot water
2 tablespoons butter
1 medium onion, finely chopped
1½ pounds lean ground beef or lamb
¼ cup parsley, finely chopped
1½ teaspoons salt
⅛ teaspoon freshly ground black pepper
1 teaspoon cinnamon
½ teaspoon crushed dried basil
1 egg, lightly beaten
¼ cup lemon juice
2 tablespoons tomato paste

1. Combine bulgur and hot water, mix well, and let stand one hour.
2. In a large frying pan, melt butter over moderate heat; add onion and sauté until tender.

3. Combine sautéed onion, bulgur, ground meat, and all other ingredients and mix thoroughly. Shape into walnut-sized balls. Brown slowly over moderate heat in butter remaining in pan, turning frequently, about 10–15 minutes. (These meatballs are delicate, so handle them gently.) Serve hot with yogurt as a sauce or dip, if desired.

Makes 40–48 meatballs
Serves 4–6 as main course

TABBOULEH

This is probably "the" national dish of Lebanon, and with good reason; it is one of the best salads in the world.

⅓ cup bulgur
¼ cup hot water
1 medium onion, grated
2 large bunches parsley, finely chopped (about 4 cups)
2 ripe tomatoes, coarsely chopped
1 tablespoon fresh mint, chopped (or crushed dried mint leaves)
⅓ cup fresh lemon juice
¼ cup olive oil
½ teaspoon salt
⅛ teaspoon freshly ground black pepper
1 head iceberg lettuce, separated into leaves

1. In a large bowl, mix bulgur with hot water; let stand one hour. Pound grated onion with pestle or back of heavy spoon into the soaked bulgur.
2. Mix parsley, tomatoes, and mint into bulgur.
3. Combine lemon juice, olive oil, salt, and pepper and beat with a fork until well blended. Pour over parsley mixture and mix well. Chill.
4. To serve: place *tabbouleh*, surrounded by lettuce leaves, on a large platter. To eat in the Lebanese manner, scoop up some *tabbouleh* with a lettuce leaf and eat with the hands.

Serves 8

LEBANESE BEAN SALAD

2–2½ cups cooked or canned red or white kidney beans, drained
½ cup parsley, chopped
1 small onion, finely chopped, or 3–4 scallions, finely chopped
1 tablespoon fresh mint, chopped, or 2 teaspoons crushed, dried mint leaves
1 large ripe tomato, coarsely chopped
1 medium cucumber, peeled and diced
¼ cup olive oil
¼ cup lemon juice
½ teaspoon salt
⅛ teaspoon freshly ground black pepper

1. Place beans, parsley, onion, mint, tomato, and cucumber in a serving bowl.
2. Combine olive oil, lemon juice, salt, and pepper and beat with a fork until creamy. Pour dressing over vegetables and mix thoroughly. Refrigerate at least 2 hours before serving. Mix again just before serving.

Serves 6

KAFTA KEBABS

1 pound lean boneless lamb
2 medium onions
½ bunch parsley
½ cup falafel mix (if unavailable, substitute ⅓ cup flavored bread crumbs)
1 teaspoon salt
¼ teaspoon freshly ground black pepper
½ teaspoon ground Syrian allspice (or ¼ teaspoon ground cloves and ¼ teaspoon cinnamon)
grated rind of 1 lemon
2 tablespoons melted butter

1. Grind lamb twice through meat grinder together with onions and parsley. Combine meat mixture with all other ingredients and mix thoroughly. Chill for at least 2 hours.
2. Form meat into 3-inch cylindrical kabobs by rolling between the palms of the hands. Grill kabobs over hot charcoal, turning once, about 4–6 minutes in all. Do not overcook. Serve hot with Arabic bread and salad.

Makes 8 kebabs
Serves 4

LEBANESE MEAT PASTRIES

1 medium onion, finely chopped
2 tablespoons butter
1 pound lean ground beef
2 teaspoons salt
dash freshly ground black pepper
1 teaspoon cinnamon
1 teaspoon crumbled dried basil
1 tablespoon tomato paste
¼ cup pine nuts
4–5 tablespoons yogurt
2 packages refrigerated unbaked biscuits (10 in each package).

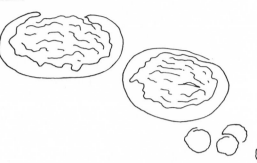

1. In a large frying pan, sauté onion in butter until soft. Turn heat high, add ground beef, and brown quickly, breaking up lumps with fork. When meat is browned, carefully drain off all liquid from pan and discard.
2. To browned meat add salt, pepper, cinnamon, basil, tomato paste, pine nuts, and just enough yogurt to bind mixture together. Mix well and set aside.
3. Remove one biscuit from tube and cut in half. With the fingers, flatten and stretch each half to form a circle approximately 1½ inches in diameter. This is most easily done right on the ungreased baking sheet on which the pastries will be baked. Repeat procedure for remaining biscuits. As you work, place biscuit circles touching each other on the baking sheet.
4. Place about one teaspoon meat mixture on each biscuit round, pressing it down and spreading carefully almost to edges. Bake in a preheated 400° oven for 10–15 minutes or until pastries are lightly browned. Serve warm, with a bowl of plain yogurt if desired.

Makes about 40 pastries

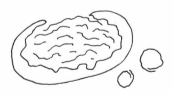

YAKNE

The Middle East (and the allied cuisines of Greece and the Balkans) is extremely fond of slow-simmered stews of meat and vegetables flavored with tomato and cinnamon. Chunks of lamb or beef, or ground meat, are used in combination with a large variety of vegetables: zucchini, peppers, cabbage, string beans, etc. *Yakne,* a very characteristic preparation, uses ground beef and eggplant.

1 large eggplant, peeled and cut in 1-inch cubes
¼ cup olive oil
1 large onion, chopped
1 pound lean ground beef
15-ounce can tomato sauce
2 teaspoons salt
⅛ teaspoon freshly ground black pepper
1½ teaspoons cinnamon

1. In a large frying pan, heat oil over high heat. Add eggplant cubes and sauté quickly, stirring, until eggplant is lightly browned. Remove eggplant from pan and set aside.
2. To same pan add one tablespoon oil, add onion, and sauté until lightly browned.
3. Add beef to pan and brown quickly over high heat. When beef is browned, carefully drain off all liquid from pan and discard.
4. To beef in pan add reserved eggplant cubes, tomato sauce, and seasonings. Mix well, then simmer, uncovered, over low heat for about one hour (or bake in a 375° oven for 40 minutes). Serve with rice or a simple pilaf.

Serves 4

KIBBEH

⅓ cup bulgur
¼ cup hot water
1 pound lean ground beef or lamb
1 medium onion, grated
8-ounce can tomato sauce
1 teaspoon salt
¼ teaspoon freshly ground black pepper
1½ teaspoons cinnamon
¼ cup pine nuts
2–3 tablespoons melted butter

1. Mix bulgur with hot water and let stand one hour. Combine bulgur with ground beef, onion, tomato sauce, salt, pepper, and cinnamon. Mix well and press flat into a greased 9- or 10-inch pie plate. Score with a sharp knife into 6 or 8 wedges.
2. Press pine nuts onto the top and pour melted butter over all.
3. Bake in a preheated 400° oven for 30 minutes. Cut into wedges along prescored lines. Serve hot, with plain yogurt as a sauce if desired.

Serves 4

MIDDLE EASTERN STUFFED EGGPLANT

2 medium eggplants
5 tablespoons olive oil
2¼ teaspoons salt
¼ teaspoon black pepper
3 tablespoons parsley, chopped
1 large onion, chopped
1 pound lean ground beef or lamb
8-ounce can tomato sauce
1½ teaspoons cinnamon
¼ teaspoon ground allspice
1 tablespoon lemon juice
¼ cup pine nuts
¼ cup dark raisins

1. Cut stem ends off eggplants, then cut eggplants in half lengthwise. With a sharp knife or spoon (a grapefruit knife is useful for this), carefully remove most of the pulp from the eggplant halves, leaving shell intact. Dice the eggplant pulp.
2. In a large frying pan, heat 4 tablespoons oil over moderate heat, then add diced eggplant and sauté slowly, stirring occasionally, until eggplant is soft and browned, about 8–10 minutes. Remove eggplant from pan and set aside. Stir in ¼ teaspoon salt, dash pepper, and parsley.
3. Add one tablespoon oil to pan and sauté onion until tender. Turn heat high, add ground meat and brown quickly. When meat is completely browned, carefully pour off all liquid from pan and discard.
4. To the meat in the pan add tomato sauce, 2 teaspoons salt, ¼ teaspoon pepper, cinnamon, allspice, lemon juice, and eggplant cubes. Simmer gently about 10 minutes or until liquid is somewhat reduced. Stir in pine nuts and raisins.
5. Stuff eggplant shells with meat mixture and place in a baking dish with water in bottom. Bake, covered, in a preheated 400° oven ½ hour. Remove cover for last 10 minutes of baking.

Serves 4

WEST AFRICA

Sub-Saharan cuisines are neither rich nor complex, perhaps because the land has always suffered from a difficult climate and a paucity of natural resources. Food is scarce and the available protein-rich foods are sadly inadequate for a large part of the population. The cuisine most well defined in terms of flavor is that of West Africa; to a large extent, it has been shaped by food products introduced after the discovery of the New World, most notably corn, tomatoes, peppers (both mild and hot), and peanuts. The peanut (commonly called groundnut) serves not only as flavoring but also as an invaluable source of protein.

The basic grains of West Africa are wheat, rice, and millet; chicken and goat are the most common meats. A variety of starchy root vegetables is used, including yam, sweet potato, and cassava, and such tropical fruits as banana, plantain, mango, and papaya. Long, slow cooking is the most characteristic technique; soups and stews are the most common dishes, often thickened with okra (gumbo). It is this particular tradition that Africa has given back so richly to the New World, specifically to the cuisines of the Caribbean and to the Creole cuisine of New Orleans.

The basic flavor principle of West African cuisine is the combination of tomatoes, peanuts, and chile peppers (frequently in staggering amounts). Onions, sweet peppers, garlic, and dried shrimp are used for variations in flavor.

WEST AFRICAN RECIPES

AFRICAN PEANUT CHICKEN SOUP
GROUNDNUT STEW

See Also:
West African Chili p. 214

AFRICAN PEANUT CHICKEN SOUP

This is a superb soup; rich, creamy and full flavored. Since African cooks traditionally grind the peanuts to a smooth paste with a mortar and pestle, it is best to use a smooth, unflavored (no salt or sugar) peanut butter.

2 medium onions, chopped
2 large red and/or green peppers, chopped
2 tablespoons oil
3–4 cloves garlic, mashed
28-ounce can tomatoes, coarsely chopped
8 cups chicken stock
¼ teaspoon pepper
¼ teaspoon crushed hot red peppers
½ cup rice
1–1½ cups cooked chicken, chopped
⅔ cup peanut butter

1. In a large pot, sauté onions, peppers, and garlic in oil over moderate to high heat until onions are just beginning to brown.
2. Add all other ingredients except rice, chicken, and peanut butter, and simmer, uncovered, over low heat for about one hour.
3. Add rice and chicken and simmer for about 10–15 minutes or until rice is tender. Add peanut butter and mix or whisk until it is completely dissolved and smooth. Heat to a simmer and serve.

Serves 8–10

GROUNDNUT STEW

2 tablespoons peanut oil
2 medium onions, chopped
2–2½ pounds lean beef, cut in 1-inch cubes
4 red and/or green sweet peppers, chopped
4 cloves garlic, mashed
15-ounce can tomato sauce (2 cups)
½ teaspoon salt
¼ teaspoon black pepper
¼ teaspoon crushed red pepper (more or less to taste)
½ cup smooth peanut butter

1. In heavy pot or Dutch oven, heat oil, add onions and sauté until onions are soft.
2. Add beef cubes and brown on all sides.
3. Add all other ingredients except peanut butter, mix well, and cook,

covered, over low to moderate heat for about 2 hours or until beef is tender.

4. Add peanut butter and stir to blend well. Continue to cook, uncovered, until sauce is reduced and thickened, about one hour. Serve stew with plain rice.

Serves 4–6

NORTH AFRICA

The area of Africa above the Sahara is socially, culturally, and economically distinct from the rest of the continent. Its affiliations lie with the Arab world of the Near and Middle East, and with the Mediterranean, and these are the traditions that have shaped its cuisine. North Africa can be divided into two separate regions: the western part, including Morocco, Algeria, and Tunisia, and the eastern part, which includes Libya and Egypt. Although many similarities exist in culinary practice between these two areas, they are each quite unique.

The basic foods of the North African diet are very similar to those of the Middle East. The most widely used grains are rice and wheat. Wheat is used in bread flour and in semolina, a processed wheat product that forms the basis of couscous. The most common meats are chicken and lamb, with some fish in immediate coastal areas. There is a wide variety of vegetables, including peppers, eggplant, chick peas, lettuce, tomatoes, cucumbers, and zucchini. The most characteristic cooking technique is that of long, slow cooking or stewing. One of the most characteristic dishes is the *tajin*, a stew of mixed meat and vegetables, so named for the clay pot in which it is cooked. Steaming grains and vegetables for *couscous* is also a widely used technique.

In northwest Africa, particularly Morocco, a wide variety of spices is used; some of the mixtures are comparable to the elaborate spice mixtures of India. One of the most common is called *ras al hanout*, but again, like curry, this does not refer to a single flavor or combination of flavors, but to individual mixtures prepared by the cook or by the spice seller. The most common spices found in both the *ras al hanout* mixture and in Moroccan cooking are cinnamon, cumin, coriander, ginger, and turmeric. Combined with onions and/or tomatoes, olives and salted lemons, these ingredients form a basic flavor principle of Moroccan cuisine. The second great flavor tradition of Moroccan cooking is the above added to a wide variety of fruits, undoubtedly a heritage from the highlands of central Asia. The garnishing herb of choice is fresh coriander leaf.

The flavoring traditions of northeast Africa are somewhat simpler. Garlic is used more heavily and mint or parsley, rather than fresh coriander leaf, are the most common garnishing and flavoring herbs. Elaborate spice mixtures generally are not made but cumin is a much-used spice.

NORTH AFRICAN RECIPES

NORTHEAST AFRICA

EGYPTIAN VEGETABLE SOUP

KEFTA (EGYPTIAN LAMB KABOBS)

NORTHWEST AFRICA

HARIRA (MOROCCAN CHICKEN AND VEGETABLE SOUP)

MOROCCAN HONEY CHICKEN

BEEF AND VEGETABLE TAJIN

MOROCCAN BAKED FISH

MOROCCAN CARROT AND PEPPER SALAD

EGYPTIAN VEGETABLE SOUP

The combination of lentils, chick peas, and mixed vegetables, flavored with cumin, mint, and garlic has been traditional in Egypt from the most ancient times; with the exception of the peppers and tomatoes, relatively recent imports from the New World, this soup may well have graced the tables of the earliest pharaohs.

28-ounce can tomatoes, coarsely chopped, or 4–5 large fresh ripe
    tomatoes, coarsely chopped
1-pound can chick peas, with juice
⅓ cup lentils
4 cups chicken stock
1 medium onion, chopped
1 medium green pepper, chopped
1–2 cups fresh greens (spinach, collard, etc.), coarsely chopped
⅓ cup parsley, chopped
¼ teaspoon pepper
2 teaspoons cumin
1 tablespoon crushed, dried mint
4 cloves garlic, mashed

1. Combine all ingredients in a large pot. Simmer for about one hour, uncovered. Enjoy.

Serves 6–8

KEFTA
(Egyptian Ground Lamb Kabobs)

3 pounds lean ground lamb
1 tablespoon salt
½ teaspoon freshly ground black pepper
1½ tablespoons cumin
6 cloves garlic, mashed
3 tablespoons crushed, dried mint
oil for frying

Garnish: fresh mint leaves

1. Combine all ingredients except oil and fresh mint leaves and knead thoroughly with the hands. Form the mixture into small cylindrical kabobs, about 3 inches by 1 inch.

2. Pour enough oil to cover the bottom of a large frying pan. Over moderate heat, fry the *kefta*, turning frequently, until they are nicely browned on the outside but still slightly pink on the inside. Serve the kabobs garnished with chopped fresh mint.

Makes about 24–30 kefta
serves 6–8

NOTE: *Kefta* are frequently served in Egypt with a plain tomato sauce, but I like them best stuffed into a pocket of fresh Arabic bread and served with yogurt or a good lemony tomato-cucumber salad.

HARIRA
(Moroccan Chicken and Vegetable Soup)

2 tablespoons olive oil
1 large onion, sliced
2 teaspoons cumin
1 teaspoon ground coriander
1 teaspoon turmeric
28-ounce can tomatoes (with juice), coarsely chopped, or 4–5 large ripe tomatoes, chopped
6 cups chicken stock
2 cups cooked or canned chick peas
2 large red and/or green sweet peppers, chopped
¼ teaspoon freshly ground black pepper
2 small zucchini, diced
1–2 cups cooked chicken, coarsely chopped
¾–1 cup vermicelli, broken in 1-inch pieces
1 tablespoon yeast, dissolved in ¼ cup warm water

Garnish: ⅓ cup fresh coriander, chopped

1. In a large pot, saute onion, cumin, coriander, and turmeric in oil for a few minutes until onion is tender.
2. Add tomatoes, stock, chick peas, peppers, and black pepper, and simmer, uncovered, for about one hour.
3. Add zucchini, chicken, and vermicelli and cook for about 10 minutes more or until vermicelli is tender.
4. Just before serving, stir in dissolved yeast. (This gives a characteristic flavor to the *Harira*.) Garnish individual servings with fresh coriander and serve.

Serves 8–10

MOROCCAN HONEY CHICKEN

4–5 pounds chicken parts
28-ounce can Italian style tomatoes, with juice, coarsely chopped, or
    4–5 large ripe tomatoes, chopped
1 onion, chopped
4 cloves garlic, mashed
6-ounce can tomato paste
1 teaspoon salt
¼ teaspoon freshly ground black pepper
1 tablespoon cinnamon
2 teaspoons ground ginger
¼ cup honey
1 teaspoon cinnamon
2 tablespoons honey
2 tablespoons toasted sesame seeds

1. In a large heavy pot or Dutch oven, combine all ingredients except last three, mix well, and cook over low to moderate heat, covered, for about one hour or until chicken is very tender.
2. Remove chicken parts from pot and set aside.
3. Cook down sauce in pot over moderate heat, stirring occasionally, until it is quite thick, almost the consistency of preserves; when it is thick enough, add the additional cinnamon and honey, and taste for salt.
4. Return chicken parts to pot and cook until chicken is just heated through. Place on serving platter, coat well with sauce, and garnish with sesame seeds. Serve with rice or bulgur pilaf.

Serves 6–8

BEEF AND VEGETABLE TAJIN

A Moroccan-Jewish dish, this *tajin* combines the traditional Moroccan mix of spices and the traditional Jewish technique of long slow cooking for the Sabbath stew.

2 tablespoons olive oil
2 large onions, sliced
4 cloves garlic, mashed
2 pounds lean boneless beef, cut in 1-inch cubes
28-ounce can Italian style tomatoes, with juice, or 4–5 large fresh
    tomatoes, coarsely chopped
2 cups cooked or canned chick peas
4 medium potatoes, peeled and cut in 1-inch cubes

4 carrots, cut in chunks
2 teaspoons salt
½ teaspoon pepper
1 tablespoon cumin
2 teaspoons paprika
2 teaspoons ginger
1 teaspoon cinnamon
1 teaspoon ground coriander

⎰1 teaspoon cinnamon⎱
⎱1 teaspoon ginger   ⎰

1. In a large heavy pot or Dutch oven, heat the olive oil over moderate heat; add onions and sauté slowly until onions are golden.
2. Add all other ingredients, mix well, cover, and cook over low heat 4–6 hours. Remove cover for last half hour of cooking to thicken sauce.
3. Taste for salt. Add one additional teaspoon each cinnamon and ginger and mix well.

Serves 4–6

MOROCCAN BAKED FISH

2–3 pounds any sea fish (halibut, swordfish, cod, sea bass, etc.), whole or in thick steaks
2 tablespoons softened butter
1 tablespoon ground cumin
1 teaspoon ground coriander
½ teaspoon cinnamon
1 clove garlic, mashed
½ teaspoon salt
dash freshly ground black pepper
1 large onion, thinly sliced

Garnish: lemon slices and fresh coriander

1. If fish is whole, have it split and eviscerated and head and tail removed.
2. Combine butter with cumin, coriander, cinnamon, garlic, salt, and pepper. Mix well and spread on all sides of fish.
3. Place fish on a large piece of heavy-duty aluminum foil and cover with onion slices. Wrap fish securely and place in a preheated 400° oven for 30–40 minutes. Unwrap fish, place carefully on serving platter, pour juices over all, and garnish with lemon slices and chopped fresh coriander, if desired.

Serves 4–6

MOROCCAN CARROT AND PEPPER SALAD

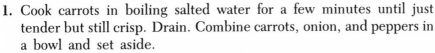

1 pound carrots, peeled and sliced
1 large sweet onion, sliced
3–4 green and red sweet peppers, sliced
4 tablespoons olive oil
2 teaspoons cumin
½ teaspoon cinnamon
1 teaspoon ginger
1 teaspoon turmeric
½ teaspoon salt
good grind fresh black pepper
juice ½ lemon

Garnish: 2 tablespoons fresh coriander, chopped

1. Cook carrots in boiling salted water for a few minutes until just tender but still crisp. Drain. Combine carrots, onion, and peppers in a bowl and set aside.
2. In a small sauce pan, combine olive oil and all seasonings except lemon juice and coriander. Stir over low heat for a few minutes. Pour oil and spice mixture over vegetables, mix well, and let stand for an hour or two (or covered, overnight, in the refrigerator, if desired).
3. Just before serving squeeze lemon juice over the vegetables and mix well. Garnish with chopped coriander. Serve at room temperature.

Serves 4–6

THE MEDITERRANEAN

If there is one food that defines Mediterranean cuisine as surely as the soybean defines Chinese cuisine, it is the olive. This fruit has flourished in the area for many thousands of years. Cured ripe (black) or unripe (green) in a salt brine, the olive is a piquant condiment, but it is the oil pressed from the ripe fruit that has become the hallmark of Mediterranean cuisine. Grades and varieties of olive oil differ from area to area: French and Italian types tend to be lighter in color, flavor, and aroma than the Spanish and Greek oils, which are darker gold in color and more robust in taste and odor.

For as long as olive oil has been used in the Mediterranean, it has been combined with a number of indigenous seasonings to form the classic flavor principles of the region. These seasonings include onions, garlic, parsley, basil, oregano, thyme, anchovies, and a variety of nuts including pine nuts, almonds, walnuts, and hazelnuts. The degree to which any of these seasonings is used varies from area to area and from dish to dish. After the discovery of the New World by the Spanish and Portuguese, however, a new set of flavoring ingredients was added to those indigenous to the Mediterranean, and these were, of course, the tomato and the bell pepper. Introduced to the Iberian peninsula in the sixteenth century, these vegetables rapidly became popular throughout the Mediterranean. Because they were a flavorful addition to sauces, they became firmly entrenched as part of the already existing flavor principles. In almost every sauce recipe, we can see the original principle (olive oil-garlic-basil, let us say), re-interpreted with the additon of the tomato and the pepper. Why the Mediterranean seized upon the tomato so ardently is not entirely clear. It may be because the fruit is grown very successfully and is cheap and easy to produce. It may be because the tomato sauce provides not only a flavorful vehicle for other ingredients, but also offers a visual appeal that Mediterranean sauces previously did not possess. It is interesting to note that, while a large part of the world chose the hot variety of the *capsicum* peppers from the New World, the Mediterranean selected primarily a milder variety, the bell pepper.

88

GREECE

Of all the countries of the European Mediterranean, Greece is the one that most clearly shows the influences of the Middle East. Unlike other regions with their tradition of leavened white bread, Greecian cooks still bake the flat, round *pita* and retain the central Asian traditions of spit-roasted meats and yogurt. When the tomato was introduced, it was combined, not with the prevailing olive oil principle, but with the more characteristically Middle Eastern spice, cinnamon.

In addition to the tomato-cinnamon principle, the flavor that best defines Greek cuisine is wild thyme (oregano), an herb that has grown uncultivated on the hillsides for centuries. This aromatic herb, in combination with olive oil and lemon, produces the characteristic taste of much of Greek cooking. It is varied frequently with the use of dill, an herb that is Middle Eastern rather than Mediterranean. Eggs substitute for the olive oil in the classic *avgolemono* (egg-lemon) sauce giving a bland taste and creamy texture.

GREEK RECIPES

TOMATO-CINNAMON PRINCIPLE

DOLMATHES (STUFFED GRAPE LEAVES)

PASTIZIO

GREEK CHICKEN

OLIVE OIL-LEMON-OREGANO

SOUPA AVGOLEMONO

CHARCOAL-BROILED SCALLOPS

BAKED FISH GREEK STYLE

SOUVLAKI

GREEK FRIED POTATOES

GREEK EGGPLANT SALAD

BAKED EGGPLANT AND ZUCCHINI

GREEK SALAD

DOLMATHES
(Stuffed Grape Leaves)

Dolmathes can be made in two ways: stuffed with meat and served hot with an egg-lemon sauce, or, as in this recipe, stuffed with rice and pine nuts and served cold as an hors d'oeuvre. They are one of the most popular and most commonly served hors d'oeuvres throughout the Balkans, Greece, and the Middle East.

30–40 grape leaves
½ cup olive oil
1 medium onion, finely chopped
½ cup raw long-grain rice
¼ cup pine nuts
3 tablespoons tomato paste
juice 1 lemon
½ teaspoon cinnamon
¼ teaspoon salt (increase to ½ teaspoon if using fresh, uncured grape leaves)
¾ cup boiling water

Garnish: lemon wedges

1. Rinse the grape leaves in warm water and drain in a colander.
2. In a medium saucepan, heat 2 tablespoons olive oil over moderate heat. Add onion and sauté until limp.
3. Add rice and pine nuts and sauté, stirring, 3–4 minutes.
4. Add tomato paste, lemon juice, cinnamon, salt, and boiling water, cover, and cook over low heat for 15–20 minutes, or until rice is tender and all liquid is absorbed. Remove from heat and let stand, covered, for one hour.
5. Placing a grape leaf right side up in front of you, place a heaping teaspoon of filling in a horizontal line along the middle of the leaf. Roll stem end of leaf up over filling, then fold in sides, then fold over top. Squeeze the stuffed rolled grape leaf gently in your hand; this will help keep it closed. Continue stuffing grape leaves until all the filling is used.
6. Pour 2 tablespoons olive oil in the bottom of a large shallow pot or frying pan. Place the stuffed grape leaves close together in a single layer in the pot. Pour over remaining ¼ cup olive oil. Place a large heavy plate or flat casserole cover over the grape leaves to keep them from unfolding while they cook.
7. Cover the pot and cook over very low heat for one hour. Let cool with plate on top of them. Remove from pan and refrigerate. (These are best made a day or two or up to a week ahead.) Bring to room temperature before serving. Serve garnished with lemon wedges.

Makes 30–40 stuffed grape leaves

PASTIZIO

1 pound pastizio noodles
1½ tablespoons butter or margarine
1 tablespoon salad oil
1 medium onion, chopped
1½ pounds lean ground beef
15-ounce can tomato sauce (2 cups)
1½ teaspoons salt
1 tablespoon cinnamon
¼ teaspoon freshly ground black pepper
1 pound ricotta or cottage cheese
2 eggs
½ teaspoon salt
2 tablespoons grated Parmesan cheese
dash pepper
¼ teaspoon grated nutmeg

1. Cook pastizio noodles in boiling salted water just until done. Drain thoroughly, mix with butter or margarine, and place in a buttered casserole.
2. In a large frying pan, heat oil and sauté onion until tender. Add ground beef and brown over high heat. When meat is thoroughly browned, carefully pour off all fat and liquid in pan and discard. To the beef, add the tomato sauce, salt, pepper, and cinnamon and cook over moderate heat until quite thick, about 15 minutes. Spoon meat mixture over noodles in casserole.
3. In a blender or food processor, blend cheeses, eggs, and other seasonings until smooth. Pour this mixture over the meat layer in casserole.
4. Bake casserole at 350° for about half an hour or until top layer is firm and just beginning to brown. Serve immediately.

Serves 6–8

GREEK CHICKEN

2–3 pounds frying chicken, cut in serving pieces
2 tablespoons butter
2 tablespoons olive oil
1½ teaspoons salt
¼ teaspoon freshly ground black pepper
16-ounce can Italian plum tomatoes
1 teaspoon cinnamon
juice 1 lemon

1. Dry the chicken pieces thoroughly with paper towels.
2. In a large frying pan, heat butter and olive oil over high heat. Add chicken pieces and brown quickly on both sides until golden. Sprinkle with salt and pepper.
3. Add tomatoes, cinnamon, and lemon juice, cover, and simmer over low heat about 30 minutes or until chicken is tender. Serve with rice.

Serves 4

SOUPA AVGOLEMONO

6 cups chicken stock
2 tablespoons fresh dill, chopped
⅓ cup orzo or *seme di melone* (tiny seed-shaped pasta) or rice
2 eggs
juice 1 large lemon

1. In a large pot heat stock with dill. Simmer over low heat ½ hour.
2. Add pasta or rice and cook 15–20 minutes or until pasta is tender.
3. Just before serving, beat eggs with lemon juice in a small bowl. Add about ½ cup hot soup slowly in a thin stream to beaten eggs, stirring constantly to prevent eggs from curdling.
4. Return egg mixture to soup pot, stirring all the while. Bring just to a simmer but do not allow to boil.

Serves 8

NOTE: Pieces of cooked chicken can be added to the *avgolemono* to make a heartier soup. It is also delicious prepared with fish stock and bits of cooked fish and/or seafood.

CHARCOAL-BROILED SCALLOPS

2 pounds sea scallops
¼ cup fresh lemon juice
¼ cup olive oil
1 tablespoon coarse or kosher salt
dash freshly ground black pepper
2 tablespoons crumbled dried oregano
2 green peppers, seeded and cut in 1-inch pieces
1 large onion, quartered and separated into layers

1. If scallops are very large, cut them in half. Place in a glass or ceramic bowl.
2. Combine lemon juice, olive oil, salt, pepper, and oregano. Beat with fork until creamy. Pour over scallops and mix well. Let stand for up to 2 hours in refrigerator.
3. Remove scallops from marinade and thread on skewers alternately with pieces of green pepper and onion. Grill over hot charcoal about 5 minutes, turning once.

Serves 4–6

BAKED FISH GREEK STYLE

2–3 pounds any fish: cut steaks, thick fillets, or whole (if whole, have fish split and eviscerated and head and tail removed)
¼ cup olive oil
juice 1 lemon
2 tablespoons crumbled dried oregano
1 teaspoon salt
dash freshly ground black pepper
1 lemon, thinly sliced
2 tomatoes, sliced
1 sweet red onion, sliced

1. Place fish in a baking dish or casserole in a single layer.
2. Combine olive oil, lemon juice, oregano, salt, and pepper and mix well. Pour over fish and let stand ½ hour.
3. Place sliced lemon, tomatoes, and onion over and around fish. Cover baking dish with aluminum foil and place in a preheated 400° oven. Bake 20–40 minutes until fish flakes easily with a fork.

Serves 4–6

SOUVLAKI

¼ cup olive oil
juice 1 lemon
2 tablespoons crumbled dried oregano
1 teaspoon salt
¼ teaspoon freshly ground black pepper
2 pounds boneless leg of lamb or lamb sirloin, cut in 1-inch cubes
1 large onion, cut in 1-inch pieces
2 green peppers, cut in 1-inch pieces

1. Combine olive oil, lemon juice, oregano, salt, and pepper and beat well with a fork.
2. Pour over lamb cubes and mix well to insure that all cubes are coated with marinade. Marinate 4–6 hours.
3. Thread lamb cubes on skewers alternately with pieces of onion and green pepper. Brush thoroughly with marinade.
4. Grill over hot charcoal, turning once, about 4 minutes on each side. Serve with fresh pita and salad.

Serves 4–6

GREEK FRIED POTATOES

4–4½ cups thinly sliced, unpeeled potatoes
2 tablespoons olive oil
2 tablespoons vegetable oil
1 large onion, chopped
1 teaspoon salt
¼ teaspoon freshly ground black pepper
2 teaspoons crumbled dried oregano
juice ½ lemon

1. Cover potato slices with cold water and let stand 2 hours. Drain thoroughly and dry as well as possible with paper towels.
2. In a large frying pan heat oils over moderate heat. Add onion and sauté 2–3 minutes.
3. Turn heat up high and add potato slices. Cook over high heat, turning constantly with spatula, about 10 minutes or until potatoes are tender but not soft.
4. Add salt, pepper, oregano, and lemon juice and fry, stirring, a few more minutes.

Serves 4

GREEK EGGPLANT SALAD

1 large eggplant
¼ cup olive oil
juice 1 lemon
1 clove garlic, mashed
1 small onion, finely chopped
1 teaspoon salt
dash freshly ground black pepper
1 tablespoon crumbled dried oregano
2 tablespoons parsley, finely chopped

1. Make several gashes in eggplant with a sharp knife, place in a pan and bake in a preheated 450° oven for 30–40 minutes or until eggplant is soft all over. Remove from oven and let cool.
2. Cut stem end off eggplant and peel off skin. Place eggplant in a bowl and mash thoroughly with a fork or heavy spoon.
3. Add olive oil gradually, mixing well after each addition.
4. Add lemon juice, garlic, onion, salt, pepper, oregano, and parsley and mix well. Serve at room temperature garnished with black olives and tomato wedges, if desired.

Serves 4–6

BAKED EGGPLANT AND ZUCCHINI

1 medium eggplant, peeled, sliced, and quartered
2 or 3 zucchini, sliced
1 large onion, sliced
½ cup olive oil
¼ cup lemon juice
1½ teaspoons salt
¼ teaspoon freshly ground black pepper
1 tablespoon crumbled dried oregano
1 clove garlic, mashed

1. Place eggplant, zucchini, and onions in a deep casserole.
2. Combine olive oil, lemon juice, salt, pepper, oregano, and garlic and beat well. Pour over vegetables.
3. Cover casserole and bake in a preheated 375° oven 40–50 minutes. Serve hot.

Serves 6

GREEK SALAD

1 head iceberg lettuce, coarsely chopped
1 cucumber, peeled and sliced
2 tomatoes, cut in eighths
1 green pepper, seeded and chopped
2 scallions, chopped
½ cup Greek black olives
¼ cup feta cheese, crumbled
½ cup olive oil
⅓ cup lemon juice
2 teaspoons crumbled dried oregano
1 teaspoon salt
⅛ teaspoon freshly ground black pepper
1 clove garlic, mashed

1. In a large serving bowl, place all the vegetables, the olives and the cheese.
2. Combine olive oil, lemon juice, oregano, salt, pepper, and garlic and beat well with a fork. Pour over salad and mix gently but thoroughly.

Serves 6–8

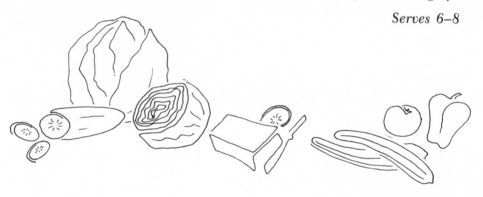

SOUTHERN ITALY

More than any other, the cuisine of southern Italy illustrates the fortuitous marriage between olive oil and the tomato. In the years following World War II, Italian food with its rich and flavorful tomato sauce quickly became the most popular "ethnic" cuisine in America; pizza and spaghetti are rivaled in popularity only by those native favorites, hot dogs and hamburgers.

The basic grain of Italy and all of the Mediterranean is wheat. It is used primarily as flour for leavened breads and for many kinds of pasta. The Italian passion for pasta is matched only by the Chinese, and perhaps for this reason is it so commonly believed that Marco Polo introduced pasta to the Italians after his travels to China in the thirteenth century. Actually, there is no mention of this in Polo's chronicles, and records show that Italy was producing pasta before trade began with China.

Other basics of Italian cuisine include a variety of vegetables— eggplant, zucchini, beans, mushrooms, leafy greens—and chicken, veal, and beef, fish and shellfish. Note that while the Greek and Middle Eastern cuisines use a great deal of lamb, the Italians rely more on beef, veal, and pork; these meats became even more important to the cuisines of northern and western Europe.

The ancient olive oil principles are still widely used in Italy, even though they are not as well known as later recipes which include the tomato. The classic oil principles, which also appear in southern France, are: the combination of olive oil, garlic, and parsley, with the frequent addition of anchovies; and the famous *pesto* (*pistou* in French), a sauce of olive oil, garlic, and fresh basil. When the tomato and the bell pepper appeared, they were combined with the above principles to form the classic tomato sauces of southern Italy.

SOUTHERN ITALIAN RECIPES

OLIVE OIL–GARLIC–PARSLEY/ANCHOVY
STUFFED PEPPER APPETIZER

ABOVE PLUS TOMATO
SPAGHETTI WITH RED CLAM SAUCE

OLIVE OIL–GARLIC–BASIL
PASTA-VEGETABLE SALAD
PESTO SAUCE
SOUPE AU PISTOU

ABOVE PLUS TOMATO
BASIC ITALIAN TOMATO SAUCE
CHICKEN CACCIATORE
CHICKEN LIVERS WITH SPAGHETTI
EGGPLANT PARMIGIANA
MARINATED GREEN BEANS

STUFFED PEPPER APPETIZER

4–5 medium sized, sweet red peppers
2 tablespoons olive oil
3 cloves garlic, mashed
2-ounce can anchovies with oil
1 cup coarse bread crumbs or corn flake crumbs
½ cup parsley, finely chopped
1 ripe tomato, chopped

1. Cut peppers in half; remove core and seeds.
2. In a medium saucepan, heat olive oil; add garlic and sauté until just beginning to turn golden.
3. Mash anchovies and oil with a fork; add this and all other ingredients to garlic and oil in pan. Mix thoroughly.
4. Stuff pepper halves lightly with crumb mixture; drizzle a little more olive oil over the tops.
5. Place stuffed peppers in a shallow oiled baking dish and bake at 350° for about 20 minutes.
6. Serve at room temperature on individual serving dishes garnished with a few sprigs of parsley.

(2 pepper halves per serving)
Serves 4–5

SPAGHETTI WITH RED CLAM SAUCE

A delicious meal that can be made in ½ hour from items off your pantry shelf. Of course, fresh clams or mussels can be used if available. The secret of the flavor is liberal amounts of fresh parsley and fresh garlic.

¼ cup olive oil
4 large cloves garlic, finely minced
28-ounce can crushed Italian style tomatoes
1 teaspoon salt
¼ teaspoon freshly ground black pepper
2 8-ounce cans minced, chopped or whole clams, with juice
½ cup parsley, finely chopped
1 pound spaghetti or linguine, cooked al dente according to package instructions

Garnish: finely chopped parsley

1. In a medium pot or skillet, heat olive oil over low heat; sauté garlic slowly, stirring, until very soft. Do not brown.
2. Add tomatoes, salt, pepper, and juice from clams. Cook over low heat, uncovered, about 20–30 minutes, stirring occasionally. Add parsley for last 10 minutes.
3. Just before serving, add clams and bring to a simmer. Serve over hot pasta, with additional parsley sprinkled on top if desired.

Serves 4

PASTA-VEGETABLE SALAD

A marvelous summer dish for lunch or the buffet table; bits of cooked chicken, ham, or seafood also can be added. Note that the sauce is a combination of a pesto and a vinaigrette. It will taste very salty by itself, but the pasta and vegetables absorb a great deal of flavor as they marinate; in fact, you may need to add a little salt just before serving.

1 pound small pasta (shells, twists, etc.)
1 pound fresh asparagus, cut in 1-inch pieces
1 small bunch broccoli, separated into small flowerets
½ pound fresh mushrooms, small whole or large sliced
1 sweet red pepper, finely chopped, or 3 tablespoons canned red pimiento, finely chopped
½ cup pitted black olives, sliced (optional)
¾ cup olive oil
¼ cup wine vinegar
4–5 cloves garlic
1 bunch fresh basil (about 1 cup tightly packed)
¼ cup grated Parmesan cheese
¼ teaspoon freshly ground black pepper
1 teaspoon salt

1. Cook pasta in boiling salted water just until tender but still firm. Do not overcook. Drain, rinse with cold water, and drain again.
2. Cook asparagus and broccoli in boiling water for just a few minutes until tender but still crisp. Drain and rinse in cold water.
3. In a blender or food processor, combine oil, vinegar, garlic, basil, cheese, salt, and pepper. Blend until smooth.
4. In a large bowl combine pasta and all vegetables. Pour sauce over and mix thoroughly. Cover and refrigerate several hours or overnight.
5. Just before serving, mix thoroughly again and taste for salt.

Serves 6–8

PESTO SAUCE

½ cup olive oil
1 cup (tightly packed) fresh basil leaves
4 cloves garlic
2 tablespoons pine nuts or walnuts
½ cup grated Parmesan cheese
small handful chopped parsley

1. Combine all ingredients in a blender and blend until smooth. Taste for salt; you may want just a dash or none at all. Serve over hot, freshly cooked pasta.

Makes enough for one pound of pasta

Cheater's Pesto (when you can't get fresh basil):

Substitute one cup (tightly packed) fresh spinach leaves, washed and drained and 3 tablespoons dried basil. This will not give you the authentic taste of the true *pesto*, but it is a very good substitute.

SOUPE AU PISTOU

½ cup dried white beans (marrow or navy)
2–3 onions, chopped
6 cups water
35-ounce can Italian style tomatoes
½ teaspoon freshly ground black pepper
6-ounce can tomato paste
½ pound string beans, cut in 1-inch lengths
2 medium potatoes, peeled and cut in ½-inch cubes

Pistou:
¼ cup olive oil
4 large cloves garlic
1 cup fresh basil leaves, tightly packed (or 3 tablespoons dried basil)
1 tablespoon salt

Garnish: garlic croutons

1. Soak beans in cold water several hours or overnight. Drain.
2. In a large pot, combine beans, onions, water, tomatoes, tomato paste, and pepper. Bring to a boil, then simmer over low heat, uncovered, for about 1½–2 hours, or until beans are tender.

3. Add string beans and potatoes and cook for another 20–30 minutes or until vegetables are tender.
4. To make *pistou:* In a blender combine olive oil, basil, garlic, and salt. Blend until smooth.
5. Stir *pistou* into simmering soup and stir for a few minutes until heated through. Serve soup garnished with a garlic crouton, if desired.

Serves 10–12

To make garlic croutons: see Onion Soup, p. 144

BASIC ITALIAN TOMATO SAUCE

¼ cup olive oil
1 large onion, chopped
3 cloves garlic, mashed
1 medium green pepper, seeded and chopped
6-ounce can tomato paste
15-ounce can tomato sauce
28-ounce can Italian style tomatoes
1 tablespoon crumbled dried oregano
1 tablespoon crushed dried basil
2 teaspoons salt
¼ teaspoon freshly ground black pepper
⅓ cup Parmesan cheese, freshly grated

1. In a heavy pot or Dutch oven, heat olive oil over moderate heat. Add onion, garlic, and green pepper and sauté, stirring, about 5 minutes.
2. Add tomato paste, sauce, tomatoes, oregano, basil, salt, and pepper. Cook uncovered over low heat for at least one hour, stirring occasionally. Just before serving, stir in cheese and mix well.

Makes about 8 cups,
enough for 1½–2 pounds of pasta

CHICKEN CACCIATORE

7 tablespoons olive oil
½ pound fresh mushrooms, sliced
2 green peppers, sliced
2–3 pound frying chicken, cut in serving pieces
1½ teaspoons salt
¼ teaspoon freshly ground black pepper
1 medium onion, chopped
2 cloves garlic, mashed
6-ounce can tomato paste
½ cup dry white wine
1 teaspoon crumbled dried oregano
2 teaspoons crushed dried basil
½ teaspoon dried thyme

1. In a large heavy frying pan or Dutch oven, heat 3 tablespoons olive oil. Add mushrooms and peppers and sauté quickly, stirring, over high heat. Remove from pan and set aside.
2. Add 4 tablespoons oil to pan. Add chicken pieces and brown on both sides over high heat. Sprinkle chicken with salt and pepper.
3. Add onion and garlic to pan and sauté another 3–4 minutes. Add tomato paste and sauté, stirring 2 minutes.
4. Add wine, oregano, basil, and thyme. Cover and cook over low heat 20–30 minutes or until chicken is tender. Remove cover, turn heat up high and reduce liquid quickly, shaking the pan.
5. Add reserved mushrooms and peppers, mix well, and serve.

Serves 4

CHICKEN LIVERS WITH SPAGHETTI

6 tablespoons olive oil
1 medium onion, chopped
4 cloves garlic, mashed
28-ounce can Italian style tomatoes, coarsely chopped
6-ounce can tomato paste
2 teaspoons salt
¼ teaspoon freshly ground black pepper
1 pound chicken livers, cut in half
2 teaspoons crumbled dried oregano
¼ cup red wine vinegar
¼ cup parsley, finely chopped
1 pound spaghetti, cooked al dente according to package instructions.

1. In a large saucepan, heat 3 tablespoons olive oil over moderate heat; add onion and 2 cloves garlic and sauté just until tender.
2. Add tomatoes, tomato paste, one teaspoon salt, and pepper. Simmer uncovered over low heat 40 minutes or more.
3. In a large frying pan heat 3 tablespoons oil. Add 2 cloves garlic and sauté 2 minutes.
4. Turn heat high, add chicken livers, and brown quickly on all sides, stirring. Add one teaspoon salt and oregano.
5. Add vinegar to pan and stir, scraping up brown bits from bottom. Simmer 2 minutes, then stir in parsley.
6. Add chicken liver mixture to tomato sauce and heat to simmering. Serve over hot cooked spaghetti.

Serves 4

EGGPLANT PARMIGIANA

At times the eggplant seems to be a sponge, with an unlimited ability to soak up the oil in which it is cooked. All too frequently the result is an unpleasantly oily dish. To control this, place a few tablespoons of oil in a large frying pan and heat over high heat. Place the eggplant slices in the pan and turn them over almost immediately so that both sides absorb a small amount of oil. Saute the slices quickly, turning frequently. The small amount of oil absorbed at the beginning of the cooking process is enough so that the eggplant will brown without sticking to the pan.

2 large eggplants, peeled and cut in ½-inch slices
6 tablespoons olive oil
1 large onion, chopped
2 cloves garlic, mashed
2 teaspoons crushed dried basil
1 teaspoon crumbled dried oregano
1 green pepper, seeded and chopped
28-ounce can Italian style tomatoes
6-ounce can tomato paste
2 teaspoons salt
¼ teaspoon freshly ground black pepper
1 pound ricotta or small-curd cottage cheese
2 eggs
½ teaspoon salt
⅛ teaspoon freshly ground black pepper
⅛ teaspoon freshly grated nutmeg
⅔ cup Parmesan cheese, grated

1. Sauté the eggplant slices in oil as described above. Set aside.
2. In a medium saucepan, sauté the onion and garlic in 3 tablespoons olive oil until translucent.

3. Add the basil, oregano, green pepper, tomatoes, tomato paste, salt, and pepper. Simmer uncovered over low heat for one hour.
4. In a blender or food processor, combine ricotta, eggs, salt, pepper, nutmeg, and half of the Parmesan. Blend until smooth.
5. To assemble: spread a few tablespoons of tomato sauce on the bottom of a large casserole or baking dish. Place ½ of the eggplant slices in the casserole, cover with ½ of the sauce and the remaining Parmesan cheese. Add rest of eggplant slices and cover with rest of tomato sauce. Pour cheese mixture over the top.
6. Bake uncovered in preheated 400° oven 30–40 minutes or until top is lightly browned and set.

Serves 8

MARINATED GREEN BEANS

1 pound green beans
2 medium onions, chopped
2 cloves garlic, mashed
¼ cup olive oil
1½ teaspoons salt
⅛ teaspoon freshly ground black pepper
1 teaspoon crushed dried basil
¼ cup parsley, chopped
1 cup fresh or canned Italian plum tomatoes, coarsely chopped

1. Snap ends off beans and remove strings, if any. Cook in boiling salted water for 2–3 minutes. Drain and place in baking dish or casserole.
2. In a small saucepan, sauté onion and garlic in olive oil until tender. Add salt, pepper, basil, parsley, and tomatoes and simmer uncovered over low heat 20 minutes.
3. Pour sauce over string beans and bake in a preheated 375° oven for 20–30 minutes. Cool. Serve at room temperature, mixing well before serving.

Serves 4

SOUTHERN FRANCE

The cuisine of Provence, a region in southern France, is similar in many ways to the cuisine of southern Italy, due undoubtedly to their common Roman heritage. This is the region of the vine and the olive, of the anchovy and the tomato, of salade Niçoise and the great bouillabaisses of Marseille. Garlic is used with less inhibition here than in the rest of France. And this is the only area of France where the bell pepper is used, clearly indicating the region's culinary affiliation with Mediterranean rather than classic French traditions.

In addition to the flavor principles already listed for southern Italy, southern France offers one that is unique; the combination of olive oil and the "herbes de Provence," a mix of thyme, rosemary, marjoram, and sage. This characteristic herb mixture is sold in little cloth bags throughout the region, along with the dried lavender for which Provence is famous. Used primarily for grilling meats and fish, this seasoning also may be used for vegetable dishes, soups, and sauces. Like the other olive oil principles, it combines beautifully with the tomato.

SOUTHERN FRENCH RECIPES

PROVENÇAL BEAN AND SAUSAGE SOUP

PROVENÇAL PÂTÉ

PROVENÇAL POT ROAST

RATATOUILLE

VEGETABLES PROVENÇAL AU GRATIN

See Also:
Bean Curd Provençal p. 211

PROVENÇAL BEAN AND SAUSAGE SOUP

2 cups dried white beans (pea, navy, marrow, etc.)
10 cups water
3 tablespoons olive oil
1 large onion, chopped
3 cloves garlic, mashed
6-ounce can tomato paste
2–3 carrots, sliced
3 stalks celery with leaves, chopped
1 teaspoon leaf sage
1 teaspoon marjoram
1 teaspoon thyme
1 teaspoon rosemary
½ teaspoon pepper
1 pound garlic or Polish-type sausage, sliced
2 teaspoons salt

1. Soak beans several hours or overnight in cold water to cover. Drain.
2. In a large pot, heat olive oil over moderate heat. Add onion and garlic and sauté until golden.
3. Add all other ingredients except sausage and salt and simmer uncovered for 1½–2 hours or until beans are tender.
4. Add sausage and salt and cook for another 20–30 minutes.

Serves 8–10

PROVENÇAL PÂTÉ

A marvelous combination of the typical herb mixture of Provence and the butter, cream, and brandy of classic French tradition.

4 tablespoons butter
1 medium onion, chopped
2 pounds chicken livers
1 teaspoon salt
½ teaspoon freshly ground black pepper
1½ teaspoons each: thyme, rosemary, marjoram, leaf sage
¼ cup brandy or Cognac
¼ cup heavy cream

1. In a medium skillet heat butter over moderate heat. Add onion and sauté until onion is soft. Add chicken livers, turn heat up slightly higher and sauté, stirring, until livers are nicely browned and firm but still a little pink on the inside. While they are sautéeing, sprinkle the livers with salt, pepper, and herbs.

2. When livers are done, remove them from pan to a food processor. To the butter and brown bits in pan add the brandy or Cognac and cook, stirring, until mixture simmers. Scrape pan well to loosen all residue stuck to the bottom. Cook for a minute or so more, stirring.
3. Add mixture from pan to the livers in food processor. Purée until smooth. Pour in heavy cream and blend again. Pour mixture into a serving bowl or terrine and chill. (You can pack the pâté into a saran-lined mold to chill. Unmold the pâté, remove the plastic wrap, glaze with a light beef and Madeira flavored aspic, and decorate with sliced mushrooms and bits of scallion and carrot for color.)

Makes about 3 cups

DAUBE DE BOEUF PROVENÇAL
(Provençal Pot Roast)

4 pound boneless beef round or rump roast
3 tablespoons olive oil
3 medium onions or 2 leeks, chopped
2 green and/or red sweet peppers, chopped
3 cloves garlic, mashed
1 cup canned or fresh tomatoes, coarsely chopped
1 tablespoon salt
¼ teaspoon freshly ground black pepper
2 teaspoons rosemary
2 teaspoons thyme
1 teaspoon marjoram
1 teaspoon leaf sage
½ cup dry white wine
½ cup pitted green olives, sliced
½ cup parsley, finely chopped

1. Dry meat thoroughly with paper towels.
2. In a large heavy pot or Dutch oven, heat olive oil over moderate heat. Add onions, peppers, and garlic and sauté, stirring, for 5 minutes.
3. Add beef and brown slowly on all sides, turning frequently.
4. Add tomatoes, seasonings, and wine; cover, and cook over low heat about 2½–3 hours. Remove meat from sauce, cool slightly, then slice. Meanwhile, continue to cook sauce until it reduces and thickens slightly.
5. Stir olives and parsley into sauce; return meat slices to pot, cover and cook until thoroughly heated through.

Serves 8

RATATOUILLE

1 large eggplant, unpeeled, cut in 1-inch cubes
2–3 zucchini, cut in ¼-inch slices
2 large onions, sliced
2 medium potatoes, peeled and cut in 1-inch cubes
1 medium red or green pepper, seeded and chopped
2–3 large ripe tomatoes, chopped, or 16-ounce can plum tomatoes, undrained
2 cloves garlic, mashed
2 tablespoons chopped fresh basil, or 2 teaspoons dried basil
1 teaspoon fennel seed
2 teaspoons thyme
1 teaspoon rosemary
1 tablespoon salt
¼ teaspoon freshly ground black pepper
¾ cup olive oil

1. Place all ingredients in a large heavy pot or Dutch oven. Mix thoroughly until all of the vegetables are coated with olive oil.
2. Cook slowly over low heat uncovered 1–1½ hours, stirring occasionally. May be served hot or cold, but I think it is best at room temperature.

Serves 6–8

VEGETABLES PROVENÇAL AU GRATIN

A lot of ingredients, but a very easy dish to prepare as everything gets thrown into one pot to cook.

1 medium eggplant, unpeeled, cut into small cubes
1 large onion, chopped
1 large green pepper, chopped
1 large potato, peeled and cut into small cubes
1-pound can chick peas, with juice
2–2½ cups fresh or canned tomatoes, chopped
¼ cup raw rice
½ cup parsley, chopped
3 cloves garlic, mashed
2 teaspoons oregano
2 teaspoons dried basil
2 teaspoons thyme
2 teaspoons rosemary
½ teaspoon salt
¼ teaspoon freshly ground pepper
⅓ cup olive oil
2–3 small zucchini, sliced
1 cup sliced fresh mushrooms
about ½ pound grated Swiss or Cheddar, or mixture of both

1. Combine all ingredients except zucchini, mushrooms, and cheese in a large pot. Mix thoroughly and cook uncovered over low to moderate heat for about one hour, stirring occasionally. Add mushrooms and zucchini for last 10 minutes of cooking. When vegetables and rice are tender and most of the juice has been absorbed, it is done.
2. To serve, turn vegetable mixture into a large shallow casserole or individual au gratin dishes. Sprinkle generously with grated cheese and run under the broiler until cheese is melted and bubbly.

Serves 6–8

SPAIN

Spain lies only miles away from Morocco across the Straits of Gibraltar. In the past it has been conquered by invaders from the Arab world, and its culinary traditions show a heavy Arabic influence. Spain also shares many of the features of Mediterranean cuisine, but frequently uses nuts (almonds, walnuts, hazelnuts) and fruits (orange, pomegranate) in its culinary preparations.

One of the classic flavor principles of Spanish cuisine is the combination of olive oil, garlic, and ground nuts. This sauce is used widely on fish, meat, and vegetable dishes and as a flavoring for soups. A second great principle is the combination of olive oil, onions, bell peppers, and tomatoes; variations in flavor are achieved with the use of orange, saffron, and garlic. The characteristic flavor of this sauce comes from slowly stewing the onions and peppers in olive oil before the tomatoes are added.

The Spanish, who are largely responsible for the introduction of the tomato and the bell pepper into Mediterranean cuisine, created a condiment that symbolizes the marriage between the Old and the New Worlds: the olive stuffed with a bit of pimiento (red pepper), one of Spain's most characteristic culinary products.

SPANISH RECIPES

GAZPACHO

SPANISH VEGETABLE SOUP

SPANISH CODFISH SOUP

CATALAN FISH AND VEGETABLE STEW

SPANISH RICE

SPANISH CHICK PEAS

ROMESCO SAUCE

GAZPACHO

Gazpacho is one of the most refreshing of summer soups. This recipe uses tomato juice as the base, but you can also use puréed ripe, fresh tomatoes when they are in season. If you do, you will need to add some salt.

2 cups tomato juice
1 cucumber, peeled and chopped
¼ cup parsley, chopped
1 green pepper, chopped
2 scallions or 1 small onion, chopped
2 cloves garlic
½ teaspoon dried crumbled oregano
juice 1 lemon
3 tablespoons red wine vinegar
1 teaspoon (more or less to taste) Tabasco sauce
salt and freshly ground pepper to taste
¼ cup olive oil

Garnish:
1 cucumber, peeled and chopped
1 large red or green pepper, chopped
3–4 scallions, chopped
1 avocado, sliced (optional)

1. In a blender combine tomato juice, cucumber, parsley, green pepper, scallions, garlic, oregano, lemon juice, vinegar, and Tabasco. Blend until smooth. Pour in a serving bowl and stir in salt, pepper, and oil.
2. Chill thoroughly. Taste for seasoning. Combine chopped vegetables to pass with soup as a garnish.

Serves 6

SPANISH VEGETABLE SOUP

¼ cup olive oil
1 large onion, chopped
2 red or green sweet peppers, chopped
28-ounce can tomatoes or 4–5 large fresh tomatoes, coarsely chopped
3 carrots, sliced
2 cups cooked or canned chick peas
6 cups chicken stock
½ teaspoon freshly ground black pepper
½ cup parsley, chopped
1 cup fresh or frozen peas

1. In a large pot, heat olive oil over low to moderate heat; sauté onion and peppers slowly, about 20 minutes, stirring occasionally.
2. Add all other ingredients except parsley and peas and simmer uncovered for about 45 minutes. Add parsley and peas and cook for another 10 minutes. Taste for salt.

Serves 8–10

SPANISH CODFISH SOUP

½ teaspoon saffron threads or powdered saffron
1 cup hot water
2 tablespoons olive oil
1 onion, thinly sliced
1 clove garlic, mashed
1 pound codfish steaks
16-ounce can Italian plum tomatoes
1 cup bottled clam juice
¼ cup parsley, chopped
1 teaspoon salt
¼ teaspoon freshly ground black pepper
1 orange

1. Soak the saffron in the hot water for ½ hour.
2. In a deep heavy pot, heat the olive oil over moderate heat, then sauté the onion and garlic, stirring, until golden.
3. Add the fish steaks and sauté briefly on both sides.
4. Add saffron water, tomatoes, clam juice, parsley, salt, and pepper. Simmer gently over low heat, uncovered, about 15–20 minutes or until fish is done.
5. With a vegetable peeler or sharp knife remove the orange part of the rind from the orange, leaving the white pith behind. Cut the rind into thin julienne strips and add to soup.
6. Remove fish from soup with slotted spoon and set aside to cool slightly. When cool enough to handle, remove all skin and bones and cut into bite-sized chunks. Return fish to soup, add the juice of the orange, and simmer until heated through.

Serves 6

CATALAN FISH AND VEGETABLE STEW

Like the French bouillabaisse which traditionally uses at least six different kinds of fish, the flavor of this stew is improved by the use of several varieties. Try a variety of firm-fleshed sea fish, plus some shrimp, clams, or mussels.

½ teaspoon saffron threads or powdered saffron
½ cup dry white wine
¼ cup olive oil
1 green pepper, seeded and cut in strips
1 sweet red pepper, seeded and cut in strips
2–3 small zucchini, sliced
1 large onion, sliced
1 clove garlic, mashed
2 pounds mixed fish fillets, large shrimp (peeled and deveined), etc.
16-ounce can plum tomatoes, with juice
½ teaspoon fennel seeds
¼ teaspoon freshly ground black pepper
½ teaspoon salt
zest of 1 orange, cut in julienne strips
juice of 1 orange
¼ cup pimiento-stuffed green olives

1. Combine saffron and wine and let stand ½ hour.
2. In a large heavy pot or Dutch oven, heat olive oil over high heat. Add peppers and zucchini and stir–fry briefly, about 1–2 minutes. Vegetables should be tender but still crisp. Remove vegetables from pot with slotted spoon and set aside.
3. In same pot over moderate heat, add onion and garlic and sauté for a few minutes. Add fish and shrimp and sauté briefly in oil.
4. Add saffron-wine, tomatoes, fennel seed, salt, pepper, orange zest and juice, and olives. Simmer gently over low heat, uncovered, about 15–20 minutes, or until fish is cooked.
5. Add reserved peppers and zucchini at the last minute and heat through. Serve with rice.

Serves 4

SPANISH RICE

3 tablespoons olive oil
1 large onion, chopped
1 red or green sweet pepper, seeded and chopped
1 cup long-grain rice
1½ cups hot chicken or fish stock
8-ounce can tomato sauce
pinch saffron threads or powdered saffron
pinch salt
⅛ teaspoon freshly ground black pepper
½ cup cooked or frozen peas

1. In a medium pot heat olive oil over low to moderate heat. Add onion and pepper and sauté slowly, stirring, until vegetables are very soft. Add rice and cook, stirring, until rice is golden.
2. Add stock, tomato sauce, saffron, salt, and pepper, mix well and cover. Cook over low heat for 15–20 minutes until rice is tender and liquid is absorbed.
3. Stir in peas and let stand, covered, for 5 minutes.

Serves 4–5

SPANISH CHICK PEAS

¼ cup olive oil (a strong fruity Spanish or Greek variety is best)
2 onions, chopped
2 red or green sweet peppers, chopped
2 cups canned or fresh ripe tomatoes, coarsely chopped
1 teaspoon salt
½ teaspoon pepper
6 cups canned or cooked chick peas, drained
1 cup parsley, finely chopped

1. In a heavy pot combine olive oil, onions and peppers. Sauté slowly over low to moderate heat, stirring occasionally, until vegetables are soft and onions are just beginning to brown, about 20–30 minutes.
2. Add tomatoes, salt and pepper, and cook over moderate heat until sauce is slightly thickened, about 20 minutes.
3. Add chick peas and parsley and cook slowly for about ½ hour, stirring occasionally, until most of the liquid has been absorbed. Cool.
4. Serve chick peas at room temperature, garnished with additional chopped parsley, if desired.

Serves 6–8

ROMESCO SAUCE

For this sauce you should use a good, strong-flavored Spanish olive oil or the taste will not be right. The Spanish use Romesco as a sauce for cooked vegetables or broiled fish, but I find it very successful also as a dip for raw vegetables and shrimp.

4 cloves garlic
30 toasted hazelnuts
1 teaspoon salt
1 medium sized tomato, very ripe
1 small dried red chile pepper, seeds removed
¾ cup olive oil
¼ cup red wine vinegar

1. Combine garlic, nuts, salt, tomato, and chile in a blender and blend until smooth. Continue blending while adding olive oil gradually, in a thin stream.
2. When all the oil is added and mixture is thick, add in vinegar, while continuing to blend.

Makes about 1½ cups

To make a delicious roast stuffed chicken with Romesco, combine an onion, a green pepper, and a couple of tomatoes, all coarsely chopped, with a small head of cauliflower, separated into flowerets, some chick peas, and green peas. Toss the vegetables with ½ cup Romesco, then stuff into a large roasting chicken (any additional vegetables can be baked in a covered baking dish). Baste the chicken with Romesco and roast. When ready to serve, remove vegetable stuffing from chicken, and add a few more tablespoons of sauce to taste.

EUROPE

Moving north from the Mediterranean with its warm semi-arid climate and into the continent of Europe, we find a very different environment both ecologically and culturally. Temperate in climate, with vast deciduous forests, river valleys, and rich pasture, this region is unequalled in its wealth of beef and pork, and of dairy products.

For our purposes, Europe can be divided basically into west and east. Western Europe includes France, Belgium, northern Italy, and parts of Germany and Austria. The eastern half of Europe can be divided further into a northern and a southern part, with the Danube River making a convenient boundary between the two. The southern half of eastern Europe, including Greece, the Balkans, and Hungary, is a wheat and wine producing area, while the northern half, including Germany, Russia, Poland, and Czechoslovakia, is a rye and beer producing area.

The basic grains of Europe—wheat in the south and center, rye in the north and east—are generally processed into flour for bread. The potato, an import from the New World, is a starch staple of great value, particularly in northern areas where it can be cultivated more easily than other crops.

Beef and veal are the most esteemed meats, and the cow provides as well the rich milk for the butter, cream, and myriad cheeses that play so important a part in the diet. Central Europe is second only to China in the cultivation of pork; the pig's natural habitat is the forest and river valley, which provide the necessary shade, moisture, and food for scavenging. Pork is quite easy to preserve and turns up in the cuisine as ham, bacon, and countless types of sausage.

Throughout the diverse cultures and traditions of Europe, meats and animal products are emphasized in the cuisine. Not only is there a greater consumption of meat and dairy products, but animal fats—butter, lard, chicken fat—rather than vegetable oils become more important in cooking. Seasonings and spices play a lesser role, with a trend toward mildly flavored foods (what we call "subtle" if we like it and "bland" if we don't!). The tendency toward subtle seasoning becomes more marked further north; the cuisines of Russia and Scandinavia, for example, are much less highly flavored than the cuisines of the Balkans and Hungary.

HUNGARY

Hungary fits the culinary pattern of central Europe in most respects. It belongs to the wheat-wine complex of southeastern Europe and produces many fine wines of its own. Traditional meats are beef and pork, with hams, bacon, and sausage playing an important role. Hungarian cuisine has taken shape from many different traditions. Because of its central geographic location, it has been open to cultural influences from all directions: from central Asia via Turkey and the Balkans, from the Mediterranean, from the beer-rye traditions of northeastern Europe, and from western Europe.

Hungary's cuisine is distinct from the European pattern in its use of hot pepper. The *capsicum* peppers, brought from the New World by the Spanish and Portuguese, are said to have been introduced into Hungary from the east via Turkey, and both the mild and hot varieties are exploited fully in Hungarian cuisine. The most familiar and most commercially valuable form of the *capsicum* is paprika, and Hungary is justifiably famous for both the rose (sweet) and hot varieties. Different types of paprika, as well as other *capsicum* peppers, appear consistently in culinary preparations.

The classic flavor principle of Hungarian cuisine is the combination of onions, lard (or bacon fat), and paprika. The paprika is used in amounts that may astonish outsiders, who are familiar with it as a garnish and coloring agent, rather than as a seasoning. Flavoring is varied with the use of garlic, caraway, and sour cream.

HUNGARIAN RECIPES

HUNGARIAN BEAN SOUP

HUNGARIAN GOULASH

NOODLE AND CABBAGE CASSEROLE

HUNGARIAN BEAN SOUP

1½ cups dried white beans (navy, pea, or marrow)
4–5 strips bacon, chopped
2 large onions, chopped
1 tablespoon paprika
3 cloves garlic, mashed
8 cups water
3 tablespoons tomato paste (½ 6-ounce can)
1 tablespoon salt
¼ teaspoon pepper
dumplings, if desired (see p. 218)

1. Soak beans in cold water to cover for several hours or overnight. Drain.
2. In a large pot, fry chopped bacon until most of the fat is rendered out. Add the onions, paprika, and garlic and sauté, stirring, until onions are soft.
3. Add water, tomato paste, and drained beans and simmer uncovered for 1–1½ hours or until beans are tender. Add salt and pepper.
4. Purée about half the beans in a blender and return to pot. Serve soup very hot with dumplings, if desired.

Serves 8

HUNGARIAN GOULASH

There are as many varieties of goulash as there are cooks in Hungary. Here is a good one that makes a. hearty winter meal.

2 tablespoons lard or salad oil
2 large onions, chopped
2 tablespoons paprika
3 large cloves garlic, mashed
6 lean pork chops
1 pound sauerkraut, drained
2–3 large carrots, sliced
2 medium potatoes, peeled and cubed
1 pound garlic or Polish type sausage, cut in chunks
1 cup beef stock
3 tablespoons (½ 6-ounce can) tomato paste
⅛ teaspoon black pepper

1. In a large heavy pot or Dutch oven, heat the lard or oil, add the onions, paprika, and garlic and sauté until the onions are soft.
2. Add the pork chops and brown lightly on both sides. Salt and pepper the chops lightly.
3. Leaving the chops at the bottom of the pot, cover them with the sauerkraut, then add the carrots, potatoes, and sausage. Pour in beef stock, tomato paste, and pepper. Cover the pot and let cook over low heat for about 2 hours. Uncover pot and let sauce thicken for last half hour or so.
4. Serve goulash with buttered noodles garnished with poppy seed.

Serves 6–8

NOODLE AND CABBAGE CASSEROLE

6 slices bacon, diced
2 medium onions, chopped
½ pound wide egg noodles*, cooked and drained
½ small head cabbage, chopped (about 4 cups)
½ pound sour cream
½ pound cottage cheese
½ teaspoon salt
good grind fresh black pepper
2 teaspoons paprika

1. In a frying pan, cook bacon over moderate heat until the fat is rendered and bacon starts to brown. Add onion and continue to fry until bacon is crisp and onions are golden.
2. Combine bacon and onions (with bacon fat) and all other ingredients except paprika and mix well. Place mixture in a buttered casserole and sprinkle generously with paprika. Bake in a 350° oven for 25–30 minutes.

Serves 4–6

*This dish is best made with homemade noodles (see recipe for fresh pasta p. 218); if made with packaged noodles, cook according to package instructions.

EASTERN EUROPEAN JEWISH CUISINE

Jewish cuisine is more a function of cultural tradition than geography; or rather, it is a product of environment mediated by culture. After displacement from their ancient homeland, the Jewish people settled in various locations throughout the Middle East, the Mediterranean, and eastern Europe. Wherever they settled they adopted many new culinary traditions while retaining the dietary laws of Leviticus that are so fundamental a part of traditional Jewish belief. In some respects the Sephardic Jews, who settled in the Middle East and the Mediterranean, had an easier time from a culinary point of view. These areas were largely Moslem and shared many of the Jewish dietary laws, including the prohibition of pork. Sephardic cooking is, in many ways, very similar to the cuisines of the host countries, as illustrated by the use of fruit and cinnamon in Moroccan Jewish cooking, of saffron in Spain, and by the use of olive oil throughout.

But for the Ashkenazi Jews, who settled in eastern and central Europe, the problem of adapting their diet to a new environment was somewhat more difficult to solve. This is, after all, the area of pork and animal fat rather than vegetable oil. Not only is pork prohibited by Jewish dietary law, but so is the mixing of meat and dairy products: lard is, of course, unusable as a cooking fat, but butter also may not be used when preparing meat. The eastern European Jews had to find another cooking fat, and discovered rendered chicken or goose fat with its very characteristic flavor and aroma. Thus, the basic flavor principle of European Jewish cooking is the combination of chicken fat and onion, with the frequent use of garlic and paprika.

Among the dietary strictures in the Old Testament is the law stating that the blood of any animal is sacred to the Lord and may not be consumed by humans. This prohibition has resulted in the practice of "koshering" meats, i.e., the salting and hanging of meat to release blood, and the practice of cooking meats for a long time to ensure that no trace of blood will be visible when eaten. The practice of overcooking meat and other foods is reinforced by the fact that no cooking is permitted on the Sabbath: from sundown on Friday until sundown on Saturday, the housewife may not light her stove. In order to have a hot meal for Saturday's dinner, it is begun before sundown on Friday and left to cook on a very low fire for the full twenty-four hour period. These slow-cooked stews, the *cholent* and the *tsimmis*, whether of meat and vegetables mixed or of vegetables alone, are characteristic preparations of Jewish cuisine, with a unique flavor and texture.

EASTERN EUROPEAN JEWISH RECIPES

GRANDMA'S CHICKEN SOUP

CHOPPED LIVER

POTATO PANCAKES

POTATO KUGEL

OLD FASHIONED BARLEY-MUSHROOM CASSEROLE

For other Jewish recipes see also:
Beef and Vegetable Tajin p. 85
Jewish Onion Boards p. 223
Challah p. 222

GRANDMA'S CHICKEN SOUP

Legend has it that the typical Jewish grandmother produced this soup simply by waving a dead fowl over a pot of boiling water. The implication is that grandma's soup, as most of her cooking, was undersalted, underflavored, and generally not very good. In defense of those grandmas who were and are excellent cooks (unfortunately, mine was not one of them), I contribute this recipe. Well prepared, this soup is a marvel of hearty, homey flavor and is the ultimate panacea for a bad cold. Made with matzoh balls, it is a traditional part of the Passover *seder*.

6–8 cups chicken stock
1 onion or 1 leek, chopped
2 carrots, diced
2 stalks celery, with leaves, diced
1 parsnip, diced
1 small bunch dill, finely chopped (about ½ cup)
good handful parsley, chopped
¼ teaspoon freshly ground black pepper
1 cup cooked chicken, chopped or shredded
1 cup thin egg noodles, or 1 recipe matzoh balls (see below)

1. In a large pot combine stock, onion, carrots, celery, parsnip, dill, parsley, and pepper. Simmer uncovered over low heat for ½ hour. Add chicken and noodles and cook just until noodles are tender. If using matzoh balls, add to soup at the last minute and heat through. Taste for salt.

Serves 8–10

Matzoh Balls:

4 eggs, well beaten
½ cup soupstock
¼ cup melted chicken fat
1 cup matzoh meal
dash freshly ground black pepper

1. Add stock and chicken fat to beaten eggs and mix well. Add matzoh meal and pepper, mix well, and let stand ½ hour. Mixture will thicken considerably.
2. Have ready a large pot of boiling salted water. Pinch off a small amount of the matzoh mixture (about the size of a small walnut) and roll lightly in the palms to form a ball. As you roll them drop balls into rapidly boiling water and let cook for 15–20 minutes. Remove from water with slotted spoon and add to chicken soup (or set aside until ready to add to soup).

Makes 20–24 matzoh balls

CHOPPED LIVER

¼ cup rendered chicken fat
2 tablespoons vegetable oil
4 large onions, thinly sliced
1 pound chicken livers
1 tablespoon salt
½ teaspoon freshly ground black pepper
½ teaspoon sugar
6 hard-boiled eggs

1. In a large frying pan, heat chicken fat and oil over moderate heat. Add onions and cook slowly, stirring occasionally, until onions are soft and a deep, dark brown (this may take 30–40 minutes). Remove onions from pan with slotted spoon and set aside.
2. Turn heat to moderately high. Add chicken livers and sauté in remaining fat until quite firm and very well browned. Add salt, pepper, and sugar for last few minutes of cooking. Remove from heat and cool slightly.
3. Grind onions, chicken livers, and hard-boiled eggs through a meat grinder, adding all scraped bits and fat from pan. Mix thoroughly. Taste for salt. If mixture is slightly crumbly, add one tablespoon additional chicken fat and blend well.
4. Chill and serve with crackers or as a sandwich spread with sliced cucumbers and Bermuda onion.

Makes about 3 cups

NOTE: If you are artistically inclined, chopped liver is a wonderful medium for sculpture. For a recent Shakespeare celebration my son sculpted the head of the great bard with a double recipe of liver, black olives for eyes, and fresh dill for hair and whiskers.

POTATO PANCAKES
(*Latkes*)

This is one of grandma's famous dishes. She would have grated the potatoes on a hand grater, but nowadays the food processor will do the job much more efficiently. It is important that the potatoes be coarsely grated; this results in a rather untidy-looking pancake with shreds sticking out here and there, but this coarse texture is part of the pancake's goodness.

8 large potatoes
1 large onion, grated
3 eggs, lightly beaten
3 tablespoons flour
1 teaspoon baking powder
1 tablespoon salt
⅛ teaspoon freshly grated black pepper
3–4 tablespoons rendered chicken fat

1. Peel potatoes and soak one hour in enough cold water to cover. Drain and dry well.
2. Grate the potatoes and then squeeze out as much moisture as possible with your hands.
3. Add grated onion and eggs to potatoes, then mix in flour, baking powder, salt, and pepper.
4. In a large frying pan heat chicken fat until sizzling. Drop large spoonfuls of potato mixture into fat and fry until brown on one side. Turn pancakes and brown on other side. Do not crowd pan while frying.
5. Serve pancakes hot, with sour cream or applesauce.

Serves 4–6

POTATO KUGEL

This is very similar to a potato pancake except that it is baked rather than fried and the texture is somewhat finer. The potatoes should be grated less coarsely than for the pancakes but not so finely that the result is a purée.

8 large potatoes
1 large onion, grated
3 eggs, lightly beaten
¼ cup flour or potato starch

1 tablespoon salt
¼ teaspoon freshly ground black pepper
½ cup melted chicken fat

1. Peel potatoes and soak one hour in enough cold water to cover. Drain and dry well.
2. Grate potatoes medium fine, then squeeze out any excess moisture with the hands.
3. Add grated onion and eggs, then stir in flour, salt, and pepper, and melted fat. Mix well. Grease baking dish with chicken fat.
4. Pour mixture into a 13 × 9 × 2–inch baking dish and bake uncovered in a preheated 400° oven 40–50 minutes or until top is browned and crisp. Cut in squares and serve hot.

Serves 6

OLD FASHIONED BARLEY-MUSHROOM CASSEROLE

¼ cup rendered chicken fat
2 medium onions, finely chopped
¾ cup medium pearl barley
2 cups chicken stock
2 tablespoons rendered chicken fat
½ pound fresh mushrooms, finely chopped
½ teaspoon salt
¼ teaspoon freshly ground black pepper
½ ounce dried European mushrooms
½ cup hot water

1. In Dutch oven or any stove-top to oven casserole, heat ¼ cup chicken fat over low to moderate heat. Add onions and cook slowly, stirring occasionally, until they are soft and a deep golden brown, about 30 minutes.
2. Add barley and sauté, stirring, about 5 minutes. Add stock, cover, and cook over low heat ½ hour.
3. Meanwhile, in a frying pan heat 2 tablespoons chicken fat over moderate heat. Add chopped fresh mushrooms, salt, and pepper and cook about 10–15 minutes or until all liquid is evaporated and mushrooms are a deep rich brown.
4. Add sautéed mushrooms, dried mushrooms, and water to barley. Stir well, then cover and place in a preheated 350° oven ½ hour or until all liquid is absorbed and barley is tender.

Serves 6

Northern and Eastern Europe

Further north in Europe the differences in culinary patterns are more striking both in terms of basic foods and of seasoning practices. This is a region of long, severe winters and short summers, with a climate suitable for growing only the most hardy of vegetables: potatoes, cabbage, beets, turnips. Mushrooms are widely used, both fresh and dried for winter use. Wheat is available but the traditional grain is rye, ground into flour or used wholemeal in the production of a wide variety of black breads. Beef, veal, and pork are the most common meats but there is a much heavier dependence on fish, both saltwater from the Atlantic and Baltic (herring and cod) and freshwater (carp, bass, pickerel, and salmon). Fish is used in soups, stews, and salads; it is eaten fresh, pickled, salted, and smoked.

As we have noted, there is a tendency in northern Europe for seasonings to decrease in intensity. Seasoning ingredients are not that numerous and are used sparingly. Onions, leeks, and garlic are well known and dill is by far the most commonly used herb. Familiar spices are caraway seed (for the ever-popular rye bread) and allspice.

The combination of any of these seasonings with sour cream forms the most characteristic flavor principles of northern and eastern European cooking. Sour cream is used as both a foodstuff and a flavoring ingredient because it has better keeping qualities than sweet cream, and it is a valuable source of both fat and protein.

NORTH AND EAST EUROPEAN RECIPES

PIROSHKI

FRESH SALMON BISQUE

RUSSIAN MUSHROOM SOUP

SWEDISH MEATBALLS

BEEF STROGANOFF

VEAL PAPRIKA WITH MUSHROOMS

UKRAINIAN BRAISED PORK

VEAL PATTIES WITH SOUR CREAM

FRESH FISH SALAD

SWEDISH HERRING SALAD

BAKED CRABMEAT IN SOUR CREAM

CHICKEN WITH SOUR CREAM AND HERBS

MUSHROOMS WITH SOUR CREAM

For other north European recipes using the sweet/sour flavor principle,
see chapter on General Principles 1 ; also
Beer rye bread p. 224

PIROSHKI

½ pound cream cheese, softened
½ pound sweet butter, softened
2 cups all-purpose sifted flour
3 tablespoons butter
2 cups fresh mushrooms, finely chopped (about ⅓ pound)
dash salt
1 small onion, minced
⅓ pound lean ground beef or veal
1 teaspoon salt
⅛ teaspoon freshly ground black pepper
3 tablespoons fresh dill, chopped, or 1 tablespoon dried dillweed
2 tablespoons tomato paste
2 tablespoons dry sherry
⅓ cup sour cream

1. Combine softened cream cheese and butter and mix until well blended. Add flour and mix thoroughly. Form into 2 balls, wrap in waxed paper, and refrigerate at least 2 hours.
2. In a large frying pan, heat 2 tablespoons butter over moderately high heat. Add mushrooms and a dash salt and sauté quickly, stirring, about ½ minute. Remove mushrooms from pan and set aside.
3. In same pan heat one tablespoon butter over moderate heat, add onion and sauté until golden. Add ground meat and brown quickly, stirring. When meat is completely browned, drain off all liquid in pan and discard. Add salt, pepper, dill, tomato paste, and sherry to ground meat and simmer uncovered over low heat about 10 minutes, stirring frequently. Mixture should be quite dry.
4. Add reserved mushrooms to pan and simmer another few minutes. Remove from heat, stir in sour cream and mix well. Place mixture in bowl and chill in refrigerator for 1–2 hours.
5. Remove one ball of chilled dough from refrigerator. Pinch off chunks of dough approximately 1 inch in size and roll each quickly into a ball with the palms of your hands. Between sheets of waxed paper roll each ball into a circle approximately 2½ inches in diameter. Place one tablespoon chilled filling on the circle and fold dough over to make a closed semicircle. Press edges of pastry with tines of fork to seal. Repeat procedure for remaining dough and filling.
6. Place filled semicircles on an ungreased baking sheet and bake in a preheated 350° oven about 12–15 minutes or until pastry is a light golden brown. Let stand a few minutes before serving.

Makes about 24 piroshki

FRESH SALMON BISQUE

2 tablespoons butter
1 medium onion, sliced
2 carrots, sliced
1 stalk celery with leaves, chopped
4 cups chicken stock
7 tablespoons dry sherry
¼ cup fresh dill, chopped, or 2 tablespoons dried dillweed
½ teaspoon salt
½–¾ pound fresh salmon
1 cup sour cream
¼ teaspoon freshly grated nutmeg

Garnish: ½ cup parsley, finely chopped.

1. In a large pot heat butter over moderate heat; add onion, carrots, and celery and sauté, stirring, 5 minutes. Add stock, 4 tablespoons sherry, dill, and salt.
2. Place salmon in pot, cover, and simmer over low heat until fish flakes easily with fork (depending on thickness of fish, from 15–30 minutes).
3. Carefully remove fish from broth with slotted spoon, set aside and allow to cool. When fish is cool enough to handle, remove all skin and bones and discard.
4. Place fish in blender or food processor with ½ cup broth from pot and all the vegetables. Purée until smooth.
5. Pour puréed mixture back into pot; stir in sour cream, nutmeg, and 3 tablespoons sherry. Heat to a simmer but do not allow to boil. Taste for salt. Serve hot, sprinkled with chopped parsley.

Serves 8

RUSSIAN MUSHROOM SOUP

2 cups beef stock
2 tablespoons tomato paste
2 tablespoons fresh dill, chopped, or 1 tablespoon dried dillweed
¼ cup dry sherry
2 tablespoons butter
1 small onion, minced
½ pound fresh mushrooms, finely chopped
½ teaspoon salt
dash freshly ground black pepper
1 cup sour cream

1. In a medium pot, heat stock with tomato paste and dill and simmer gently uncovered for 20 minutes. Add sherry and remove from heat.
2. In a frying pan melt butter over moderate heat, then add onion and sauté until just tender.
3. Add chopped mushrooms and sauté, stirring, 3–4 minutes. Add salt and pepper and remove from heat.
4. Add mushroom mixture to soup and simmer for 10 minutes. Just before serving, add sour cream and blend in thoroughly. Heat to a simmer but do not allow to boil.

Serves 4–6

SWEDISH MEATBALLS

2 slices stale white bread
⅓ cup milk
2 tablespoons butter
1 medium onion, minced
1 pound lean ground beef
½ pound ground veal
1½ teaspoons salt
1¼ teaspoons ground allspice
½ teaspoon Tabasco sauce
dash freshly ground black pepper
1 egg, lightly beaten
1 tablespoon flour
⅔ cup sour cream
½ teaspoon Tabasco sauce

1. Cut bread into small cubes and soak in the milk for 10 minutes.
2. In a large frying pan, heat the butter over moderate heat and sauté the onion just until tender.
3. Combine the ground beef and veal with the bread and milk, sautéed onion, one teaspoon salt, one teaspoon allspice, ½ teaspoon Tabasco, pepper, and egg. Mix thoroughly and shape into small balls.
4. Place meatballs in pan over moderate heat and brown well on all sides, turning frequently. Remove meatballs from pan and set aside.
5. To drippings in pan add flour and mix well. Cook 2–3 minutes, stirring. Add sour cream, ½ teaspoon salt, ¼ teaspoon allspice and ½ teaspoon Tabasco. Cook gently, stirring constantly, over low heat for 2–3 minutes. Add meatballs, mix well until heated through, and serve.

Serves 4–6

BEEF STROGANOFF

This can be prepared several ways depending on the cut of meat. Less tender cuts (stewing beef, chuck, round steak, etc.) must be stewed in the sauce until tender. The most extravagant version—and, I think, the best—uses beef tenderloin or tenderloin tails, which need only the briefest of stir-frying.

5 tablespoons butter
2 pounds beef tenderloin or tenderloin tails, cut in ¼-inch slices
½–¾ pound fresh mushrooms, sliced
few drops lemon juice
1 medium onion, finely chopped
1 clove garlic, mashed
1 cup beef stock
¼ cup dry sherry
3 tablespoons tomato paste
¼ cup fresh dill, chopped, or 2 tablespoons dried dillweed
1 teaspoon salt
¼ teaspoon freshly ground black pepper
1 cup sour cream

1. In a large frying pan, heat 2 tablespoons butter over moderate heat. When butter is foaming, add ⅓ of the beef slices and stir-fry quickly until beef is lightly browned on both sides. Do not overcook. Remove browned beef from pan and continue to brown rest of meat in 2 batches. Do not attempt to brown all the meat at once. Remove beef from pan and set aside.
2. Add 2 tablespoons butter to pan. When foaming, add sliced mushrooms and sauté quickly, stirring. Sprinkle with lemon juice, remove from pan and set aside.
3. Melt one tablespoon butter over moderate heat; sauté onion and garlic until wilted. Add the beef stock, sherry, tomato paste, dill, salt, and pepper and simmer uncovered about 10 minutes.
4. Return beef and mushrooms to sauce in pan and cook, stirring, over moderate heat until heated through.
5. Stir in the sour cream, mixing well. Bring just to a simmer but do not allow to boil. Serve with buttered noodles if desired.

Serves 4–6

VEAL PAPRIKA WITH MUSHROOMS

1 pound veal scallopini or veal tenders, cut into thin slices
¼ cup butter
½ pound fresh mushrooms, sliced
juice ½ lemon
1¼ teaspoons salt
⅛ teaspoon freshly ground black pepper
1 medium onion, finely chopped
1 large clove garlic, mashed
dash freshly ground black pepper
1 tablespoon sweet Hungarian paprika
1 cup sour cream

1. Dry veal slices thoroughly with paper towels and set aside.
2. In a large frying pan heat 2 tablespoons butter over moderately high heat. Add mushrooms and stir quickly, sprinkling them with lemon juice, ¼ teaspoon salt, and pepper. Remove mushrooms from pan and set aside.
3. Add 2 tablespoons butter and melt over moderate heat. Add onion and garlic and sauté for a few minutes until tender.
4. Turn heat up high, add veal slices and brown quickly. Add one teaspoon salt, dash pepper, and paprika, stirring to coat meat well. Turn heat low, cover pan, and simmer for 10 minutes.
5. Add mushrooms and sour cream, stirring to blend well. Bring just to a simmer but do not allow to boil. Serve with buttered noodles or buttered new potatoes.

Serves 4

UKRAINIAN BRAISED PORK

2–2½ pounds lean boneless pork loin
2 tablespoons butter
½ teaspoon salt
¼ teaspoon freshly ground black pepper
2 medium onions, sliced
2 cloves garlic, mashed
1 tablespoon caraway seeds
1 cup beef stock
½ cup sour cream

1. Remove all excess fat from pork. In a heavy pot or Dutch oven heat butter over moderate heat. Add pork and brown slowly on all sides. Sprinkle with salt and pepper.
2. To pot add onions, garlic, caraway seeds, and stock. Cover and cook over low heat 2–2½ hours or until meat is fork tender. Remove pork from pot and cool slightly. Cut in slices.
3. Meanwhile, turn heat up under pot and cook rapidly until sauce is reduced to about ⅔ cup. Return sliced meat to pot and simmer about 10 minutes.
4. Just before serving, remove meat slices from pot with slotted spoon and place on serving dish. Add sour cream to sauce in pot and whisk in thoroughly. Heat just to a simmer but do not allow to boil. Pour sauce over meat. Good served with sweet and sour red cabbage and apples.

Serves 4–6

VEAL PATTIES WITH SOUR CREAM

1½ pounds ground veal
1 egg
1 small onion, grated
1¼ teaspoons salt
¼ teaspoon freshly grated black pepper
½ teaspoon ground allspice
2 tablespoons butter
flour for dredging
1 clove garlic, mashed
2 tablespoons fresh dill, chopped, or 2 teaspoons dried dillweed
1 cup sour cream

1. Combine ground veal, egg, onion, salt, pepper, and allspice. Mix well and form into 8 patties.
2. Heat butter in a large frying pan over moderate heat. Dredge patties in flour and sauté on both sides until golden brown. Remove from pan, set aside and keep warm.
3. To pan add garlic and sauté briefly. Add dill and sour cream, scraping up any brown bits that stick to the bottom of the pan. Bring just to a simmer but do not allow to boil. Pour sauce over patties and serve.

Serves 4

FRESH FISH SALAD

1½–2 pounds any firm white fish (haddock, halibut, cod, etc.)
1 small onion, sliced
1 stalk celery with leaves, sliced
1⅛ teaspoons salt
dash white pepper
juice 1 lemon
1 cup celery, finely chopped
⅓ cup mayonnaise
⅓ cup sour cream
2 tablespoons chives, finely chopped
2 tablespoons fresh dill, finely chopped or 2 teaspoons dried dillweed
⅛ teaspoon freshly ground black pepper

Garnish: lemon slices, cucumber slices

1. In a medium to large pan place fish, onions, sliced celery, one teaspoon salt, white pepper, ½ of the lemon juice, and enough cold water just to cover fish. Simmer over low heat, uncovered, until fish flakes easily with fork. Remove fish from broth and cool thoroughly. Remove any skin and bones.
2. Flake the fish into a bowl and combine with chopped celery.
3. In a small bowl combine mayonnaise, sour cream, chives, dill, ⅛ teaspoon salt, black pepper, and rest of lemon juice. Mix thoroughly, then pour dressing over fish and mix gently but well.
4. Chill before serving. Taste for lemon and salt. Serve on a bed of fresh greens; garnish with lemon and cucumber slices.

Serves 4–6

SWEDISH HERRING SALAD

2-pound jar pickled herring with onion
1 large tart apple, peeled, cored, and diced
2 boiled potatoes, peeled and diced
3–4 small cooked or canned beets, diced
2 hard-boiled eggs, separated
1½ cups sour cream
⅓ cup fresh dill, chopped
Garnish: sprigs of fresh dill

1. Drain herring and onions thoroughly; chop fine. Combine with diced apple, potatoes, beets, and egg whites, finely chopped.
2. Gently mix sour cream and dill into mixture. Mound onto a serving platter and garnish with egg yolks, mashed finely or sieved, and sprigs of fresh dill. Serve with rye or pumpernickel bread and butter.

Serves 6–8 as an appetizer

BAKED CRABMEAT IN SOUR CREAM

1 pound fresh crabmeat
2 tablespoons butter
1 scallion, finely chopped
3 tablespoons parsley, finely chopped
3 tablespoons chives, finely chopped
1 tablespoon dill, finely chopped, or 1 teaspoon dried dillweed
½ teaspoon salt
dash white pepper
juice ½ lemon
½ cup sour cream
½ cup grated Swiss Gruyère or Emmenthal cheese

1. Pick over crabmeat to remove any bits of cartilage.
2. In a frying pan melt butter over moderate heat. Add scallion, parsley, chives, and dill. Sauté a few minutes, stirring.
3. Add crabmeat, salt, pepper, and lemon juice and sauté a few minutes more. Remove from heat and stir in sour cream.
4. Place crab mixture in a shallow buttered baking dish or in buttered individual ramekins and top with grated cheese.
5. Heat in a preheated 400° oven for 10 minutes, then run under the broiler for a few seconds until cheese is lightly browned.

Serves 4

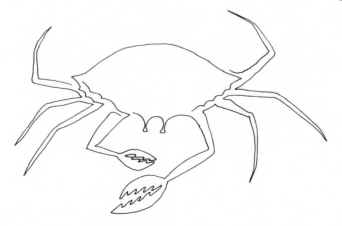

CHICKEN WITH SOUR CREAM AND HERBS

2 tablespoons butter
3–4 pounds chicken parts, or 3 chicken breasts, cut in half
2 leeks, white parts only, cleaned and chopped
2 stalks celery with leaves, chopped
2 carrots, sliced
1 teaspoon salt
¼ teaspoon freshly ground pepper
1 tablespoon fresh or freeze-dried chives
1 tablespoon marjoram
1 chicken bouillon cube, or 1 teaspoon granulated chicken bouillon
1 cup sour cream

Garnish: additional chives

1. In large frying pan or Dutch oven, melt butter over moderate heat. Brown chicken parts lightly on both sides. Add all other ingredients except bouillon and sour cream and cook, covered, over low heat for 40–45 minutes until chicken is tender.
2. Remove chicken from pot, set aside and keep warm while preparing sauce.
3. Add bouillon cube to liquid that has accumulated in pan. Cook rapidly over high heat until liquid is reduced to about ½ cup. Turn heat low and stir in sour cream until well blended. Return chicken parts to sauce and heat until simmering.
4. Garnish chicken with additional chives and serve immediately, with noodles, if desired.

Serves 4–6

MUSHROOMS WITH SOUR CREAM

1 pound fresh mushrooms
2 tablespoons butter
1 small onion, minced
1 clove garlic, mashed
1 teaspoon salt
dash freshly ground black pepper
juice ½ lemon
2 tablespoons dry sherry
1 tablespoon fresh dill, chopped, or 1 teaspoon dried dill seed
½ cup sour cream
½ teaspoon paprika

1. Wipe mushrooms with a damp cloth, cut off tough stem ends, and slice.
2. In a large frying pan, heat butter until foaming over moderately high heat. Add onion, garlic, and mushrooms and sauté quickly, shaking pan frequently.
3. Sprinkle salt, pepper, and lemon juice over mushrooms and cook a few minutes longer.
4. Add dill and sherry and cook quickly until liquid is almost completely reduced.
5. Stir in sour cream, mix well, and bring to a simmer. Remove from heat, pour into serving dish, and sprinkle with paprika.

Serves 4

FRANCE

Almost all cultures produce some type of fermented, alcoholic beverage based on readily available plant products: rice in the Orient; barley, malt, and hops in northern Europe; corn mash in America. The Mongols of central Asia concocted an alcoholic drink made from mare's milk; called *koumiss,* it was reputed to be quite pleasant in both taste and effect.

But nowhere has the production of wines and distilled spirits reached such distinction as in France where, from Roman times, the grape vine seems to have found the ideal ecological and sociological niche. Climate, soil, and selected varietal grapes combine to produce the great vintages of the Bordeaux and Burgundy regions, of the Champagne country, and the Rhône Valley.

The great wine tradition in France and the tradition of fine spirits—Cognac, Benedictine, Chartreuse, Grand Marnier, etc.—no doubt was fostered by the great monasteries. There, many of the sons of the nobility, accustomed to the good life, perpetuated a tradition of fine food and drink, spending much time developing secret recipes for coaxing greatness from the grape.

Great effort was expended from early times in exploiting the second great source of France's culinary wealth, dairy products. The quality and flavor of French butter and cream are unexcelled, and much the same conditions that led to the development of the great wines led also to the production of an immense variety of fine cheeses. These two food categories—wines and dairy products—are fundamental to French cuisine.

As is the case with other temperate cuisines, spices are not used heavily but, rather, select herbs—thyme, parsley, tarragon, onion, shallot, garlic—are judiciously used. Piquancy is provided by a number of subtly flavored vinegars and mustards, products which are also derived from the wine tradition.

The basic foods of France are similar to those of the rest of central Europe; wheat, used almost exclusively in the form of refined white flour for bread; potatoes and a variety of root and leafy vegetables; beef, veal, pork and a variety of pork sausages, and poultry. The egg is of highest importance in French cuisine, both as a primary ingredient in omelets, crepes, soufflés, and quiches, and as a binding and enriching agent in many of the great sauces.

Several fundamental cooking techniques should be pointed out. The first is the making of stocks for use in soups and sauces. Meat, fish or poultry, bones, vegetables, and herbs are simmered for hours to produce richly flavored broths; these broths may then be further cooked and reduced to produce the thick, highly concentrated pastes or jellies used as the basis of many sauces.

The second technique is the blending and cooking of butter and flour to make a *roux*, a thickening agent for sauces.

The third technique is deglazing. When sautéeing foods over moderate heat in oil or butter, there are brown bits that remain at the bottom of the pan rich in color and flavor. Deglazing is simply the adding of liquid to the pan, scraping up the residue and cooking it to produce a sauce. These three techniques are fundamental to French culinary practice, and each is crucial to the making of sauces. And after all, the sauce is the most distinctive feature of classic French cuisine.

Two clear flavor principles emerge in French cooking. The first is the combination of wine with herbs; the second is the combination of butter, and/or cheese with wine and/or stock. Variation is achieved with the use of an immense variety of wines and cheese, and by the use of such additional ingredients as mustard, lemon, vinegar, and tomato. One important regional variation (in addition to the Mediterranean, see p. 106) must be noted. In Normandy, apples, apple cider, and apple brandy (Calvados) are substituted for the wine and herbs. This rich dairy region also produces what is thought to be the finest butter, cream, and Camembert cheese in the world.

FRENCH RECIPES

CHICKEN STOCK

BEEF OR VEAL STOCK

FISH STOCK

ONION SOUP GRATINÉE

CREAM OF CAULIFLOWER SOUP

MARINATED MUSHROOMS

MARINATED MUSSELS

COUNTRY PÂTÉ

MOUSSELINE OF CHICKEN LIVERS

BOEUF BOURGUIGNON

FILLET OF BEEF WITH MUSHROOM SAUCE

HERBED VEAL STEW

CALVES LIVER IN MUSTARD SAUCE

CASSOULET

PORK CHOPS NORMANDY

CHICKEN WITH APPLES AND CREAM

SEAFOOD RAVIGOTE

SHRIMP WITH CLAM SAUCE

SAUCE VINAIGRETTE

MARINATED LEEKS AND ASPARAGUS

MARINATED MIXED VEGETABLES

ON THE MAKING OF STOCK

There are three basic steps in making a good homemade stock: 1) slow simmering of bones, meat, vegetables, and seasonings in a large quantity of water for several hours or more to extract every possible bit of flavor from the ingredients; 2) rapid boiling down, or reducing, of stock to concentrate the flavor; 3) straining and skimming to obtain a clear concentrated liquid. It is important to remember that even though the ingredients are going to be cooked to death, they should be fresh and of good quality to start with. The pot in which they are cooked should be large enough to provide maximum circulation, and all ingredients should be placed directly in the water. The use of little cheesecloth bags to tie up spices and so forth is a nuisance and does not allow for full development of flavor. There are two basic kinds of stock—white and brown. White stocks, generally of poultry or fish, are those in which all the ingredients are placed directly in the water and cooked as described above, resulting in a lightly colored stock. Brown stocks, generally of beef or veal, are those in which the bones and meat are browned slowly in butter or fat before the water is added: browning provides the stock with additional flavor and a rich brown color. Butter, not oil, should be used in this browning process, not only for flavor but for ease in skimming fat off the chilled stock.

NOTE: In making stock for Oriental soups that are going to be flavored with salting agents such as soy sauce or fish sauce, follow recipes as given but cut down sharply on salt or eliminate altogether.

CHICKEN STOCK

4–5-pound stewing chicken, cut in pieces, or 4–5 pounds assorted
  chicken parts: necks, backs, etc.
4 quarts cold water
2 large onions or 2 large leeks, chopped
3–4 carrots, sliced
3–4 stalks celery with leaves, sliced
½ cup parsley, chopped
1–2 parsnips, sliced
2 tablespoons coarse or kosher salt
12 peppercorns
½ teaspoon turmeric

1. Place chicken, vegetables, and seasonings in a large pot and cover with cold water. Bring to boil, then simmer uncovered over low heat for 3–4 hours.
2. Strain thoroughly and taste for salt.
3. Chill, then skim off any congealed fat. Stock is now ready to use.

Makes about 8 cups

BEEF OR VEAL STOCK

2 tablespoons butter
4–5 pounds beef or veal bones, with some meat attached, if possible
1 tablespoon sugar
2 large onions, chopped
3–4 stalks celery with leaves, chopped
3–4 carrots, chopped
4 quarts boiling water
2 tablespoons coarse or kosher salt
12 peppercorns
½ cup parsley, chopped
2 bay leaves
1 small lemon, sliced

1. In a large pot melt butter over low to moderate heat. Add bones and brown slowly, turning frequently. Sprinkle bones with sugar and continue browning for about ½ hour.
2. Add onions, celery, and carrots and continue to cook, stirring, about 5 minutes.
3. Add water and all other ingredients and cook uncovered over low heat for 3–4 hours. Occasionally skim off any scum that may rise to the surface.
4. Strain thoroughly, then taste for salt. Chill, then skim off any congealed fat. Stock is now ready to use.

Makes about 8 cups

NOTE: To make a glace de viande, or concentrated seasoning base for soups and sauces, boil down prepared stock until it is reduced by about half. Continue to cook, stirring, until it is quite thick and syrupy. Store, covered, in the refrigerator.

FISH STOCK

3–4 pounds fish (heads, tails, flesh, shrimp shells, lobster shells, etc.)
4 quarts water
2 tablespoons coarse or kosher salt
12 peppercorns
1 bay leaf
1 lemon, sliced
2 large onions, sliced
3–4 carrots, sliced
3–4 stalks celery with leaves, sliced
½ cup parsley, chopped

1. Place all ingredients in a large pot. Bring to the boil, then simmer uncovered over low heat for 2–3 hours.

2. Strain thoroughly, then return to pot and boil rapidly for about 15 minutes. Taste for salt. If a stronger flavor is desired the stock can be fortified with bottled clam juice and/or some lemon juice.

Makes about 8 cups

ONION SOUP GRATINÉE

3 tablespoons butter
4 large onions, thinly sliced
1 teaspoon sugar
6 cups beef stock
¼ teaspoon freshly ground black pepper
garlic croutons (see below)
2 cups grated Gruyère cheese (or cheddar, or a mixture of both)

1. In a heavy pot melt butter over low to moderate heat; add onions and sugar and sauté slowly, stirring occasionally, until onions are soft and well browned.
2. Add beef stock and pepper and simmer for 30 minutes.
3. To serve: ladle hot soup about ⅔ to the top of individual onion-soup or oven-proof bowls. Top with a garlic crouton and cover generously with grated cheese. Run under the broiler until cheese is melted and bubbly and just beginning to brown.

Serves 6–8

To make garlic croutons: cut 6–8 ½-inch slices of day-old French bread. Brush both sides of slices lightly with 3–4 tablespoons melted butter that has been mixed with 1 clove garlic, mashed, or ½ teaspoon granulated garlic. Bake croutons in a 350° oven for 10–12 minutes.

CREAM OF CAULIFLOWER SOUP

2 tablespoons butter
1 medium onion, sliced
1 medium cauliflower, coarsely chopped
4 cups chicken stock
¼ teaspoon white pepper
¼ teaspoon freshly grated nutmeg
½ cup light cream
1 cup grated Gruyère, Cheddar, or mixture of both

1. In a medium-sized pot heat butter over moderate heat; add onion and sauté until onion just begins to turn golden.
2. Add cauliflower and stir briefly in the onion-butter.
3. Add chicken stock and pepper, bring to a simmer and cook

uncovered about 15–20 minutes until cauliflower is tender. Cool slightly.
4. Purée cauliflower and onion in a blender or food processor until smooth, then return to pot. Stir in nutmeg and cream.
5. Bring soup to a simmer over low heat, stirring occasionally. Just before serving, stir in grated cheese and blend until smooth.

Serves 8

MARINATED MUSHROOMS

Always good at a cocktail party or on a buffet table. Try mixing them with black olives or boiled shrimp, or mixing them into a tossed green salad.

1 pound uniformly-sized small fresh mushrooms
⅓ cup olive oil
3 tablespoons red wine vinegar
1 shallot or 1 scallion, minced
1 clove garlic, mashed
1 teaspoon Dijon mustard
1 teaspoon salt
good dash freshly gound black pepper
3 tablespoons parsley, chopped

1. Wipe mushrooms with a damp cloth and cut off tough ends of stems.
2. Combine all other ingredients and beat well with a fork or shake in a tightly covered jar. Pour over mushrooms.
3. Mix well and marinate several hours in refrigerator.

Makes 3–4 cups

MARINATED MUSSELS

3 cups shelled freshly steamed or canned mussels, drained
⅓ cup olive oil
5 tablespoons red wine vinegar
½ teaspoon salt
good dash freshly ground black pepper
1 teaspoon Dijon mustard
2 scallions, finely minced
1 clove garlic, mashed
2 tablespoons fresh dill, finely chopped
2 tablespoons parsley, finely chopped
1 tablespoon chives, finely chopped

Garnish: fresh greens, lemon wedges

1. Place mussels in a glass or ceramic bowl.
2. Combine all other ingredients and beat well with a fork to blend. Pour over mussels and mix gently. Cover and refrigerate several hours.
3. Serve on fresh greens with a wedge of lemon.

Serves 6 as an appetizer

COUNTRY PÂTÉ

This coarse-grained, home-style pâté can be made 3 or 4 days in advance.

1 pound chicken livers
3 eggs
1 pound ground veal
1 pound ground bulk sausage meat
1 tablespoon salt
1 teaspoon ground allspice
2 cloves garlic, mashed
1 teaspoon cracked black pepper
¼ cup Cognac
1 pound fresh pork fat, sliced, or 1 pound thick-sliced bacon, blanched in boiling water for 10 minutes and drained
2 ounces Prosciutto or Smithfield ham, sliced in thin strips

1. Place chicken livers in a blender or food processor and purée until they are liquid.
2. In a large bowl beat eggs lightly. Add puréed livers, ground veal, sausage, salt, allspice, garlic, pepper, and Cognac. Mix thoroughly.
3. Line the bottom and sides of a large loaf pan (13 × 4½ × 2½ inches) or terrine with the pork fat, reserving a few slices for the top. Place half the pâté mixture in pan, pressing down well with back of spoon. Place the Prosciutto strips on top of the pâté. Cover with remaining pâté mixture, pressing down well. Place remaining pork fat slices over the top. Cover pan tightly with aluminum foil.
4. Place pâté pan in a larger pan filled with enough water to come to a third of the way up the side. Bake in a preheated 300° oven for 2 hours.
5. Remove from oven and place some heavy weights on top of the foil. This will cause excess fat to overflow into the larger pan, and the pâté will compress as it cools. Allow pâté to cool with weights on top.
6. Remove weights. Remove pâté from pan and carefully peel off fat slices. Wrap pâté in foil and refrigerate. Serve cold, cut in thin slices, with good bread, sweet butter, and sour gherkins.

Serves 6–8

MOUSSELINE OF CHICKEN LIVERS

¼ cup butter
2 scallions or 1 small onion, minced
1 large clove garlic, finely minced
1 pound chicken livers, cut in half
1 teaspoon salt
¼ teaspoon freshly ground black pepper
½ teaspoon ground allspice
1 tablespoon parsley, chopped
¼ cup Madeira
2 tablespoons butter, softened

1. In a large frying pan melt butter over moderate heat. Add the scallions and garlic and sauté just until wilted.
2. Turn heat up, add chicken livers and sauté, stirring, until the livers are browned on all sides.
3. Add salt, pepper, allspice, and parsley and stir. Then add the Madeira. Bring to a simmer, scraping up all bits from the bottom of the pan.
4. Remove chicken livers from pan with slotted spoon and set aside. Continue to cook sauce rapidly until liquid reduces by about half. Remove from heat and allow to cool slightly.
5. Purée livers and sauce in blender or food processor until smooth. Beat in 2 tablespoons softened butter. Pack mixture into small bowl or crock, cover tightly and refrigerate. Serve with crackers or melba toast.

Makes about 2 cups

BOEUF BOURGUIGNON

2 pounds boneless beef cut in 1–1½-inch cubes
3 tablespoons vegetable oil
2 leeks, finely chopped
3 cloves garlic, mashed
3 carrots, cut in chunks
2 teaspoons salt
12 peppercorns
½ cup parsley, chopped
2 teaspoons thyme
4 tablespoons tomato paste
1 cup red Burgundy wine (or any dry red wine)
1 cup small white onions, peeled
½ pound fresh mushrooms, small whole or large sliced

1. Dry beef cubes thoroughly with paper towels.
2. In a heavy pot heat oil over moderate heat. Add beef cubes and brown slowly on all sides, turning frequently.
3. Add leeks, garlic, and carrots and cook for another few minutes, stirring. Add salt, peppercorns, parsley, thyme, tomato paste, and wine. Mix well, cover, and cook over low heat 2–3 hours until beef is tender.
4. Uncover, add onions and mushrooms for last ½ hour of cooking.

Serves 4–6

FILLET OF BEEF WITH MUSHROOM SAUCE

2 tablespoons butter
1 medium onion, minced
1 carrot, chopped fine
1 stalk celery with leaves, chopped fine
3-pound fillet of beef, trimmed
1 teaspoon salt
¼ teaspoon freshly ground black pepper
2 tablespoons butter
½ pound fresh mushrooms, sliced
2 tablespoons butter
2 tablespoons green peppercorns
½ cup Madeira wine
¼ cup beef stock
1 tablespoon Dijon mustard
2 tablespoons parsley, finely chopped

1. In a medium frying pan, heat 2 tablespoons butter over low heat. Add onions, carrots, and celery and stir until vegetables are thoroughly coated with butter. Remove from heat.
2. Butter a roasting pan that can be heated on top of the stove as well as in the oven. Place the fillet in the roasting pan. Sprinkle beef with ½ teaspoon salt and ¼ teaspoon pepper and spread with 2 tablespoons softened butter. Surround beef with buttered vegetables. Roast in a preheated 450° oven 15 minutes. Lower oven heat to 350° and roast 30 minutes more for rare.
3. In same frying pan used for vegetables, heat 2 tablespoons butter over moderate to high heat. Add sliced mushrooms and sauté quickly, stirring, about one minute. Remove from heat and set aside.
4. In a small bowl, crush peppercorns with a pestle or heavy spoon and set aside.
5. When fillet is done, remove from roasting pan and set aside. Keep warm.
6. Pour Madeira and beef stock into roasting pan and set over low heat. Stir well to scrape up all brown bits from bottom of pan. Add

mustard, crushed peppercorns, ½ teaspoon salt, and ¼ teaspoon pepper. Cook, stirring, about 2–3 minutes until slightly reduced. Stir in parsley and sautéed mushrooms and heat through.

7. Carve fillet into serving slices. Pour hot sauce over the fillet and serve.

Serves 6–8

HERBED VEAL STEW

2 tablespoons olive oil
3 tablespoons butter
2 cups sliced fresh mushrooms
2 cups sweet frying peppers, cut in ½-inch strips
2 pounds boneless veal cubes
1 medium onion, chopped
1 teaspoon salt
¼ teaspoon freshly ground black pepper
1 clove garlic, mashed
1 teaspoon dried tarragon
1 medium-sized ripe tomato, chopped
½ cup dry white vermouth
1 tablespoon flour
2 tablespoons parsley, finely chopped
few drops lemon juice

1. In a large heavy pot, heat one tablespoon oil and one tablespoon butter over moderate to high heat. Add mushrooms and peppers and sauté quickly, stirring, a few minutes. Remove from pan and set aside.

2. Dry veal cubes thoroughly with paper towels. In same pot heat one tablespoon oil and one tablespoon butter over high heat. Add onion and sauté a few minutes. Add veal cubes and brown quickly on all sides.

3. Add salt, pepper, garlic, tarragon, tomato, and vermouth. Mix well, cover, and cook over low heat 1½–2 hours until veal is very tender. Add reserved mushrooms and peppers and cook, covered, 10 minutes more.

4. Remove meat and vegetables from pot with slotted spoon and set aside. In a small pot heat one tablespoon butter over moderate heat. Add one tablespoon flour and mix well. Cook, stirring constantly, over moderate heat for 2 minutes. Add parsley and mix well.

5. Add flour mixture to sauce in pot and whisk thoroughly over low heat until well blended and smooth. Return meat and vegetables to sauce and cook, stirring, just until heated through. Sprinkle in lemon juice and serve.

Serves 4–6

CALVES LIVER IN MUSTARD SAUCE

The success of this dish will depend largely on the quality and freshness of the liver, so buy the best.

1 pound calves liver, cut in thin slices
flour for dredging
3 tablespoons clarified butter
salt and pepper
2 shallots, finely minced, or small onion, finely minced
¼ cup dry white wine
1 tablespoon Dijon mustard
¼ cup light cream
2 tablespoons parsley, chopped
few drops lemon juice

1. Remove membranes and all tough connective tissue from liver. Dredge lightly with flour.
2. In a medium skillet melt butter over moderate heat. Add liver slices and sauté a few minutes on each side, until lightly browned on the outside and just slightly pink on the inside. Remove liver from pan and set aside. Salt and pepper the liver lightly.
3. If there is no butter left in the pan, add one tablespoon. Sauté shallot or onion in butter until soft. Add wine and mustard, then cream, and stir to blend. Bring just to a simmer, sprinkle in lemon juice and parsley. Spoon sauce over liver and serve.

Serves 2–3

CASSOULET

One of the great bean dishes of the world—and wonderful fare for a cold winter night.

1 pound dried white beans (Great Northern or marrow)
1 medium onion, peeled
4 whole cloves
¼ teaspoon freshly ground black pepper
1 carrot, sliced
¼ cup parsley, chopped
1 stalk celery with leaves, chopped
1 tablespoon salt

½ pound bulk sausage meat
½ pound garlic or Polish sausage, sliced
1 medium onion, chopped
2 cloves garlic, mashed
½ cup dry white wine
8-ounce can tomato sauce
½ teaspoon salt
⅛ teaspoon freshly ground black pepper
2 teaspoons thyme
1 teaspoon dried basil
1 cup pieces cooked pork
1 cup pieces cooked poultry (duck, goose, turkey, or chicken)
¼ cup butter
½ cup dry bread crumbs
⅓ cup parsley, chopped

1. Soak beans overnight in enough cold water to cover. Drain.
2. Stick 2 cloves in each end of the onion. Place the onion, beans, pepper, carrot, parsley, and celery in a large pot; pour in about 2 quarts cold water. Simmer uncovered over low heat about 1½–2 hours or until beans are tender. Add one tablespoon salt for last ½ hour of cooking.
3. Drain beans, reserving cooking liquid, which should measure about 1½–2 cups. Discard clove-studded onion.
4. In a large frying pan, brown sausage meat and sausage slices. Remove from pan and set aside.
5. Drain all but one tablespoon fat from pan. Add onion and garlic and sauté until golden. Add wine, tomato sauce, ½ teaspoon salt, pepper, thyme, and basil, then add reserved bean liquid. Cook uncovered over low heat for about 15 minutes, scraping up all brown bits from bottom of pan. You should have about 2 cups of sauce.
6. In a deep casserole, alternate layers of beans and combined mixed meats. Pour sauce into casserole.
7. In a small frying pan melt butter, add bread crumbs and parsley and sauté, stirring, for a few minutes.
8. Spread bread crumb mixture evenly over the top of the casserole. Cover and bake in a preheated 350° oven about one hour. Remove cover for last 10 minutes of baking.

Serves 8

PORK CHOPS NORMANDY

2 tablespoons salad oil
6–8 lean pork chops
¼ cup cider
1½ tablespoons butter
1 medium onion, sliced
2 apples (Winesap or Granny Smith), peeled, cored, and sliced
1½ tablespoons flour
¾ cup unfiltered apple cider (not apple juice)
1 teaspoon beef bouillon or 1 beef bouillon cube
good grind black pepper, dash salt
2–3 tablespoons Calvados (apple brandy)

1. In a large frying pan, heat oil and brown chops quickly on both sides. Remove chops as they brown to a shallow baking dish; salt and pepper lightly. Add ¼ cup cider to baking dish, cover, and bake chops for 40–50 minutes at 350° until they are tender.
2. Drain off oil remaining in pan; add butter. Over moderate heat sauté onion and apples until just tender and beginning to turn golden. Add flour, mix well, and cook for another 2–3 minutes.
3. Add cider, whisk well to blend, and cook until mixture just comes to a simmer and thickens. Add bouillon, salt, and pepper and mix well. Add Calvados, heat through, and remove from heat.
4. Remove pork chops from baking dish and place on serving platter. Spread sauce over the chops and serve immediately.

Serves 4–6

CHICKEN WITH APPLES AND CREAM

3–4 pounds boneless chicken breasts
flour for dredging
3–4 tablespoons clarified butter
salt and pepper
2 tablespoons butter
1 medium onion, finely chopped
2 apples (Winesap or Granny Smith), peeled, cored, and sliced
1½ tablespoons flour
¾ cup unfiltered apple cider
1 chicken bouillon cube or 1 teaspoon granulated chicken bouillon
dash salt and pepper
¼ cup Calvados (apple brandy)
⅔ cup heavy cream

1. Remove any skin from chicken breasts. Cut breasts in half, then pound between sheets of waxed paper into uniform thickness, about ¼-inch thick.
2. Dredge chicken pieces lightly with flour; heat clarified butter in a large skillet and sauté chicken over moderate heat until golden brown. Remove chicken from pan as it browns, salt and pepper each piece lightly, set aside and keep warm while preparing sauce.
3. Add 2 tablespoons butter to pan and sauté onion and apples until tender. Add flour, mix well, and cook for another 2–3 minutes.
4. Add cider, bouillon, salt and pepper, mix well and bring to a simmer. Stir in Calvados, then the heavy cream and stir until well blended and very hot. Pour sauce over chicken and serve.

Serves 6–8

SEAFOOD RAVIGOTE

1 head romaine or curly endive, washed, dried, and chilled
1 pound cooked shrimp, peeled and deveined
1 pound cooked lobster meat, cut in chunks
1 pound lump crabmeat
14-ounce can artichoke hearts, drained and cut in half
¾ cup olive oil
¼ cup white wine vinegar
2 teaspoons Dijon mustard
1 teaspoon salt
¼ teaspoon freshly ground black pepper
2 tablespoons fresh dill, chopped
2 tablespoons parsley, finely chopped
1 tablespoon chives, chopped
2 scallions, finely chopped
1 tablespoon capers

1. Line a large salad or serving bowl with romaine or endive leaves.
2. In a quart jar with a tight-fitting cover, combine oil, vinegar, mustard, salt, pepper, herbs, and capers. Cover tightly and shake thoroughly.
3. Pour dressing over combined seafood and mix gently but thoroughly. Place seafood in lettuce-lined bowl and serve.

Serves 6–8

SHRIMP WITH CLAM SAUCE

8-ounce can minced clams
1½ pounds boiled shrimp, peeled and deveined
2 tablespoons butter
3 tablespoons scallions, finely minced
1 tablespoon chives, chopped
1½ tablespoons flour
½ cup Chablis or other medium dry white wine
¼ teaspoon salt
good dash white pepper
½ cup heavy cream
1⅓ cups grated Gruyère or Emmenthal cheese

1. Drain minced clams, reserving clam juice, which should measure about ½ cup. Combine shrimp and clams and set aside.
2. In a medium saucepan melt butter over moderate heat. Add scallions, chives, and flour and sauté, stirring constantly, for about 2 minutes.
3. Pour in wine and clam juice and whisk rapidly until mixture is smooth. Continue to cook, stirring, until sauce thickens and comes just to a boil.
4. Add salt, pepper, heavy cream, and one cup of the cheese. Cook, stirring, until cheese is melted and sauce is smooth.
5. Remove sauce from heat and stir in shrimp and clams. Mix well, then pour into a buttered shallow casserole or au gratin dish or individual ramekins. Sprinkle with remaining cheese.
6. Place in a 400° oven for 15–20 minutes until bubbly. If desired, run under the broiler for a few seconds to brown cheese slightly.

Serves 4 as main course
6 as appetizer

TWO MARINATED VEGETABLE SALADS VINAIGRETTE

The Vinaigrette

¾ cup olive oil
¼ cup wine vinegar
2 teaspoons Dijon mustard
1 teaspoon salt
⅛ teaspoon freshly ground black pepper
1 large clove garlic, mashed

Combine all ingredients in a jar with a tightly fitting cover and shake well.

Marinated Leeks and Asparagus

1 pound fresh asparagus
2 medium leeks

1. Trim tough ends from asparagus. Cut off stem end and upper green parts from leeks. Discard. Wash leeks thoroughly and cut into quarters lengthwise. Cook leeks and asparagus in boiling water to cover for a few minutes or until asparagus are tender. Drain thoroughly. Pour on a generous amount of dressing, mix gently, and let stand for a couple of hours. Serve at room temperature.

Serves 6

Marinated Mixed Vegetables

2 medium potatoes, peeled and cubed
1 small head cauliflower, broken into flowerets
½ pound small fresh mushrooms, cleaned and trimmed of stem ends
6–8 canned or fresh cooked artichoke hearts, cut in half
½ pound string beans, cut in 1-inch pieces
¼ cup parsley, finely chopped

1. Cook potatoes, cauliflower, and string beans in boiling salted water just until tender. Do not overcook. Drain thoroughly.
2. Combine cooked vegetables with artichokes and mushrooms in a large bowl. Pour over a generous amount of vinaigrette and mix thoroughly. Let stand for a couple of hours. Before serving taste for salt and dressing; you may need to add some more at this point. Garnish with parsley and serve at room temperature.

Serves 8

NORTHERN ITALY

The cuisine of northern Italy is similar in many respects to that of France: indeed, France owes much of its culinary distinction to traditions brought from Italy by Catherine de Medeci in the sixteenth century. During that period veal, fish, and chicken, artichokes and asparagus all were popularized, and desserts became glorified creations.

Still, northern Italy retains the fundamentally Italian love of pasta and garlic and although tomatoes and peppers are used, it is not as heavily as in the Mediterranean cuisine. Butter and cream are widely used, but the butter is frequently mixed with olive oil. Wine is essential in the preparation of many sauces, but Italian taste seems to prefer the flavor of the sweeter wines like Marsala, rather than the drier cooking wines of France. Parsley, oregano, and basil are the preferred cooking herbs.

The clearest flavor principle is the combination of wine vinegar and garlic; lemon, nuts, capers, and anchovies are added for variation.

NORTHERN ITALIAN RECIPIES

GARLIC-STUFFED EGGS

CHICKEN IN GARLIC-VINEGAR SAUCE

CALVES LIVER VENETIAN STYLE

SHRIMP IN LEMON-GARLIC SAUCE

GARLIC RICE

CAULIFLOWER IN GARLIC SAUCE

GARLIC-STUFFED EGGS

6 large eggs
1 tablespoon butter
1 tablespoon olive oil
4 cloves garlic, finely minced
2 tablespoons red wine vinegar
⅛ teaspoon salt
⅛ teaspoon freshly ground black pepper
3 tablespoons parsley, finely chopped

1. Place eggs in a saucepan with cold water to cover. Simmer over low heat, uncovered, for 5 minutes. Cover pot, turn off heat, and let stand 15 minutes. Run cold water into pot. Cool eggs slightly, then shell.
2. Cut eggs in half lengthwise. Carefully scoop out yolks and place in a small bowl. Mash thoroughly.
3. In a small frying pan heat butter and oil over moderate heat. Add garlic and sauté, stirring, about ½ minute until garlic just begins to brown. Do not allow garlic to burn.
4. Add vinegar and simmer about 2 minutes, shaking pan frequently. Remove from heat and cool slightly.
5. To mashed yolks add vinegar-garlic mixture, salt, pepper, and parsley. Mix well, then spoon yolk mixture into reserved egg white shells. Refrigerate.

Makes 12 stuffed egg halves

CHICKEN IN GARLIC-VINEGAR SAUCE

2½–3½-pound frying chicken, cut in serving pieces
¼ cup olive oil
4 cloves garlic, finely minced
1½ teaspoons salt
¼ teaspoon freshly ground black pepper
¼ cup red wine vinegar
1 teaspoon crumbled dried oregano
¼ cup parsley, chopped

1. Dry chicken pieces thoroughly with paper towels.
2. In a large frying pan heat olive oil over moderate heat; add garlic and sauté, stirring, 2 minutes. Add chicken pieces, and brown on all sides until golden. Sprinkle chicken with salt and pepper.
3. Add the vinegar, oregano, and parsley. Cover and cook over low heat about 20–30 minutes or until chicken is tender. Turn chicken occasionally while cooking.

Serves 4

CALVES LIVER VENETIAN STYLE

2 pounds calves liver, thinly sliced
2 tablespoons olive oil
1 tablespoon butter
1½ teaspoons salt
¼ teaspoon freshly ground black pepper
4 cloves garlic, finely minced
⅓ cup red wine vinegar
1 teaspoon crumbled dried oregano
2–3 tablespoons parsley, chopped

Garnish: 2 lemons, quartered

1. Remove any skin or membrane from the liver.
2. In a large frying pan, heat oil and butter over moderate heat until sizzling. Add liver and sauté quickly on both sides until tender and slightly pink on the inside, about 2–3 minutes. Sprinkle liver with salt and pepper and transfer to heated serving platter.
3. Add garlic to pan and sauté 2 minutes. Add vinegar and oregano and simmer about 5 minutes. Stir in parsley, mix well, and pour over liver. Serve garnished with lemon wedges.

Serves 4–6

SHRIMP IN LEMON-GARLIC SAUCE

4 large cloves garlic, finely minced
3 tablespoons butter
2 tablespoons olive oil
3 pounds raw shrimp, peeled and deveined
2 teaspoons salt
⅛ teaspoon freshly ground black pepper
juice 2 small lemons
2–3 tablespoons parsley, chopped

1. Over low heat in large frying pan, sauté garlic in butter and oil until soft but not browned.
2. Turn up heat, add shrimp and sauté quickly until tender, about 3 minutes.
3. Add salt, pepper, and lemon juice. Heat to sizzling, sprinkle with chopped parsley, and serve immediately.

Serves 6

GARLIC RICE

2 tablespoons butter
2 tablespoons olive oil
4 cloves garlic, finely minced
1 cup long-grain rice
2 tablespoons red or white wine vinegar
2 cups hot beef stock
¼ cup parsley, chopped

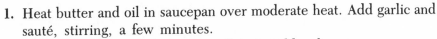

1. Heat butter and oil in saucepan over moderate heat. Add garlic and sauté, stirring, a few minutes.
2. Add rice and sauté, stirring until it is golden brown.
3. Add vinegar and stock. Cover and cook over low heat 15–20 minutes until rice is tender and all liquid is absorbed. Stir in chopped parsley and serve.

Serves 4–5

CAULIFLOWER IN GARLIC SAUCE

1 medium head cauliflower
2 tablespoons butter
2 tablespoons oil
4 cloves garlic, finely minced
1 teaspoon salt
⅛ teaspoon freshly ground pepper
2 tablespoons red wine vinegar
2 tablespoons water

1. Cut leaves and tough stem from cauliflower; separate head into small flowerets.
2. Heat butter and oil in a large saucepan and sauté garlic, stirring, just until starting to brown. Add cauliflower and sauté, stirring, a few more minutes.
3. Add salt, pepper, vinegar, and water; cover, and cook over low heat about 10 minutes. Shake pan over high heat to reduce sauce at very end.

Serves 4

NOTE: Other vegetables such as broccoli, mushrooms, green beans, potatoes, etc., can be added or substituted. Leftovers are good in a tossed salad.

MEXICO

When the conquistadores arrived in Mexico looking for gold and pepper, little did they know what an impact their discovery would have on the eating habits of the Old World. The Indians of Mexico, they found, lived on a diet composed largely of thin flat cornmeal bread, which the Spanish called *"tortillas"* (little cakes), a variety of beans and squashes, and sauces made of tomatoes and chile peppers. After its importation into Europe, the tomato was integrated as a fundamental culinary element in many of the cuisines of Europe, the Mediterranean, and the Middle East. The *capsicum* peppers, of which the chile pepper is one, had even greater success. Conservatively estimated, half a billion people, perhaps even one quarter of the world's adult population, eat some variety of chile pepper every day! In addition to corn, beans, and squashes, tomato and peppers, the New World offered chocolate, vanilla, peanuts, potatoes, avocados, and the turkey.

Mexico has remained amazingly constant to a set of culinary traditions many thousands of years old; fossilized botanic remains testify to this fact. The corn and beans that graced the aboriginal table remain today as the basis of the Mexican diet and they are eaten together at almost every meal. There is good reason for this: together, corn and beans provide the full complement of amino acids, the protein elements necessary for growth and body repair.

The chile pepper is still the cornerstone of Mexican seasoning practice. There are literally hundreds of varieties that are used with great subtlety in this cooking tradition. Of the red, green, yellow, and orange chiles, some are violently pungent, others moderately so, some mild; they may be used fresh, dried, or pickled. There are many varieties of tomato as well; they may be used either red or green, fresh or cooked into sauce.

Of the many foods introduced by the Spanish to Mexico, the most widely accepted are wheat, rice, beef and dairy products, pork, and chicken. The Spanish also brought with them the technique, apparently unknown to pre-Columbian Mexico, of rendering fat from meat, and of cooking food in fat or oil. This technique of frying was accepted enthusiastically by the Mexicans, who cooked primarily by slow stewing, or simmering in liquid. The major seasoning introduced by the Spanish was the family of citrus fruits, and many varieties of lemon, lime, and orange are widely used in Mexican cooking today.

160

Two major flavor principles can be extracted from Mexican cuisine. The first is the age-old combination of tomatoes and chile pepper; the second is the comparatively newer combination of lime and chile. Either principle may be varied with the use of a number of seasoning ingredients: garlic, cinnamon, cumin, oregano, onion, saffron, achiote, and a variety of seeds and nuts. Fresh coriander leaf is very widely used as a garnishing herb.

One great regional variation, that of the cuisine of the Yucatan, should be noted. The same basic foods are used here as in the rest of Mexico, but influences from Europe, the Caribbean, and America gave rise to the unique combination of sour orange, garlic, and achiote. This principle is used frequently in Yucatec cuisine when cooking in the ancient *pib*, or earth pit.

MEXICAN RECIPES

LIME-CHILE

CEVICHE

GUACAMOLE

MEXICAN STUFFED EGGS

SOPA DE LIMA

RED SNAPPER VERA CRUZ

TOMATO-CHILE

TARASCAN TOMATO SOUP

MEXICAN BLACK BEAN SOUP

LOIN OF PORK IN RED ADOBO SAUCE

SOUR ORANGE–GARLIC–ACHIOTE

COCHINITA PIBIL

POLLO MOTULEÑO

CEVICHE

Ceviche is a traditional Mexican dish that occurs in many versions in parts of South America and the South Pacific. The fish or seafood is cooked not by heat but by marination in citrus juice. The acid in the juice breaks down the connective tissue in the fish as does heat, so that when it is served, the fish is as fully cooked as though it has been baked in an oven.

1 pound boneless white fish fillets, cut in thin strips, or 1 pound bay scallops
juice 3 lemons
juice 3 limes
3 tablespoons olive oil
1 large ripe tomato, chopped
2–3 tablespoons fresh coriander leaf, chopped (cilantro)
1 small onion or 3 scallions, chopped
1 small fresh red chile pepper, seeded and finely chopped, or 2 tablespoons chopped canned serrano chiles
1 teaspoon salt
dash freshly ground black pepper
10 pitted green olives, halved

1. Combine fish or scallops with lemon and lime juices in a glass or ceramic bowl. Mix well. Be sure fish is entirely covered with juice. Cover and refrigerate 6–8 hours or overnight.
2. Before serving, drain off most of juice. Add oil, tomato, cilantro, onion, chile pepper, salt, pepper, and olives. Mix well. Serve in small custard cups or dessert dishes.

Serves 4–6 as an appetizer

GUACAMOLE

The avocado is indigenous to Mexico, where it is cheap and plentiful. Mashed up in the form of guacamole, it is featured in many Mexican meals as a salad, a sauce, and as a filling for tacos.

2 medium-sized ripe avocados
juice 1 lime
juice ½ lemon
1 large clove garlic, mashed
2 scallions, minced

1½ tablespoons canned green chili pepper, finely minced
½ teaspoon salt
dash freshly ground black pepper
½ teaspoon chili powder
2 tablespoons coriander leaf (cilantro) or parsley, finely chopped

1. Peel and pit the avocados. Mash with a fork until smooth. Stir in all other ingredients and mix well. If not serving immediately, cover surface closely with plastic wrap.
2. Serve at room temperature with corn chips or fried tortillas.

Makes about 3 cups

MEXICAN STUFFED EGGS

6 large eggs
3 tablespoons mayonnaise
2 tablespoons lime juice
1 teaspoon canned jalapeño pepper, finely minced (seeds removed)
1 scallion, finely minced
2 tablespoons cilantro or parsley, finely chopped
¼ teaspoon salt
dash freshly ground black pepper
¼ teaspoon cayenne pepper

1. Place eggs in medium saucepan with enough cold water to cover. Bring pot to boil, turn heat low and simmer uncovered for 5 minutes. Cover pot, turn off heat, and let stand 15 minutes. Run cold water into pot. Shell eggs.
2. Cut eggs in half lengthwise. Carefully scoop out yolks, place in bowl and mash well.
3. Add all ingredients except the cayenne pepper. Mix well, then heap egg yolk mixture into reserved egg white shells. Sprinkle each with a dash of cayenne pepper. Chill.

Makes 12 stuffed eggs

SOPA DE LIMA

6 cups chicken stock
juice 1 large lemon
2 tablespoons cilantro, chopped, or ¼ cup parsley, chopped
pinch crushed dried red peppers
1 can mild green chile, minced
¼ cup vegetable oil
6 corn tortillas, cut in thin strips
1 cup cooked chicken, cut in thin strips
½ cup cooked pork, cut in thin strips (optional)
3 scallions, chopped
½ unpeeled lime, finely chopped

1. In a large pot, heat chicken stock and add to it lemon juice, cilantro, red peppers, and chile. Simmer uncovered over low heat 15 minutes.
2. Before serving, fry tortilla strips in hot vegetable oil until lightly browned and crisp. Drain on paper towels. Add tortilla strips, chicken, pork, scallions, and lime to soup and heat through.

Serves 8

RED SNAPPER VERA CRUZ

1 medium onion, chopped
1 green pepper, seeded and chopped
1 stalk celery, chopped
1 carrot, chopped
2 tablespoons vegetable oil
16-ounce can Italian plum tomatoes, or 2 large ripe tomatoes
¼ cup lemon or lime juice
1 clove garlic, mashed
½ teaspoon ground cumin
½ teaspoon oregano
2 tablespoons cilantro or parsley, finely chopped
2 teaspoons salt
dash freshly ground black pepper
2 pounds red snapper fillets
10 green olives, pitted and halved
4½-ounce can small shrimp, rinsed in cold water and drained

1. Slowly sauté onion, green pepper, celery, and carrot in oil until tender but not browned. Add tomatoes, lemon juice, garlic, cumin, oregano, cilantro, salt, and pepper.

2. Carefully place fish fillets in sauce, cover pan, and simmer gently until fish is just done, about 10 minutes.
3. Add the olives and shrimp to the sauce and heat through. Serve with rice.

Serves 6

TARASCAN TOMATO SOUP

Named for the Tarascan Indians of the State of Michoacan, west of Mexico City, this is a wonderful soup—rich, smooth, and delicious.

2 tablespoons salad oil
1 medium onion, chopped
3 cloves garlic, mashed
2 medium green or sweet red peppers, chopped
1-pound can dark red kidney beans, with juice
1 cup fresh or canned tomatoes, chopped
4 cups chicken stock
6-ounce can tomato paste
2 large *ancho* chiles, seeded and cut in thin strips
1 teaspoon oregano
½ teaspoon black pepper
1–1½ cups shredded mild cheddar cheese
2 cups corn chips or tortilla chips, coarsely crumbled

1. In a large pot heat oil; add onion, garlic, and peppers and sauté until onion is just beginning to brown.
2. In a blender or food processor, blend beans with juice and tomatoes until smooth.
3. To onions in pot add stock, puréed beans, and all other ingredients except cheese and corn chips. Cook over low heat, stirring occasionally, for about 45 minutes.
4. Just before serving, place a small handful of grated cheese at the bottom of individual soup bowl. Ladle hot soup over, then garnish with corn chips. Serve immediately.

Serves 6–8

NOTE: In the beautiful city of Uruapan, where I first ate this soup, it came garnished with a large dollop of sour cream. That seemed a bit like gilding the lily to me, but try it if you like.

MEXICAN BLACK BEAN SOUP

1 cup dried black beans
1 tablespoon vegetable oil
½ cup ham or Canadian bacon, diced
1 large onion, chopped
2 carrots, chopped
2 stalks celery, chopped
3 cloves garlic, mashed
2 quarts water
½ teaspoon freshly ground pepper
1 teaspoon crumbled dried oregano
1 bay leaf
1 teaspoon ground cumin
1 teaspoon chili powder
¼ teaspoon crushed dried red peppers
1 cup tomatoes, coarsely chopped
1 tablespoon salt
⅓ cup cream sherry

1. Soak beans overnight in enough cold water to cover. Drain.
2. In a large pot heat oil; add ham and sauté a few minutes.
3. Add onion, carrots, celery, and garlic and sauté 3–4 minutes.
4. Add drained beans, water, and all other ingredients except salt and sherry. Simmer uncovered 1½–2 hours or until beans are tender. Add more water if necessary during cooking.
5. When beans are tender stir in salt and remove pot from heat. Cool slightly, then purée in blender or food mill. Stir in sherry, bring to a simmer, and serve.

Serves 8

LOIN OF PORK IN RED ADOBO

2 tablespoons sesame seeds
2 tablespoons pumpkin seeds (pepitas)
4 tablespoons ground *ancho* chiles, or 4 large *ancho* chiles, seeds and stems removed and cut in small pieces
1 teaspoon cinnamon
12 whole cloves
1 tablespoon cumin seeds
1 teaspoon salt
4–5 medium-sized very ripe tomatoes
¼ cup cider vinegar
2 tablespoons oil
3–4 pounds lean boneless loin of pork

1. In a blender combine all ingredients except the oil and pork. Blend until smooth.

2. In a heavy pot or Dutch oven, heat oil over high heat. Add pork loin and brown quickly on all sides.
3. Add sauce from blender and stir over high heat for a few minutes. Lower heat, cover pot, and cook for 1½–2 hours or until pork is very tender.
4. Remove pork from pot and slice. Continue to cook sauce over high heat until it is reduced and thickened. Spoon sauce over pork and serve with fresh tortillas.

Serves 6–8

COCHINITA PIBIL
(Roast Suckling Pig Cooked in a Pit)

This is an ancient and classic dish of the Yucatan. The *pib*, or earth pit, is one of the oldest known cooking techniques, and is not unique to Mexico. It was probably very widely used throughout the world by hunting and gathering groups, and survives today in such diverse forms as the Indian clambake of the northeast coast of America, and the Hawaiian luau. Basically, it is a hole or trench dug in the earth or sand that is lined with red-hot stones. The food is wrapped protectively in some material that retains moisture and does not burn easily (such as seaweed or banana leaves), placed in the pit and covered with another layer of hot stones. In effect, this method slowly steam-cooks the food, allowing it to retain its natural moisture and succulence. Before the Spanish conquest, the Indians probably cooked wild game and turkey using this technique and, indeed, turkey, either whole or in parts, is very good prepared this way.

Most of us, of course, do not have access to an earth pit, but I think the following method produces quite respectable results. To prepare this dish I use a large, covered, earthenware casserole and cook the meat in a slow oven for a long time. Since this method results in meat that is very tender and very moist, it is not necessary to buy an expensive cut.

4–6-pound whole pork shoulder or butt
¼ cup orange juice
¼ cup lemon juice
6 large cloves garlic
24 black peppercorns
2 tablespoons ground achiote
1 teaspoon oregano
1 teaspoon cumin
1 teaspoon salt

1. With a sharp knife trim the skin off the pork and as much of the fat as possible. Make deep incisions on all sides of the meat.
2. In a blender, combine all the other ingredients and blend until

smooth. Pour this sauce all over the meat in the casserole, rubbing it well into the incisions. Cover and let marinate in the refrigerator overnight.

3. Cook, covered, in a 300° oven for 4–5 hours. Remove the meat from the casserole and cut the meat off the bones. Chill the sauce and discard the fat that has accumulated on the top.

4. Reheat the meat in the skimmed sauce and serve.

The best way to serve *cohinita pibil* and the way it is served most frequently in the Yucatan is in the form of *panuchos*. These are fried tortillas, covered with a layer of mashed refried beans, topped with the pork cooked in its sauce, and garnished with sweet and sour onions. It is very messy to eat and very delicious.

To make the sweet and sour onions, slice 3 large onions, cover with water and simmer for about 5 minutes. Drain the onions, then combine with ¼ cup vinegar and one tablespoon sugar. Let marinate for several hours.

Serves 8–10

POLLO MOTULEÑO

A classic dish from the Yucatan. It is frequently served with slices of fried plantain.

2 tablespoons lard or salad oil
3–4 pounds chicken parts
1 medium onion, chopped
3 cloves garlic, mashed
1 cup (8-ounce can) tomato sauce
¼ cup sour orange juice (combine 2 tablespoons orange juice with 2 tablespoons lemon juice)
1 teaspoon ground cumin
1 teaspoon oregano
¼ teaspoon salt
dash freshly ground pepper
1 teaspoon ground achiote or adobo paste (see p. 251)
¼ cup ham, finely chopped

Garnish: ½ cup fresh cooked or frozen peas

1. Heat lard or oil in large frying pan or pot; brown chicken parts on all sides. Remove chicken parts from pan as they brown, salt and pepper lightly and set aside.

2. In same pan, sauté onion and garlic until lightly browned. Add all other ingredients except peas and mix well. Return chicken parts to sauce and cook uncovered over low to moderate heat for about 30–40 minutes until chicken is tender. Garnish with peas and serve.

Serves 6

GENERAL PRINCIPLES I

SWEET-SOUR

Most flavor principles, with their bonds of seasoning ingredients, can be linked to specific geographic areas: fish sauce and coconut milk in Southeast Asia, sour cream and dill in Scandinavia, and so forth. But there are some flavor principles so widely disseminated, one cannot say that they are unique to any specific culture or location.

The first of these is the sweet and sour principle, a flavoring used throughout the world, and with good reason. The sourness is provided by acidic substances of various kinds: vinegar (literally, "sour wine"), citrus fruits such as lemon and lime, and other acidic fruits like tamarind. The acidic flavor gives zest to foods and, when used in small amounts, heightens other flavors. In larger amounts, acid, like salt, inhibits the growth of bacteria and thus is useful in the preservation of foods. But the amounts or concentrations of acidic juices necessary to prevent spoilage may have an overwhelming taste and an unpleasant effect on the palate. Its effect needs to be diluted with other flavoring ingredients, and sugar provides the perfect balance. This combination results in the flavor we call sweet/sour.

The sweet/sour principle accounts for a large number of familiar pickled products: pickled herring, pickled vegetables, relishes, condimental sauces like ketchup, and chutneys. Other seasonings typical of any given tradition are easily incorporated into this principle: the sweet/sour in Chinese cuisine frequently uses gingerroot and garlic; the sweet/sour in central Asia uses cinnamon; and, in northern Europe, onion and dill are added.

An interesting variation of sweet/sour is the combination of hot and sour. Here the sugar is omitted and hot peppers and/or chile are substituted. This principle is not as widespread as sweet/sour and is found primarily in Asian cooking in such preparations as Chinese hot and sour soup, Korean *kim chee* (fermented spiced cabbage), and certain dishes characteristic of Bombay.

SWEET/SOUR RECIPES

RED CABBAGE SOUP

CHINESE HOT AND SOUR SOUP

SPICY CHINESE BEEF

SAUERBRATEN

SOUR BEEF CURRY

STEAMED PORK BALLS SWEET-SOUR

SWEET AND SOUR STUFFED CABBAGE

PICKLED FISH

OLD FASHIONED CUCUMBER SALAD

INDONESIAN CUCUMBER SALAD

APRICOT CHUTNEY

GREEN APPLE CHUTNEY

CANTALOUPE CHUTNEY

CAPONATA

SWEET AND SOUR PLUM SAUCE

See also:
Swedish Herring Salad p. 135

RED CABBAGE SOUP

In this traditional favorite of eastern Europe, beets can be substituted for the cabbage to produce borscht. Like borscht, this soup can be garnished with sour cream if desired.

2 tablespoons butter
1 medium onion, thinly sliced
1 tart green apple, cored and thinly sliced
2 cups red cabbage, coarsely shredded or chopped
4 cups beef stock
¼ cup cider vinegar
¼ cup lemon juice
¼ cup firmly packed brown sugar
1 teaspoon white sugar
1 teaspoon salt
¼ teaspoon black pepper
½ teaspoon ground ginger
⅓ cup raisins

1. In a large pot melt butter over moderate heat; add onion and apple and sauté, stirring, until tender.
2. Add cabbage and sauté another 3 minutes. Add the stock, vinegar, lemon juice, sugars, salt, pepper, ginger, and raisins. Cook uncovered over low heat for 45 minutes. Serve hot or chilled, garnished with sour cream if desired.

Serves 6–8

CHINESE HOT AND SOUR SOUP

A specialty of northern China, as evidenced by the use of soy bean paste (*miso*) and sesame oil. The vinegar and several kinds of pepper give the soup its hot and sour flavor. The chewiness of the shredded ingredients provides a good textural contrast to the slightly viscous quality of the soup. This recipe was developed by Paul Rozin.

¼ cup dried tree ears
6 medium dried Chinese mushrooms
16 dried tiger lily buds
8 cups chicken stock (homemade or canned)
⅔ cup raw pork, finely shredded
6-ounce cake fresh bean curd (tofu), cut in ¼-inch dice
2 teaspoons soy sauce
4 teaspoons miso
2 cloves garlic, finely minced
1 teaspoon sugar
1 teaspoon salt
½ teaspoon freshly ground black pepper
⅛ teaspoon ground Szechuan pepper
5–7 tablespoons rice wine vinegar or 5–6 tablespoons distilled white
    vinegar
6 tablespoons cornstarch
½ cup cold water
2 eggs, beaten
1 tablespoon sesame oil

1. Place tree ears, mushrooms, and tiger lily buds in a bowl and cover with warm water. Let stand ½ hour. With a sharp knife remove hard center core from mushrooms and discard. Shred mushrooms and tree ears. Cut lily buds into 1-inch long pieces.
2. In a large pot combine stock, tree ears, mushrooms, lily buds, pork, bean curd, soy sauce, miso, garlic, sugar, and salt. Simmer gently over low heat for 20 minutes
3. Stir in black pepper, Szechuan pepper, and vinegar. (The amount of vinegar is critical but cannot be specified precisely. The soup should have a distinct but not overwhelming sour taste.)
4. Just before serving bring soup to the boil. Dissolve cornstarch in cold water; add this paste gradually to the soup, stirring, until soup is slightly thickened. Not all the paste may be needed, so add it carefully at the end.
5. Remove soup from heat and add beaten eggs. Allow a few seconds for the eggs to start congealing, then stir. This should result in light strands of egg in the soup

6. Stir in sesame oil and serve. (This soup is delicious reheated the next day.)

Serves 10–12

SPICY CHINESE BEEF

1½–2 pounds boneless beef, cut in 1-inch cubes
3 tablespoons soy sauce
3 tablespoons dry sherry
3 tablespoons Chinese plum sauce
1 tablespoon red wine vinegar
1 teaspoon sugar
3 tablespoons peanut oil
2 cloves garlic, finely minced
1 tablespoon gingerroot, finely minced
¼ teaspoon crushed dried red peppers

1. Dry beef cubes thoroughly with paper towels; cut off any excess fat.
2. In a small bowl combine soy sauce, sherry, plum sauce, vinegar, and sugar, and mix well.
3. In a heavy pot or Dutch oven, heat peanut oil over high heat. Add garlic, gingerroot, and red peppers and stir fry a few seconds. Add beef cubes and brown quickly on all sides.
4. Add sauce mixture, cover, and cook over low heat 2–2½ hours or until beef is very tender. Serve with plain rice.

Serves 4–6

SAUERBRATEN

2 cups cider vinegar
2 cups water
⅓ cup dark brown sugar
½ teaspoon ground cloves
½ teaspoon ground allspice
1 tablespoon salt
½ teaspoon freshly ground black pepper
6 peppercorns
1 bay leaf
2 large onions, chopped
2–3 carrots, chopped
2–3 stalks celery, chopped
4–5-pound boneless beef round or rump roast
2 tablespoons vegetable oil
1 cup sour cream

1. In a saucepan combine vinegar, water, sugar, cloves, allspice, salt, pepper, peppercorns, bay leaf, onions, carrots, and celery. Bring just to a simmer, stirring.
2. Place roast in a large glass, enamel or ceramic bowl or pan. Cool marinade slightly, then pour over roast. Cover and refrigerate 5–7 days, turning the meat once a day.
3. When ready to cook, remove roast from marinade and dry thoroughly with paper towels. Reserve marinade and vegetables.
4. In a large heavy pot or Dutch oven, heat oil over moderate to high heat. Add roast and brown quickly on all sides.
5. Turn heat low. Remove peppercorns and bay leaf from marinade, then add chopped vegetables and ½ cup marinade to roast in pan.
6. Cover and cook over low heat for 2 hours, adding more marinade if necessary.
7. Remove roast from pot and allow to cool slightly. Cut in thin slices.
8. Return sliced meat to cooking liquid and cook over low heat one hour. When ready to serve, remove meat slices to platter. Add sour cream to liquid in pot and stir to make a sauce. Heat thoroughly but do not allow to boil. Pour sauce over meat and serve.

Serves 8–10

SOUR BEEF CURRY

2 pounds boneless beef, cut in 1–1½-inch cubes
3 tablespoons mustard oil or vegetable oil
2 medium onions, chopped
4 cloves garlic, finely minced
2 teaspoons gingerroot, finely minced
1 teaspoon mustard seeds
1½ teaspoons ground cumin
1 teaspoon turmeric
1 bay leaf, crumbled
1 tablespoon salt
¼ teaspoon freshly ground black pepper
¼ teaspoon ground cloves
¼–½ teaspoon crushed dried red peppers
¼ teaspoon crushed cardamom seeds or ground cardamom
½ cup red wine vinegar

1. Dry beef cubes thoroughly with paper towels.
2. In a large heavy pot or pan heat oil over moderate heat. Add onion,

garlic, gingerroot, and all seasonings except vinegar. Sauté, stirring, about 5 minutes.

3. Add beef cubes, and brown on all sides, stirring.
4. Add vinegar, cover, and cook over low heat 1½–2 hours or until beef is tender and all the liquid is reduced. This is a dry curry; in the cooking process all the liquid evaporates and the "oil comes out." Serve with plain rice and fruit chutney.

Serves 4–6

STEAMED PORK BALLS SWEET-SOUR

1 pound lean ground pork
3 tablespoons soy sauce
2 tablespoons dry sherry
¼ teaspoon salt
1 teaspoon gingerroot, finely minced or ½ teaspoon ground ginger
1 teaspoon sugar
2 cloves garlic, mashed
11-ounce can mandarin orange sections
1 tablespoon sugar
¼ cup distilled white vinegar
1 teaspoon soy sauce
1 teaspoon cornstarch

1. Combine ground pork, 3 tablespoons soy sauce, sherry, salt, gingerroot, sugar, and garlic. Mix thoroughly and form into 12 large balls.
2. Place balls on a steamer rack or in a heatproof plate that will fit on top of a pot ½ filled with boiling water. Cover plate with aluminum foil. Steam balls over low heat 15–20 minutes or until they are thoroughly cooked through.
3. In a small saucepan, combine juice from orange sections, one tablespoon sugar, 3 tablespoons vinegar, and one teaspoon soy sauce. Heat to simmering.
4. Combine cornstarch with one tablespoon vinegar and add to sauce. Cook, stirring, until thickened and clear.
5. Add steamed balls and orange sections to sauce and heat to simmering.

Serves 3–4

SWEET AND SOUR STUFFED CABBAGE

Another traditional eastern European dish, this is best made a day or two in advance since its flavor improves with age. It can also be frozen.

1 large head green cabbage
2 quarts boiling salted water
1½ pounds lean ground beef
⅓ cup cooked rice
2 teaspoons salt
⅛ teaspoon black pepper
1 teaspoon ground ginger
1 egg, lightly beaten

1. Carefully remove 10–12 whole outer leaves from the cabbage. Place leaves in boiling salted water for 5 minutes. Drain, rinse in cold water, and drain again. Set aside while preparing stuffing.
2. Mix beef, rice, salt, pepper, ginger, and egg.
3. Place a large spoonfull of meat mixture on the center of a cabbage leaf. Fold bottom of leaf up over filling, then fold top of leaf down. Fold in both sides and secure the stuffed cabbage leaf with a wooden toothpick. Place stuffed cabbage leaves in the following sauce:

35-ounce can Italian plum tomatoes
2 large onions, sliced
¼ cup lemon juice
¼ cup cider vinegar
½ cup dark brown sugar
2 teaspoons ground ginger
1½ teaspoons salt
¼ teaspoon black pepper
½ cup dark raisins

1. Place all sauce ingredients in a large pot and bring to a simmer.
2. Place stuffed cabbage leaves carefully in sauce, cover, and cook over low heat for one hour. If serving immediately, uncover pot and cook sauce down rapidly until it is quite thick.

Serves 4–6

PICKLED FISH

2 pounds fresh salmon, bass, pickerel, or salmon trout, cut in steaks or
   uniform thick slices
1½ cups distilled white vinegar
½ cup water
1 large onion, sliced
1 carrot, sliced
1 stalk celery, sliced
½ cup sugar
1 tablespoon salt
6 peppercorns
1 bay leaf

1. Combine fish with vinegar, water, onion, carrot, celery, sugar, salt,
   peppercorns, and bay leaf in a large shallow pan. Simmer, covered,
   over low heat until fish is just tender, about 10–15 minutes.
2. Cool fish in broth, then cover and refrigerate for at least 24 hours.
3. Remove bay leaf and peppercorns before serving. Serve chilled.

Serves 6 as an appetizer or first course

OLD FASHIONED CUCUMBER SALAD

4 cucumbers, peeled and thinly sliced
2 tablespoons salt
½ cup white or cider vinegar
3 tablespoons sugar
good dash freshly ground black pepper
1 medium onion, thinly sliced

Garnish: 2 tablespoons fresh dill, chopped (optional)

1. Place sliced cucumbers in a glass or ceramic bowl, add salt, and mix
   well. Refrigerate 1–2 hours.
2. Rinse cucumber slices thoroughly in cold water and drain well.
3. Mix vinegar, sugar, and pepper. Pour over cucumber and onion
   slices and mix well. Chill for several hours. Garnish with chopped
   dill if desired.

Serves 4

INDONESIAN CUCUMBER SALAD

4 cucumbers
2 carrots
2 scallions, finely chopped
1 teaspoon salt
1 clove garlic, finely minced
2 teaspoons gingerroot, finely minced
1½ teaspoons turmeric
pinch crushed dried red peppers
⅓ cup water
¼ cup distilled white vinegar
¼ cup sugar

1. Peel cucumbers and cut into narrow strips, discarding center pulp and seeds. Cut carrots into narrow strips.
2. Combine scallions, salt, garlic, gingerroot, turmeric, red peppers, and water. Simmer over low heat 10 minutes. Remove from heat, add vinegar and sugar, mix well and pour over cucumber and carrot strips.
3. Marinate several hours or overnight in refrigerator. Serve chilled.

Serves 8

APRICOT CHUTNEY

4 pounds ripe apricots
¼ cup salt
3 quarts water
2 cups cider vinegar
1½ cups sugar
2 large onions, sliced
4 cloves garlic, sliced
1 cup dark and/or golden raisins
2 teaspoons gingerroot, finely minced, or 1 teaspoon ground ginger
1 teaspoon crushed dried red peppers
4-ounce package crystallized ginger, chopped

1. Pit and slice apricots. Place in a large bowl. Mix water and salt and pour over apricots. Mix well and let stand overnight. Drain.
2. In a large pot combine drained apricots with vinegar, sugar, onions, garlic, raisins, gingerroot, and red peppers. Simmer uncovered over low heat 1–1½ hours, stirring occasionally and skimming off any foam that may rise to the surface. Cook until thick, clear, and golden brown.
3. Add chopped crystallized ginger to mixture for the last 5 minutes of cooking. Pack simmering chutney into hot sterilized jars and seal immediately. (Or pour into clean jars, cover, and store in refrigerator.) Let stand at least one week before serving.

Makes about 6 pints

GREEN APPLE CHUTNEY

6 cups tart green apples, cored and sliced, unpeeled
2 limes, chopped
2 lemons, chopped
2 green tomatoes, chopped
2 large onions, sliced
1 cup golden raisins
4 cloves garlic, chopped
2 cups cider vinegar
1½ cups sugar
4 teaspoons gingerroot, finely minced or 2 teaspoons ground ginger
2 teaspoons salt
1 teaspoon crushed dried red peppers

1. Combine all ingredients in a large pot. Cook uncovered over moderate heat, stirring occasionally, about 1–1½ hours or until mixture is thick and golden brown.
2. Pour simmering chutney into hot sterilized jars and seal immediately. (Or pour into clean jars, cover, and store in refrigerator.) Let stand at least one week before serving.

Makes about 6 pints

CANTALOUPE CHUTNEY

This recipe developed when my local grocer was selling overripe melons at six for a dollar—and I can't resist a bargain! If you like chutneys, try this one; it has a wonderful, unique flavor quite different from the usual mango or apricot.

3–4 medium sized ripe cantaloupes
¼ cup salt
1 quart water
¼ cup fresh gingerroot, finely shredded
2 cups cider vinegar
1 cup sugar
2 cinnamon sticks
1 cup golden raisins
¼ teaspoon crushed red pepper
½ cup lime juice

1. Peel and seed melons and cut into small cubes. Mix water and salt, pour over melon cubes, mix well, and let stand overnight.
2. Drain melon cubes and combine in a large heavy pot with gingerroot, vinegar, sugar, and cinnamon sticks. Cook uncovered over moderate heat about 45 minutes until thick and syrupy.
3. Add raisins, red pepper, and lime juice and cook for another 15 minutes. Pour into sterilized bottles and seal. (If you don't want to go through the sterilization, simply pour into clean bottles, cover, and store in the refrigerator after cooling.)

Makes about 3 pints

CAPONATA

An Italian mixed vegetable relish made with typical Mediterranean seasonings in addition to the sweet-sour principle.

1 medium to large eggplant, unpeeled, cut in ½-inch cubes
1 large onion, chopped
1 large green pepper, seeded and chopped
2 medium ripe tomatoes, chopped
2 stalks celery, chopped
1 cup sliced fresh mushrooms

⅓ cup pimiento-stuffed green olives, halved
4 cloves garlic, mashed
½ cup olive oil
⅓ cup red wine vinegar
1 tablespoon salt
3 tablespoons sugar
¼ teaspoon freshly ground black pepper
1 teaspoon crumbled dried oregano
1 teaspoon crushed dried basil
1 tablespoon capers

1. Combine all ingredients in a large pot and mix thoroughly. Cook uncovered over low heat, stirring occasionally, about one hour or until mixture is soft and all the liquid has cooked away. Cool, then refrigerate.
2. Serve chilled or at room temperature as a salad, relish, or spread. Well covered, it will keep in the refrigerator for at least a week.

Serves 6–8

SWEET AND SOUR PLUM SAUCE

This is a specialty of the Caucasus where it is used on grilled meats and kebabs. Almost any variety of plum will do, but the Italian prune plums are easy to pit and very inexpensive in the summer. When the fruit is available, make yourself a supply for the rest of the year. Not only is it wonderful on roast meats, particularly pork, and poultry, but it makes a wonderful sauce for ice cream.

2 pounds Italian prune plums
¼ cup lemon juice
1 cup sugar
1 teaspoon ground ginger
1 teaspoon cinnamon

1. Cut plums in half, remove pits, and place in a heavy pot.
2. Add all other ingredients and cook over moderate heat about 45–50 minutes, until sauce is thick and syrupy.
3. Ladle into sterilized jars and seal, or pour into clean jars, cover, and refrigerate.

Makes about 3 cups

GENERAL PRINCIPLES II

CULTURED MILK

The second widespread flavor principle is the combination of a cultured milk product such as cheese, yogurt, or buttermilk with an herb or spice. This principle is not nearly as universal as the sweet/sour principle, but it is ccmmon enough to be considered a general rather than a culturally specific principle. It is found in parts of southern Europe, the Balkans, Greece, Turkey, the Middle East, central Asia, Afghanistan, and India; it is not part of the cuisines of Mexico, South America, aboriginal America, the Orient, or Africa. Clearly, the cultured milk principles occur where there is a tradition of dairying.

Why, if the primary product of dairying is milk, does this principle so consistently employ cultured dairy products rather than fresh milk? First, cultured dairy products can be stored for longer periods of time without spoilage. Second, because of their solid or semi-solid form, not only are they a more concentrated source of nutrition, but they are easier to store and transport. But most importantly, cultured dairy products satisfy nutritional needs more adequately than fresh milk.

Human infants, like the young of other mammals, are born with an enzyme (lactase) necessary to the digestion of milk sugar (lactose) found in mother's milk. As the child begins to wean the enzyme gradually declines and in many adults disappears entirely, so that the person is no longer capable of properly digesting fresh milk. The culturing of milk with various controlled enzymes and bacillae has much the same effect as the lactase enzyme in an infant's digestive system: culturing breaks down the lactose in the whole milk and makes the product digestible for the adult. It is for this reason so many dairying groups culture their milk for use in the form of yogurt and cheese. And no doubt the flavor of these products, very different from that of fresh milk, is a further incentive.

Many of these dairying traditions originated in the highlands of central Asia, where sheep and goats and later cows first were domesticated. The principles were spread both east and west by pastoral nomads and warlike tribes. Their milk culturing practices were introduced as far east as China, where the tradition was rejected, and as far west as central Europe. In India, which was invaded many times by Aryan nomads from central Asia, dairy culturing became very strong in the north, less so in the south.

The cheeses used in this principle are for the most part "fresh" cheeses cultured with enzymes but not cured for long periods of time; they include such varieties as cottage cheese, pot cheese, farmer's cheese, ricotta, feta, and Indian *panir*. The cheeses and yogurt all combine with seasonings typical of a given tradition: cinnamon and/or dill in central Asia, the Balkans, and Greece; mint and parsley in the Middle East; garlic, cumin, and coriander in India.

Sour cream is also a cultured milk product, but its use is more limited geographically than the use of yogurt. It is used as a principle ingredient almost exclusively in northern and eastern Europe (see p. 127).

CULTURED MILK RECIPES

PERSIAN CUCUMBER SOUP

TURKISH SPINACH SOUP WITH WALNUTS

CHEESE BOREK

SPINACH PIE

ITALIAN MEATBALLS

ARMENIAN ONION-LAMB CASSEROLE

YOGURT FISH

DILLED EGGPLANT SPREAD

YOGURT RICE

RAITA (INDIAN CUCUMBER-YOGURT SALAD)

PERSIAN CUCUMBER SOUP

A refreshing and nourishing summer soup.

2 cups yogurt
1 cup milk
¼ cup fresh dill, chopped, or 2 tablespoons dried dillweed
2 scallions, chopped
2 tablespoons chives, chopped
2–3 tablespoons parsley, chopped
1 large cucumber, peeled and chopped
1 teaspoon salt
good dash freshly ground black pepper

Garnish: 1 medium cucumber, peeled and chopped

1. Place yogurt, milk, dill, scallions, chives, parsley, cucumber, salt
   and pepper in blender. Blend until smooth. Chill thoroughly.
2. Pour soup into serving bowls and garnish with additional chopped
   cucumber.

Serves 6

TURKISH SPINACH SOUP WITH WALNUTS

3 tablespoons olive oil
1 medium onion, chopped
3 cloves garlic, mashed
1 pound spinach, washed and trimmed
6 cups chicken stock
½ teaspoon freshly ground black pepper
½ cup parsley, finely chopped
⅓ cup fresh dill, finely chopped or 3 tablespoons dried dillweed
½ cup orzo or rice
1 cup yogurt

Garnish: ½ cup walnuts, coarsely chopped

1. In a heavy pot heat olive oil; add onion and garlic and sauté over
   moderate heat until onion is golden. Add spinach and cook until
   wilted. Remove spinach from pot and chop finely or purée.
2. Return spinach to pot and add all other ingredients except orzo,
   yogurt, and walnuts. Simmer uncovered for about 30 minutes.
3. Add orzo or rice and cook for about 10 minutes or until tender.
   Whisk yogurt into soup and heat to the simmer.

4. Ladle soup into individual bowls and garnish with a tablespoon of chopped walnuts.

Can also be served cold.

Serves 6–8

CHEESE BOREK

A Turkish dish that is popular throughout the Middle East, Greece, and the Balkans. Thin, strudel-like leaves of filo pastry are stuffed with a creamy cheese herb mixture.

½ pound feta cheese, finely crumbled
1 cup creamed cottage cheese
3 eggs, lightly beaten
3 scallions, finely minced
¼ cup parsley, finely chopped
¼ teaspoon freshly ground black pepper
¾ cup melted butter
20 sheets filo pastry (about ½ pound)

1. Combine cheeses, eggs, scallions, parsley, pepper, and one table-spoon melted butter. Mix thoroughly.
2. Keep extra filo sheets covered with a damp cloth while working, as they dry out very quickly. Place one sheet filo, long side across, in front of you. Brush lightly but completely with melted butter. Place another sheet on top of it and brush again with butter. Repeat, using 10 sheets in all.
3. Spoon half of cheese filling down the center of filo sheets to within one inch of both short sides. Fold long side up over filling, then brush that surface completely with melted butter. Fold short sides in, then brush them with melted butter. Continue to roll from the long side closest to you. Brush again with butter. Continue until pastry is completely rolled and closed and all sides are brushed thoroughly with butter. Place rolled pastry, seam side down, on a buttered baking tray. Repeat with rest of filo sheets and filling to make another roll. Place the second roll on the baking sheet at least 3 inches from the first one.
4. Bake in a preheated 375° oven for about 40 minutes or until the rolls are puffed and a light golden brown. Let stand for 5 minutes, then transfer to a serving platter and slice. Serve hot.
   These can be prepared, except for the baking, early in the day. Cover prepared rolls closely with a cloth and refrigerate. Bring to room temperature before baking.

Makes 2 12-inch rolls; each roll serves 6 as an appetizer

SPINACH PIE

3 eggs
1 pound creamed cottage cheese
¼ pound feta cheese, crumbled
2 tablespoons grated Parmesan cheese
2 tablespoons melted butter
¼ cup parsley, chopped
¼ cup fresh dill, chopped
10-ounce package frozen chopped spinach, defrosted and well drained
   (squeeze out all water with your hands)
½–1 teaspoon salt
¼ teaspoon freshly ground black pepper
2 unbaked 8-inch pie shells

1. In a large bowl beat eggs well, add cheeses and mix thoroughly.
2. Stir in melted butter, parsley, dill, spinach, salt, and pepper and mix
   well. Pour mixture into pie shells and bake in a preheated 375° oven
   until set and lightly browned, about ½ hour.
3. Cut into wedges and serve warm.

Makes 2 pies; serves 12

ITALIAN MEATBALLS

1½ pounds lean ground beef, or a mixture of ground beef, veal, and pork
½ cup flavored Italian-style bread crumbs
2 eggs, lightly beaten
½ cup grated Parmesan cheese, or a combination of grated Parmesan
   and Romano
⅓ cup parsley, finely chopped
⅓ cup Ricotta or puréed cottage cheese
1 teaspoon crumbled dried oregano
2 teaspoons crushed dried basil
1½ teaspoon salt
¼ teaspoon freshly ground black pepper
¼ teaspoon freshly grated or ground nutmeg
2 tablespoons olive oil for sautéeing

1. In a large bowl, combine the ground meat with all the ingredients
   except the oil. Mix thoroughly with the hands, then chill slightly.
2. Form meat mixture into balls about the size of a small plum.
3. In a large frying pan heat olive oil over moderate heat. Brown balls
   slowly on all sides, turning frequently.

4. Remove meatballs from pan with a slotted spoon. Add to Italian tomato sauce (see p. 102) and simmer over low heat for ½ hour.

Makes about 35 meatballs
Serves 6

NOTE: To make a big hit with the younger set, make the meatball mixture as described above, but instead of making it in small balls, shape the mixture with your hands into one gigantic meatball, patting it to make it perfectly round and smooth. Brown the ball slowly on all sides in a large pot or deep skillet, using a large spatula to turn it. After the meatball is browned on all sides, carefully pour off all but about one tablespoon fat from the pan. Add onions, peppers, and garlic as described in recipe for Italian Tomato Sauce, p. 102, and sauté, stirring. Add all other sauce ingredients, mix well, cover and cook over low heat for 1–1½ hours, turning meatball carefully in the sauce once or twice during cooking. Present the giant meatball on a platter of hot freshly cooked pasta to your youngest child and watch his or her eyes! Then carve the meatball into slices, spoon the sauce over all, and serve.

ARMENIAN ONION-LAMB CASSEROLE

1 cup rice
1 cup beef stock
1 pound onions (about 4–5 medium) sliced
2–3 tablespoons butter
1 small onion, chopped
1½ pounds lean ground lamb
1½ cups yogurt
½ cup fresh dill, chopped or 2 tablespoons dried dillweed
1 teaspoon cinnamon
¼ teaspoon pepper

1. Cook rice in beef stock until all the liquid is absorbed. Keep covered and set aside.
2. In a large frying pan melt butter over moderate heat. Add sliced onions and cook for just a few minutes until onions are completely coated with butter and just beginning to turn soft. Remove from pan and set aside.
3. In same frying pan, sauté the chopped onion until soft; there should be enough butter left to coat bottom of pan. Add ground lamb and brown over high heat. When lamb is completely browned, carefully drain all liquid from pan and discard. Into lamb mix parboiled rice and all other ingredients except sautéed onions. Mix well. Taste for salt.
4. In a buttered casserole place half the lamb mixture. Top with all the sautéed onions; salt and pepper the onions lightly. Place rest of lamb mixture on top of onions. Cover casserole and bake in a 350° oven for 25–35 minutes. Serve with Arabic bread and salad.

Serves 6

YOGURT FISH

1½–2 pounds fish fillets (sole, flounder, perch, etc.)
1 cup yogurt
4 cloves garlic, mashed
2 tablespoons crushed dried mint leaves
dash freshly ground pepper
flour for dredging
4 tablespoons clarified butter, *ghee*, or salad oil
2 limes, quartered, and fresh mint leaves for garnish

1. Combine yogurt, garlic, mint, and pepper and spoon over fish fillets in a pan, making sure each fillet is thoroughly coated. Marinate 1–2 hours.
2. Heat butter, *ghee*, or oil in a large frying pan over moderate heat. Dredge coated fillets in flour, then fry a few minutes on each side until golden. Salt the fried fillets lightly, then serve immediately with fresh lime and mint for garnish.

Serves 3–4

DILLED EGGPLANT SPREAD

1 large eggplant
3 tablespoons olive oil
1 small bunch dill, about ½ cup finely chopped
3 cloves garlic, mashed
½ teaspoon salt
couple good grinds black pepper
⅓ cup chopped walnuts
½ cup crumbled feta cheese

1. Pierce eggplant in 3 or 4 places with a sharp knife. Roast over a charcoal fire, turning occasionally, until soft; or bake on a tray in a very hot oven, 450–500° about ½ hour until soft.
2. When eggplant is cool, peel off skin and discard. Purée eggplant pulp in blender or food processor with dill, olive oil, garlic, salt, and pepper.
3. Place mixture in bowl and stir in walnuts and feta cheese. Serve at room temperature with triangles of Arabic bread or crackers.

Makes about 2 cups

YOGURT RICE

3 tablespoons butter
1 small onion, chopped
1 cup long-grain rice
1¾ cups hot chicken stock
3 tablespoons fresh mint, chopped, or 1 tablespoon crumbled dried
    mint leaves
3 tablespoons parsley, finely chopped
good dash freshly ground black pepper
½ cup yogurt

1. In a medium saucepan heat butter over moderate heat. Add onion
   and sauté until golden.
2. Add rice and sauté, stirring, until rice is golden brown and all the
   butter has been absorbed.
3. Add hot stock, cover, and cook over low heat about 15–20 minutes
   or until all liquid is absorbed.
4. Stir in mint, parsley, pepper, and yogurt. Mix well, cover, and let
   stand 5–10 minutes.

Serves 4–5

RAITA

A cooling and refreshing salad to serve with heavily spiced foods.

2 cucumbers
1 small onion
2 cups yogurt
2 cloves garlic, mashed
½ teaspoon salt
good dash freshly ground black pepper
3 tablespoons fresh mint, chopped, or 1 tablespoon crumbled dried
    mint leaves

1. Peel cucumbers and grate coarsely. Grate onion.
2. Add cucumbers and onion to yogurt. Stir in garlic, salt, pepper, and
   mint and mix well. Chill thoroughly before serving.

Serves 4–6

GENERAL PRINCIPLES III

SMOKING

The third general principle is not a seasoning but the ancient technique of smoking. Its origins may never be established clearly, but we know that it could not have developed until man learned to use and control fire. The unique flavor of smoked foods has been a desirable one throughout culinary history.

Smoking undoubtedly was first used as a technique for preserving foods for storage; foods that have been dehydrated by exposure to air and heat are less susceptible to bacterial contamination. But smoking also provides a characteristic flavor, depending on the fuel used. As a preservative technique, it is used primarily by cultures that have access to large amounts of wood for burning, such as the forest areas of central Europe, the northwest coast of America, and even the tropical rain forests of the Amazon where some tribes use it to preserve fish. It does not show up as a primary culinary technique in traditionally fuel-short areas such as China or India.

The technique of smoking is used almost exclusively with meat and fish and, to a lesser extent, cheese: it is almost never used for curing vegetables. Although it still is widely utilized as a curing technique in rural and agricultural areas the smoked flavor and texture have come to be appreciated in more sophisticated cuisines. Most of us have no need to preserve our meat and fish, but we certainly enjoy the taste of sausage, ham, bacon, kippered salmon, smoked whitefish, etc. Even in China, where smoking has never been primary technique, the flavor is used to season foods in such preparations as marinated smoked hard-boiled eggs, and chicken smoked over tea leaves.

If you like smoked foods, you can build yourself a real smokehouse. Or, there are a number of small electric smokers on the market. But if it's the flavor and texture you're after rather than need to preserve your food, try the following recipes. (Liquid smoke is widely available in supermarkets, and much to my amusement, almost always placed on the "gourmet" shelf. It is curious that one of the oldest flavorings known to man has now suddenly become a special and exotic ingredient!)

SMOKED FOOD RECIPES

SMOKED FISH
SMOKED FISH PÂTÉ 1
SMOKED FISH PÂTÉ 2
SMOKED BEEF STRIPS

SMOKED FISH
(The Easy Way)

2 tablespoons liquid smoke
2 tablespoons soy sauce
½ teaspoon sugar
1–2 pounds fresh fish fillets (salmon, turbot, etc.), cut in ½–¾-inch slices
1 tablespoon vegetable oil

1. In a shallow pan large enough to hold the fish fillets in a single layer, combine liquid smoke, soy sauce and sugar. Mix well.
2. Place fish fillets in marinade and let stand at room temperature at least 2 hours and as long as 4 hours. Turn fillets frequently so that marinade penetrates as much as possible.
3. Brush both sides of fish with vegetable oil, then place skin-side down on an oiled rack set over a pan.
4. Bake in a preheated low 275° oven about 45 minutes. Cool, then refrigerate. Serve at room temperature.

Serves 6 as an appetizer

And now, two recipes using your own phony homemade smoked fish:

Smoked Fish Pâté 1

1 pound any white fish (turbot, haddock etc.), smoked according to previous recipe
1 pound cream cheese, softened
2 tablespoons bottled white horseradish

1. Mash or finely flake smoked fish; combine with softened cream cheese and horseradish. Blend thoroughly with the back of a spoon. Spoon into a serving dish or mold and chill. Serve, garnished with cucumber slices and lemon, as a spread for crackers or thinly sliced pumpernickel.

Makes about 2 cups

Smoked Fish Pâté 2

1 pound salmon fillet, smoked according to previous recipe
½ cup (8 ounces) sour cream
½ pound cream cheese, softened
2 tablespoons fresh dill, finely chopped
1 tablespoon fresh or freeze-dried chives, finely snipped

1. Coarsely flake smoked salmon and combine with sour cream in a food processor. Blend until smooth. Add cream cheese, dill, and chives, and blend again until smooth.
2. Spoon into a serving dish or mold and chill. Garnish with a few sprigs of fresh dill and serve as a spread for bagels or thinly sliced pumpernickel.

Makes about 2 cups

SMOKED BEEF STRIPS

½ pound lean boneless beef (top round or sirloin)
2 tablespoons liquid smoke
2 tablespoons soy sauce
¼ teaspoon sugar
vegetable oil

1. Cut beef against the grain into thin strips (no more than ⅛-inch thick). This is easier to do if the meat is partially frozen. Remove all excess fat.
2. In a glass or ceramic bowl combine liquid smoke, soy sauce, and sugar. Mix well, add beef strips, and mix thoroughly with marinade. Let stand 2 hours, stirring occasionally.
3. Lay beef strips out, not touching each other, on a lightly oiled rack set over a pan. Bake in a preheated low 275° oven for 30 minutes. Let cool, then refrigerate. Serve as an hors d'oeuvre.

Makes 24–30 beef strips

CROSSROADS CUISINE

Crossroads cuisines develop when several distinct culinary traditions merge to form a unique style of cooking. Through trade, migration, war, or any form of cross-cultural contact, culinary elements have integrated particularly in areas vulnerable to outside cultural influence. Each of the cuisines of Indonesia, Malaysia, and the Philippines has been shaped to some degree by the traditions of Southeast Asia, China, and India. One can almost trace the routes of spice-bearing Arab and Indian traders by observing where curries have been integrated into the cuisine.

This cultural give-and-take is not always well-balanced. India, with her ancient and traditional wealth of aromatic herbs and spices, has given more to other cuisines than she has absorbed from outside cultures. West African traditions have been shaped largely by ingredients from other parts of the world. Some cultures are remarkably resistant to new or "foreign" elements. Both France and China, for example, are distinctly insular in terms of their culinary traditions. Then, again, if you have a good thing going, why tamper with it?

Many factors are involved in a culture's receptiveness to new ideas and new ingredients. These factors may concern nutritional needs or they may have aesthetic, social, or psychological import. When the Spaniards conquered Mexico, for example, they brought with them many goods and ingredients from the Old World. Those accepted enthusiastically by the Mexicans tended to be basic food items (beef, pork, rice) and new cooking techniques (frying in oil or fat), rather than seasoning ingredients. The basic Mexican diet may have been deficient in animal meat and fat; since pre-Columbian times, however, they have had a strong and satisfying flavor principle of chile pepper and tomato. Spain, on the other hand, tended to take less from Mexico in terms of basic foods (corn and beans, for example) than of flavoring ingredients (tomatoes and peppers). Spanish cuisine may have needed new ingredients to enhance the flavor and visual appeal of traditional seasonings.

The following recipes illustrate how specific flavor principles and other culinary traditions have crossed cultural boundaries to form new principles and new traditions.

CROSSROADS RECIPES

INDONESIA
INDONESIAN VEGETABLE SCRAMBLE

PHILIPPINES
PORK ADOBO

BALKANS
BALKAN VEGETABLE CAVIAR WITH CHEESE
STUFFED CABBAGE

TURKEY
IMAM BAYILDI

ITALY
BAGNA CAUDA

UNITED STATES
CHILI
CREOLE SEAFOOD
DIRTY RICE

INDONESIAN VEGETABLE SCRAMBLE

The spicy sauce includes two distinct flavor principles: soy sauce-molasses-peanut, and a typical curry of ginger-cumin-turmeric.

3 tablespoons dark soy sauce
1 teaspoon dark brown sugar
1½ tablespoons peanut butter
1 teaspoon cumin
1 teaspoon turmeric
½ teaspoon ground coriander
3 tablespoons peanut oil
2 large cloves garlic, mashed
1 tablespoon gingerroot, minced
1 medium onion, chopped
¼ teaspoon crushed dried red peppers

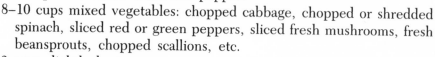

8–10 cups mixed vegetables: chopped cabbage, chopped or shredded spinach, sliced red or green peppers, sliced fresh mushrooms, fresh beansprouts, chopped scallions, etc.
3 eggs, lightly beaten

1. In a small bowl combine soy sauce, sugar, peanut butter, cumin, turmeric, and coriander and mix to form a smooth paste. Set aside.
2. In a large frying pan or wok, heat oil over high heat. Add garlic, gingerroot, onion, and hot pepper and stir-fry until mixture starts to smell good. Add seasoning paste and stir-fry a few minutes longer.
3. Add vegetables, tougher ones like cabbage first, tender ones like mushrooms and beansprouts later, and stir-fry until done but still crisp.
4. Add eggs and stir-fry until dry. Serve immediately with plain rice, if desired.

Serves 6

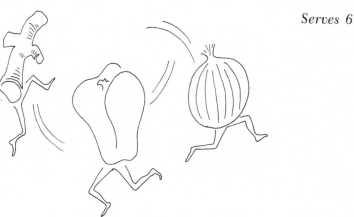

PHILIPPINE ADOBO

The cooking of the Philippines vividly illustrates the integration of many culinary traditions; from China, Southeast Asia, India, and, most strongly, from Spain, which has had a significant influence on the culture. In this recipe we see the soy sauce of China, the coconut milk of Southeast Asia, the olive oil and saffron of Spain, as well as the characteristically Spanish technique of long slow cooking. The *adobo* (the name is Spanish as well) is a national dish that has many variations; in some the meat is fried after it has cooked in liquid, but I find that initial frying is easier and produces much the same results.

a good pinch of saffron threads
½ cup hot water
2 tablespoons olive oil
3–3½ pounds chicken parts, cut in small serving pieces
1½ pounds boneless lean pork, cut in 1-inch cubes
6 cloves garlic, mashed
⅓ cup rice wine vinegar
2 tablespoons soy sauce
1 bay leaf, crumbled
¼ teaspoon freshly ground black pepper
½ cup coconut milk (see p. 40)

1. Soak saffron threads in hot water for ½ hour.
2. In a large heavy pot or deep skillet with a cover, heat olive oil over moderate heat. Brown chicken pieces and pork cubes.
3. Add saffron water, garlic, vinegar, soy sauce, bay leaf, and pepper, cover, and cook over low heat for about an hour or until meat is very tender. Remove meat from pot and rapidly cook down sauce until it is very thick.
4. Stir in coconut milk, return chicken and pork to pot and cook until completely heated through. Garnish with tomato wedges, if desired, and serve with plain rice.

Serves 6

BALKAN VEGETABLE CAVIAR WITH CHEESE

The Balkan States and Greece, which lie in the southeast corner of Europe, illustrate the ideal conditions for the development of "crossroads" cuisine. Accessible by numerous land and sea routes, their geographic location opens them to cross-cultural contact from central Europe, the Mediterranean, and from the Middle East. In this recipe at least two of those traditions are combined: the stewing of onions and peppers in olive oil from the Mediterranean; and the combination of dried mushrooms, sour cream, and cottage cheese of eastern and central Europe. There are many recipes for vegetable "caviars" from this region, and they are so named because they approximate the rich flavor of caviar with ingredients that are readily available and far less expensive.

½ ounce dried mushrooms
warm water
¼ cup olive oil
1 large onion, coarsely chopped
2 large red or green peppers, coarsely chopped
¾–1 pound fresh mushrooms, coarsely chopped
4 cloves garlic, mashed
1 teaspoon salt
good grind fresh black pepper
¼ teaspoon crushed dried red peppers
⅓ cup fresh dill, chopped (or 2 tablespoons dried dillweed)
8 ounces cottage cheese
8 ounces sour cream

1. Soak dried mushrooms in warm water to cover for about ½ hour. Drain and chop fine, discarding any tough bits of stem.
2. In a heavy skillet or pot, heat olive oil over moderate heat. Add onions, peppers, mushrooms, and garlic and sauté slowly, stirring occasionally. Continue to cook until all the liquid from the vegetables has evaporated and the vegetables are thick and cooked down. This should take about 20–30 minutes.
3. When all the liquid has cooked away and vegetables are stewing in the oil, add dried mushrooms, salt, black and red pepper, and dill. Continue to cook for another 10 minutes. Remove from heat and cool.
4. Stir in cottage cheese and sour cream and mix well. Taste for salt. Chill and serve as a spread on crackers or thinly sliced pumpernickel.

Makes about 4 cups

STUFFED CABBAGE

A traditional favorite of Greece, the Balkans, and the Middle East, this dish combines two very strong flavor principles: tomato-cinnamon and lemon-dill.

1 large head green cabbage
2 quarts boiling salted water
1½ pounds lean ground beef
1½ teaspoons salt
¼ teaspoon freshly ground black pepper
1 teaspoon cinnamon
2 tablespoons fresh dill, chopped or 2 teaspoons dried dillweed
½ cup cooked rice
1 egg, lightly beaten
1 cup chicken stock
1 cup fresh or canned tomatoes
¼ cup lemon juice
1 teaspoon salt
2 tablespoons fresh dill, chopped or 2 teaspoons dried dillweed

1. Remove 12–15 whole outer leaves from cabbage. Place leaves in boiling salted water for 3 minutes. Drain, rinse in cold water, and drain again.
2. In a large bowl combine ground meat, 1½ teaspoons salt, pepper, cinnamon, dill, rice, and egg. Mix thoroughly with the hands.
3. Place a heaping tablespoon of filling on the center of a cabbage leaf. Fold bottom of leaf up over filling, fold top down, then fold sides in. Fasten stuffed cabbage envelop with a wooden toothpick.
4. In a large pot combine stock, tomatoes, lemon juice, one teaspoon salt, and dill. Bring to a simmer.
5. Place stuffed cabbage leaves carefully in sauce, cover, and cook over low to moderate heat about 40 minutes.
6. Uncover pot and cook rapidly to reduce sauce.

Serves 6

IMAM BAYILDI

With a heritage belonging to both Europe and Asia, Turkey has always played a significant role in the exchange of culinary elements. In this classic recipe for marinated eggplant several distinct flavor principles have merged: the lemon-parsley of the Middle East, the olive oil-tomato-garlic of southern Italy, and a touch of sweet-sour. The typical Spanish technique of slowly cooking onions in olive oil is included here as well. According to tradition, the name "The Imam Fainted" was given to the dish either because it is so delicious or because so much costly olive oil is used in its preparation. Both are true!

4–5 small (baby) eggplants (3–5 inches long)
salt
1–2 cups olive oil (generally about 1½ cups is about right)
3 large onions, sliced
4 cloves garlic, mashed
35-ounce can Italian plum tomatoes, drained
½ cup parsley, finely chopped
juice 2 lemons
1 teaspoon salt
⅛ teaspoon freshly ground black pepper
2 teaspoons sugar

1. Cut stem ends off eggplants and cut in half lengthwise. Do not peel. On the peel side of each half make 2 or 3 small gashes with a knife, being careful not to cut all the way through the eggplant.
2. Place eggplant halves on a large platter or tray and heavily salt both sides of each half. Allow to stand ½ hour. At the end of this time wipe all excess salt and moisture from eggplant.
3. Cover the bottom of a large frying pan with olive oil. Over moderate heat, sauté eggplant halves on both sides until lightly browned. Add more oil as needed. As the halves finish browning, transfer them cut sides up to a large shallow baking dish or casserole.
4. When all the eggplant is browned, add more oil to the pan. Add the sliced onions and cook slowly until they are soft and dark golden brown. This may take up to ½ hour.
5. Add the garlic, tomatoes, parsley, lemon juice, salt, pepper, and sugar to the onions, and simmer over moderate heat for 10 minutes.
6. Pour this sauce mixture over the eggplant halves, then generously anoint the top with more olive oil. Cover and bake in a preheated 400° oven 30–40 minutes. Remove cover for last 10 minutes of baking.
7. Allow to cool, then marinate in refrigerator several hours or overnight. (This may be prepared up to 2 days ahead of time). Serve at room temperature.

Serves 6–8

BAGNA CAUDA

This dish was first prepared for me in Mexico City by an eastern European Jew who got the recipe from an Italian living in Stockholm.* The history of the recipe is not nearly as complicated as the route it took to get into this book! It shows the amalgamation of two separate traditions, northern and southern Italian. The olive oil, garlic, and anchovies belong clearly to the Mediterranean complex, while the cream is central European. *Bagna Cauda*, which means "hot bath," can be served as a first course, as a cocktail party dip, or as a late evening light meal.

6 whole heads (not cloves) garlic
2 cups heavy cream
2-ounce can anchovy fillets (with oil)
½ cup pecans, finely chopped
¼–⅓ cup olive oil
3 cups assorted raw vegetables: carrot sticks, celery sticks, radishes, cauliflowerets, zucchini strips, etc.
1 pound boiled shrimp, peeled and deveined
1 small loaf crusty French bread, cut in cubes

1. Separate garlic heads into cloves; peel cloves and chop finely.
2. In a chafing dish or electric skillet combine garlic with cream and simmer over low heat for 10 minutes, stirring frequently.
3. Mash anchovies with their oil into garlic mixture and simmer another 5 minutes. Stir in the pecans, then add enough oil to make the mixture smooth and creamy.
4. Arrange a platter of vegetables, shrimp, and bread cubes. Keep garlic mixture hot over low heat while guests dunk vegetables, etc. into dip.

Serves 6–8

* With thanks to Dr. Ezio Giacobini, who provided the recipe.

CHILI

As the archetypal "melting pot," the United States has spawned many new culinary traditions. The distinctive cuisine of the Southwest, aptly called "Tex-Mex," combines culinary traditions from Mexico with indigenous Indian traditions and European elements.

Chili, the dish of spiced meat and beans, is the Tex-Mex classic. The major seasoning is chili powder, a commercial blend of spices (garlic, oregano, cumin, chile pepper) that approximates the flavor of traditional

Mexican cuisine in much the same way that commercial curry powders approximate the flavor of Indian cuisine. Chili powder as such does not exist in Mexico, but is a wholly American invention. There are hundreds of regional and ethnic versions of chili, all of which claim to be "authentic." In Cincinnati, with its large Greek population, chili is heavily seasoned with cinnamon, a spice that is not used in the Tex-Mex version. (For a wholly new version, which would no doubt cause diehard Tex-Mexers to choke on their chiles, see recipe for West African Chili, p. 214).

2 tablespoons vegetable oil
1 large onion, chopped
1 large red or green pepper, chopped
1½ pounds lean ground beef
4 cloves garlic, mashed
15-ounce can tomato sauce
1-pound can tomatoes, with juice
1 teaspoon salt
¼ teaspoon freshly ground black pepper
1 heaping teaspoon ground cumin
1 heaping teaspoon crumbled dried oregano
1 tablespoon chili powder
½ teaspoon crushed dried red peppers (more or less to taste)
1 pound can red kidney beans, drained
1 pound can whole kernel corn, drained

Garnish: chopped onions, chopped fresh chile pepper, and grated Cheddar cheese

1. In a large frying pan heat oil over moderate heat. Add onion and peppers and sauté until starting to brown.
2. Add ground beef, turn heat up, and brown quickly, crumbling with fork. When meat is completely browned, drain off all liquid in pan and discard.
3. Add all other ingredients and cook uncovered over low to moderate heat for at least one hour. Chili tastes better the longer it cooks. Allow to cook until almost all of the liquid is cooked away and mixture is thick.
4. Serve chili with rice or tortillas and provide bowls of chopped onions, chopped fresh chile peppers, and grated Cheddar cheese for garnishes.

Serves 6

CREOLE SEAFOOD

The Creole cookery of New Orleans is a true blend of many culinary traditions, including French, Spanish, African, and native American. The slow sautéeing of onions, peppers, and garlic, and the forthright seasonings are typically Spanish, while the butter, wine, and thyme are more characteristically French. The seafood and rice, both plentiful in the Gulf Coast and Bayou country, are the basis of Creole cuisine; Tabasco sauce, a unique regional product, is an oft-used seasoning.

To make a true gumbo, the dish may be thickened with okra, an African import, or with gumbo *filé*, the powdered bark of the Sassafras tree, an ingredient derived from native American Indians. Gumbo *filé* is stirred into the stew after it has been removed from the heat, or passed around the table for diners to use at their own discretion. The gumbo is best made with a variety of seafood; bits of hot or garlic sausage may also be added.

2 tablespoons butter
1 large onion, sliced
1 large red or green pepper, sliced
2 large cloves garlic, mashed
2 stalks celery, sliced
28-ounce can tomatoes, coarsely chopped
½ cup white wine
1 teaspoon salt
¼ teaspoon freshly ground black pepper
1 teaspoon celery seed
2 teaspoons thyme
½ cup parsley, chopped
½ teaspoon (more or less to taste) Tabasco
2 pounds any or all of the following: fresh shrimp, oysters, crabmeat or any boneless white fish

1. In a large pot melt butter; sauté onion, pepper, garlic, and celery slowly over low heat until vegetables are soft.
2. Add all other ingredients except fish and seafood and cook over low to moderate heat for 40–50 minutes, stirring occasionally.
3. Add fish and seafood and cook until done. Serve over plain rice.

Serves 4–6

NEW ORLEANS DIRTY RICE

Despite its picturesque name, this dish is simply a New Orleans version of stuffing, one that will give your Thanksgiving bird a certain distinction. I find it most useful as a buffet dish to feed a large number of hungry people, particularly teenagers. Although I generally make it with shrimp or oysters (or both if you want to be lavish), it is also good with leftover chicken and giblets.

3 cups long-grain rice
6 cups chicken stock
2 pounds bulk pork sausage
3 tablespoons butter
1 bunch scallions, chopped (white and green parts)
2 medium green peppers, chopped
2 stalks celery with leaves, chopped
4 cloves garlic, mashed
2 teaspoons thyme
2 teaspoons leaf sage
1 teaspoon allspice
2 bay leaves, crumbled
½ teaspoon pepper
½ cup parsley, chopped
1–2 teaspoons Tabasco, to taste
1 pound cooked shrimp, or 10–12 ounces fresh oysters, or 2 cups cooked chicken and/or giblets, chopped

1. Cook rice in chicken stock until all liquid is absorbed. Keep covered and set aside.
2. In a large frying pan brown sausage meat, crumbling the sausage as you cook it. When sausage is completely browned, remove it from pan with a slotted spoon and set aside. Pour off all but about 2 tablespoons of sausage drippings.
3. To sausage drippings in pan add butter and melt over moderate heat. Add scallions, peppers, celery, and garlic and sauté until vegetables are soft.
4. Combine cooked rice, sausage, vegetables, and butter from pan, and all other ingredients. Mix thoroughly and taste for salt—you may need a dash or two. Turn mixture into a large buttered casserole. Cover and bake at 350° for 30–40 minutes or until steaming hot.

Serves about 16

CREATIVE CUISINE

Whenever I lecture about cuisine, and more specifically about flavor principles, someone in the audience is bound to ask: "Well, why not oysters in chocolate sauce or ice cream with fried onions?" The question really is: why do some flavors and foods seem to "go together" and some do not? Is there some scientific basis for, let us say, the combination of soy sauce and gingerroot that makes it "better" than soy sauce and oregano? The answer, I think, is no; custom, tradition, and familiarity all invest certain flavoring combinations with meaning and with a positive value.

Naturally, one cannot put together any arbitrary set of seasoning ingredients and come up with something good. Ultimately, when one steps outside of established ethnic traditions the success of any preparation is dependent on the individual's sense of what will work and what won't. What tastes good to you may not taste good to me; I am fairly sure, for example, that the combination of honey, dates, fish sauce, and cumin would not particularly delight my family's palate, but apparently it did please the ancient Romans who used it as a sauce for boiled ostrich.

Creative cuisine means using one's own cooking sense, one's taste and knowledge, to create recipes that are not only new and different, but good-tasting. There are many ways to do this, but the most expedient approach is to abstract the critical features of any ethnic cuisine and reapply them in a new way. For example, take a characteristic flavor principle from one cuisine (Indian curry, let us say) and use it with a characteristic cooking technique of another cuisine (Chinese stir-fry). Or take a basic food item from one cuisine (Oriental bean curd) and prepare it with a flavor principle from another cuisine (Provençal olive oil-tomato-herb). Or, combine two very different flavor principles (Chinese and French) in the same dish. The possibilities, you will begin to see, are almost endless, and the quality of the results limited only by your ingenuity and your own taste. The following recipes illustrate some of the ways to be creative by using the salient characteristics of various ethnic cuisines and reinterpreting them in new ways.

RECIPES FOR CREATIVE CUISINE

COLD SPINACH SOUP
CHINESE FISH PÂTÉ
ROAST PORK WITH APRICOT SAUCE
STEAK WITH BROWN CREAM SAUCE
VIETNAMESE HAMBURGERS
INDONESIAN PEANUT CHICKEN SALAD
BEAN CURD PROVENÇAL
STIR-FRIED VEGETABLE CURRY
STIR-FRIED CARROTS
SPICED COLLARD DIP
YOGURT-DILL SALAD DRESSING
WEST AFRICAN CHILI

COLD SPINACH SOUP

The Russians and the Chinese may not be able to come together politically, but in this recipe, willy-nilly they form an alliance of two very different flavor principles.

1 tablespoon peanut oil
2 teaspoons gingerroot, finely minced
1 pound fresh spinach, washed and stripped of tough stems
4 scallions, chopped
4 cups chicken stock
1 tablespoon soy sauce
3 tablespoons dry sherry
1 cup sour cream
2 tablespoons chives, finely chopped

1. In a large pot heat oil over high heat. Add gingerroot and stir-fry about 20 seconds. Add spinach and scallions and stir-fry about 1–2 minutes.
2. Add stock, soy sauce, and sherry. Simmer over low heat, uncovered, about 10 minutes.
3. Remove from heat and let cool. Purée in blender with ¾ cup of the sour cream. Chill thoroughly.
4. Just before serving, add chives and mix thoroughly. Garnish each serving with a blob of sour cream.

Serves 6–8

CHINESE FISH PÂTÉ

A French cooking technique combines with a Chinese flavor principle to produce a very unusual and very good pâté.

1 pound fresh carp (skin and bones removed), or 1 pound fresh shrimp, peeled and deveined
2 ounces fresh pork fat
2 eggs, lightly beaten
4 tablespoons sesame oil
1 teaspoon gingerroot, finely minced
1 clove garlic, finely minced
1 tablespoon soy sauce
2 tablespoons dry sherry
½ teaspoon salt
½ teaspoon sugar
1 slice gingerroot (about size and thickness of a quarter)

1. Grind the fish or shrimp with the pork fat twice through meat grinder. Combine with eggs.
2. In a small frying pan heat 2 tablespoons sesame oil over high heat. Add minced gingerroot and garlic and stir-fry about 20 seconds.
3. Add soy sauce, sherry, salt, and sugar and simmer gently a few minutes. Remove from heat and cool slightly. Add soy sauce mixture to fish.
4. Put 2 tablespoons sesame oil in a 3-cup mold and tilt mold so that oil films bottom and sides. Spoon fish mixture into mold, pressing down with back of spoon to ensure that there are no air pockets. Place slice of gingerroot on top of fish, then cover mold tightly with aluminum foil.
5. Place mold in a larger pan containing enough hot water to come about halfway up side of mold. Place pan in a preheated 325° oven for 40–50 minutes or until pâté is firm and resilient to the touch.
6. Cool pâté in mold, then run a sharp knife around the edge and unmold onto serving plate.
7. Serve chilled, cut in slices and garnished with shredded carrot and cucumber.

Serves 4–6

ROAST PORK WITH APRICOT SAUCE

A combination of Western and Oriental flavoring ingredients that go particularly well with pork. This is a superb and very easy company dish.

4–5 pound boneless lean rolled roast of pork
3 cloves garlic, cut in slivers
½ teaspoon salt
⅛ teaspoon freshly ground black pepper
10–12-ounce jar apricot preserves
⅓ cup soy sauce
2 cloves garlic, mashed
¼ teaspoon crushed dried red peppers
2 tablespoons dark brown sugar

1. With a small sharp knife make small gashes at regular intervals in roast; insert garlic slivers. Sprinkle roast with salt and pepper. Roast in a preheated 350° oven 2½–3 hours.
2. In a small saucepan combine preserves, soy sauce, garlic, peppers, and brown sugar. Simmer 5 minutes stirring. Baste roast with this mixture several times during roasting period.
3. When pork is done, let rest for 10 minutes, then cut in thick slices. Serve with remainder of sauce.

Serves 8–10

STEAK WITH BROWN CREAM SAUCE

Two great cuisines, French and Chinese, contribute both cooking techniques and flavor principles to this unusual and delicious dish.

6 4-ounce fillets mignons or club steaks
¼ cup butter
1 cup beef stock
¼ cup dry sherry
1 tablespoon soy sauce
1 teaspoon gingerroot, finely minced
2 cloves garlic, finely minced
1½ tablespoons flour
⅓ cup heavy cream
3 scallions, chopped

1. In a large frying pan heat 2 tablespoons butter over moderate heat. Add steaks and sauté about 2 minutes on each side for medium rare. Remove steaks from pan and keep warm while preparing sauce.
2. Combine stock, sherry, and soy sauce and pour into same pan. Stir over moderate heat, scraping up any brown bits from bottom of pan. Remove from heat.
3. In a medium saucepan heat 2 tablespoons butter over moderate heat. Add gingerroot and garlic and sauté for a few minutes.
4. Add flour and cook, stirring constantly, for 2 minutes.

5. Pour in sauce from frying pan and whisk rapidly until mixture is smooth. Cook, stirring constantly, until sauce thickens and begins to boil. Stir in cream and cook to simmering.
6. Pour sauce over steaks and garnish with chopped scallions.

Serves 4–6

VIETNAMESE HAMBURGERS

Foreigners tend to be somewhat contemptuous of the American dependence on the hamburger. If they are judging by the mass-produced fast-food variety, their disdain is justfied. But a juicy, well-prepared burger is a true delight, and this version represents the best of two worlds.

1 pound lean ground beef
1 tablespoon *nuoc mam*
1 teaspoon crumbled lemon grass
1 large clove garlic, mashed
good pinch crushed hot red peppers

1. Mix all ingredients thoroughly and form into patties. Broil over hot charcoal, turning once.
2. Serve on crusty hard rolls, with crisp lettuce leaves and scallions or sliced mild onion for garnish. Pass additional *nuoc mam*, crushed hot pepper, and of course, ketchup.

Makes 4 hamburgers

INDONESIAN PEANUT CHICKEN SALAD

Here is another good example of a traditional dish redone for the modern buffet. It is probably the most successful chicken salad I've ever made, so if you're bored with the usual mayonnaise and celery combination, try this one—it's always a big hit.

¾ cup dark soy sauce
¾ cup water
1 tablespoon lemon juice
¼ cup molasses
6 cloves garlic, mashed
¼ teaspoon crushed red peppers
¾ cup peanut butter
½ cup chopped peanuts
6–7 pounds boneless chicken breasts
2 20-ounce cans pineapple chunks, drained
8 ounce can water chestnuts, drained and sliced

1. In a medium saucepan combine soy sauce, water, lemon juice, molasses, garlic, and red peppers. Simmer, stirring, for a few minutes. Add in peanuts and peanut butter and stir over low heat until well blended.
2. Spread chicken breasts on a large foil-lined baking tray. Brush generously with sauce. Bake in a 400° oven for about 30 minutes or until done. Cool slightly, then cut the chicken into bite-sized chunks.
3. Combine chicken, pineapple chunks, and water chestnuts in a large bowl. Pour remaining sauce over and mix thoroughly. Chill.
4. Mound chicken salad on a large serving platter. Garnish with any and all of the following: melon chunks, cherry tomatoes, hard-boiled egg wedges, cucumber slices, red and green pepper strips.

Serves 16–20

BEAN CURD PROVENÇAL

Here is a good example of one way in which a culinary element can be lifted out of its traditioal setting and redone in another, quite different, culinary tradition. Bean curd (*tofu*) is a protein-rich food developed in the Orient many thousands of years ago, but as an Oriental food product, it does not have to be cooked and flavored in an Oriental fashion. Here bean curd reappears in a richly flavored herb and tomato sauce that complements its bland flavor and pasta-like texture.

2 tablespoons olive oil
1 medium onion, chopped
1 large ripe tomato, coarsely chopped
8-ounce can (1 cup) tomato sauce
½ teaspoon thyme
½ teaspoon marjoram
½ teaspoon leaf sage
½ teaspoon rosemary
¼ teaspoon oregano
⅛ teaspoon freshly ground black pepper
¼ teaspoon salt
1 cup fresh mushrooms, sliced
1 pound firm bean curd, cut in small cubes
2–3 tablespoons parsley, chopped

1. In a medium skillet, heat olive oil and sauté onion until golden. Add tomato, tomato sauce, and all seasonings and simmer uncovered for about 20 minutes, stirring occasionally.
2. Add mushrooms and bean curd and cook for another 5–6 minutes until thoroughly heated. Garnish with parsley and serve.

Serves 4

STIR-FRIED VEGETABLE CURRY

This recipe combines a Chinese and an Indian flavor principle, with the characteristic Chinese technique of stir-frying.

6–8 cups assorted fresh vegetables: snow peas; onions, quartered and separated into layers; broccoli flowers and stems, sliced; sliced mushrooms; sliced carrots; sliced celery; red and green pepper strips; asparagus tips, etc.
3 tablespoons soy sauce
3 tablespoons dry sherry
½ teaspoon sugar
1 teaspoon cornstarch
¼ cup peanut or vegetable oil
2 teaspoons gingerroot, finely minced
3 cloves garlic, finely minced
1 teaspoon ground cumin
½ teaspoon ground turmeric
½ teaspoon ground coriander
¼ teaspoon crushed dried red peppers

1. Choose an assortment of 4 or 5 vegetables that complement each other in color and texture. Separate less tender vegetables (onions, broccoli stems, carrots, etc.) from tender vegetables (mushrooms, etc.).
2. Combine soy sauce, sherry, sugar, and cornstarch, mix thoroughly and set aside.
3. In a large frying pan or wok heat oil over high heat. Add gingerroot, garlic, cumin, turmeric, coriander, and red peppers. Stir-fry about ½ minute.
4. Add less tender vegetables and stir-fry 1–2 minutes. Add rest of vegetables and stir-fry 1–2 minutes.
5. Add soy sauce mixture and heat quickly, stirring constantly, until sauce is slightly thickened and all vegetables are coated and heated through.

Serves 6

STIR-FRIED CARROTS

A Middle Eastern flavor principle and a Chinese cooking technique. Very easy and very good.

1 pound carrots
2–3 tablespoons vegetable oil
juice 1 lemon
¼ cup parsley, finely chopped

1 tablespoon fresh mint, chopped, or 2 teaspoons crushed dried mint
leaves
½ teaspoon salt

1. Scrape carrots and cut into rounds about ⅛-inch thick.
2. In a large frying pan or wok heat oil over high heat. Add carrots and
   stir-fry 2–3 minutes.
3. Remove carrots from pan with slotted spoon and place in serving
   dish. Add lemon juice, parsley, mint, and salt and mix well. Serve
   immediately.

Serves 4

SPICED COLLARD DIP

Here, a classic Indian main course dish (see p. 60) is reinterpreted for
the large party or cold buffet table. It makes a very unusual and
delicious dip for an assortment of raw vegetables.

1 pound fresh collard greens (or spinach)
2 tablespoons oil
1 medium onion, chopped
1 tablespoon mustard seeds
1 tablespoon gingerroot, finely minced
4 cloves garlic, minced
1 teaspoon cumin
¼ teaspoon crushed dried hot pepper
½ teaspoon ground coriander
1½ cups yogurt
½ teaspoon salt
¼ cup oil
juice 1 lime
2–3 tablespoons fresh coriander, chopped (optional)

1. Remove tough stems from collard greens. Wash leaves thoroughly,
   drain, then cook in the water clinging to the leaves for a few minutes
   just until wilted. Drain and squeeze as much water as possible from
   greens.
2. In a small frying pan heat oil, add onion, mustard seeds, gingerroot,
   and garlic and fry over moderate to high heat until mustard seeds
   start to pop. Stir in cumin, chile, and coriander and fry for a few
   minutes more.
3. Scrape all spice mixture from frying pan into blender or food
   processor, add cooked greens and purée until smooth. Add yogurt
   and salt and blend again.
4. Slowly pour in oil and continue blending until slightly thickened.
   Stir in lime juice and coriander, if desired. Chill.

Makes about 2½ cups

YOGURT-DILL SALAD DRESSING

Also good as a dip for raw vegetables or as a sauce for cold poached fish.

1 cup yogurt
3 tablespoons mayonnaise
1 tablespoon lemon juice
¼ cup fresh dill, chopped or 2 tablespoons dried dillweed
⅓ cup parsley, chopped
2 tablespoons fresh or freeze-dried chives
2 cloves garlic
¼ teaspoon freshly ground black pepper
½ teaspoon salt
3–4 chopped scallions

1. Combine all ingredients in a blender or food processor and blend until smooth. Chill.

Makes about 1½ cups

WEST AFRICAN CHILI

A familiar Southwest American preparation goes exotic by using a typical west African flavor principle.

2 tablespoons oil
1½–2 pounds lean ground beef
1 large onion, chopped
2 large red or green peppers, coarsely chopped
15-ounce can (2 cups) tomato sauce
1 teaspoon salt
¼ teaspoon pepper
½ teaspoon (more or less to taste) Tabasco
2 cups fresh, frozen, or canned corn kernels
½ cup smooth peanut butter

1. In a large frying pan, sauté onion in oil over moderate to high heat until beginning to brown. Add ground beef and brown over high heat.
2. When meat is completely browned, carefully pour off and discard all liquid from pan. Add peppers, tomato sauce, salt, pepper, hot pepper sauce and mix well. Cook over low to moderate heat about 30 minutes until slightly thickened. Add corn, mix well, and cook another 10 minutes.
3. Add peanut butter, blend in well, and heat until just bubbly. Taste for salt. Serve over plain rice or as a stuffing for green peppers, onions, or large zucchini shells.

Serves 6–8

BREADS

Most cultures have a basic grain or starch that is fundamental to the diet. It is a food staple that is eaten at almost every meal and provides both nutritional and psychological "bulk." These basic foods include rice in the Orient and India, wheat and barley in central Asia and the Middle East, yams and cassava root in sub-Saharan Africa, potatoes and rye in northern Europe, corn in Mexico, and so forth. I call this category of foods "bread," although clearly not all of the above fit our traditional, more limited notion of bread as a baked milled-grain product. They are all alike, however, in that they are all plant products, whether grains or starchy roots, and they all seem to serve a similar psychological function. A Frenchman would be as lost without his crusty loaf of white bread as a Japanese without his bowl of rice or a Mexican without his tortilla. These products generally are bland in flavor, light in color, and seem to be an essential accompaniment to the other foods and sauces typical of any culinary tradition. Included in this section, then, are recipes for basic grain dishes, as well as pasta and the more traditional "breads."

Bread-baking is an ancient art. It began with the discovery that ground seeds or grains can be mixed with water and baked in hot ashes or on hot stones to provide a nourishing and satisfying meal. The flat, unleavened "griddle" bread survives today in such forms as Mexican corn tortillas, Indian wheat chapattis, and Jewish matzohs.

Leavened bread was probably discovered in the Near or Middle East at least four or five thousand years ago; in this area bread wheat was first discovered and cultivated. This strain of wheat is high in gluten, the element that gives flour the capacity to expand as the growing yeast organisms produce bubbles of carbon dioxide.

If you have never baked bread, it will take a little time to get used to the proper "feel" of the dough. It should be smooth and elastic and neither so moist that it sticks to your hands nor so dry that it crumbles and breaks off in pieces. The liquids used in preparing bread dough should always be very warm to the touch but not unpleasantly hot. Hard wheat or bread flour is excellent for most breads, but all-purpose unsifted flour works very well. Since yeast requires warmth and moisture to grow, any unused yeast should be stored tightly covered in the refrigerator, where it will keep for a long time.

For griddle breads, use an ungreased clay, cast iron, or heavy aluminum griddle that can take the direct flame of a gas or electric burner. For hot stone or brick oven breads (Arabic bread, *nan*) it is worth investing in a baking stone made of unglazed clay or stoneware, or some unglazed baking tiles. Preheated in a very hot oven, these baking stones or tiles will give you much the same results as a hot brick oven, and are also very useful for pizza and other similar baked foods.

Bread baking is one of the most satisfying acts of cooking, because the fruit of one's labors is, indeed, the "staff of life." And besides, home-baked bread smells and tastes better than practically anything you can buy.

BREAD RECIPES

BASIC RICE PILAF

BULGUR PILAF

FRESH PASTA

TOMATO PASTA

SPINACH PASTA

ARABIC BREAD

NAN

CHAPATTIS

TORTILLAS

CHALLAH

JEWISH ONION BOARDS

BEER-RYE BREAD

VERMONT JOHNNYCAKE

BASIC RICE PILAF

There are many different varieties of rice, all of which provide different textures and flavors. The best all-purpose rice, I find, is the enriched converted long-grain, which needs no rinsing before or after cooking, and which cooks up into firm, separate grains. For plain rice, just use twice as much water as rice, and add a pinch of salt.

3 tablespoons butter
1 small onion, chopped
1 cup converted long-grain rice
2 cups hot chicken stock

1. In a medium saucepan melt butter over moderate heat. Add onion and sauté for a few minutes until golden.
2. Add rice and sauté, stirring, about 5 minutes or until rice is golden and all the butter is absorbed.
3. Add hot stock, cover, and cook over low heat 15–20 minutes or until all the liquid is absorbed. Fluff rice up with a fork and serve.

Serves 4–5

BULGUR PILAF

1 medium onion, chopped
3 tablespoons butter
1 cup bulgur
½ teaspoon ground (rubbed) sage
½ teaspoon cinnamon
2 cups hot chicken stock

1. Sauté onion in butter until just golden. Add bulgur and cook, stirring, until it is a light golden color.
2. Add sage, cinnamon, and hot stock. Cover and cook over low heat 15–20 minutes or until all liquid is absorbed.
3. Remove from heat and allow to stand, covered, 5 minutes. Fluff up with fork before serving.

Serves 4–6

FRESH PASTA

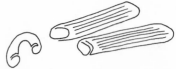

Like making homemade bread, making fresh pasta is one of those culinary ventures that, once mastered, will fill you with delight and self-satisfaction. Like bread baking it takes a little practice and getting used to the "feel" of the dough—not too sticky, not too dry. The dough can be rolled and cut for almost any pasta shape, or pinched off in small pieces to make dumplings. There are a number of hand-operated and electric pasta machines on the market, none of which to my mind is completely satisfactory; but if you have one, by all means use it, following the manufacturer's directions. If not, try it by hand. Here's how:

2 cups flour
1 scant teaspoon salt
2 eggs
2 teaspoons oil
2 teaspoons water

1. In a large bowl mix flour and salt, then make a well in the middle. Put the eggs, water, and oil in the well, then mix the wet ingredients into the flour with the hands. Knead the mixture with the fingers and heel of the hand until it forms a ball that is not too sticky and not too crumbly. If it seems too sticky add a little flour; if too dry add a little water, no more than a teaspoon at a time.
2. Cover the ball of dough with a towel and let it rest for about ½ hour.
3. On a floured board roll out the dough as thin as possible. With a sharp knife cut it into desired shapes and lengths; then let it dry for about an hour.
4. Cook pasta in boiling salted water for a few minutes. *Fresh pasta cooks very quickly*, so start testing for doneness after just a few minutes. Drain, and serve with butter, cheese, or your favorite sauce.

Makes about one pound

TOMATO AND SPINACH PASTA

The following variations on fresh pasta are more for color and visual appeal than for flavor; the light green spinach pasta, the orange tomato pasta, and the creamy white plain pasta look wonderful when combined with, say, a *pesto* sauce as a spectacular buffet dish.

To make the tomato pasta; follow recipe for fresh pasta, substituting 3 tablespoons canned tomato paste for the water. Mix as directed. If it seems too dry, add a little warm water, one teaspoon at a time.

To make the spinach pasta: increase flour to 2½ cups. Wash 6 ounces (about 4 cups) fresh spinach leaves, drain, then cook with just the water clinging to the leaves for a few minutes, just until the spinach is wilted. Purée the spinach in a blender or food processor, then squeeze out as much liquid as possible. Add spinach purée to eggs and oil in place of the water and proceed as directed.

ARABIC BREAD

Arabic bread, or *pita*, is the archetypical descendent of breads that originally were baked on hot stones or slabs of rock or clay. For best results, then, it is important to have your oven and baking tray thoroughly preheated and at a high temperature. If you have some unglazed tiles or a baking stone, by all means use them, although an ungreased metal tray will also work. This is a very easy bread to make and tastes wonderful hot from the oven.

1 tablespoon granulated yeast, or 1 cake compressed yeast
1 tablespoon sugar
2 cups hot water
5–6 cups white flour (for a more earthy loaf, you can substitute 2 cups whole wheat flour for 2 cups of the white)
2 teaspoons salt
sesame seeds

1. Combine yeast, sugar and ½ cup of the hot water in a large bowl and let stand for a few minutes. Add the rest of the water, 2 cups of flour, salt, and beat until smooth.
2. Add the rest of the flour to make a smooth, elastic dough. Knead thoroughly. Cover dough with a towel and let rise in a warm place for about an hour or until doubled in bulk.
3. Punch dough down. Let rest for 10–15 minutes. Divide into six equal balls. Roll each ball into a circle about 6–7 inches in diameter,

making sure that the circle is slightly thicker around the edges than in the center. As you roll, sprinkle some sesame seeds over the surface so that they are rolled into the dough.

4. Place each circle on a hot tray or tile in a preheated 450° oven for 10–12 minutes or until it is puffy and lightly browned on the top. Remove from oven and continue with rest of loaves.

Makes 6 loaves

NAN

Nan is a round, rather flat, leavened bread similar in appearance to Arabic bread, but richer because of the butter and yogurt in the dough. It is a specialty of northern India and traditionally is baked in the *tandoor*, a brick or stone oven heated very hot with charcoal at the bottom. The loaves of *nan* are baked directly on the hot side walls of the oven; to approximate this technique you should preheat your oven very hot and bake the *nan* on a preheated baking stone or tiles.

½ cup warm water
1 tablespoon sugar
1 tablespoon granulated yeast or 1 cake compressed yeast
4 tablespoons butter
1 cup yogurt
2 teaspoons salt
½ cup water
5½–6½ cups flour
1 large onion, slivered
2–3 tablespoons melted butter

1. In a large bowl combine warm water, sugar, and yeast; stir and let stand for a few minutes.
2. Combine butter, yogurt, salt, and water and heat until butter is melted. Cool until warm but not hot to the touch. Add yogurt mixture to yeast mixture.
3. Add 2 cups flour to the liquid mixture and beat well. Add enough more flour to make a smooth elastic dough. Knead thoroughly. Cover with a cloth and let rise in a warm place for about one hour or until doubled in bulk.
4. Punch dough down and divide into 4 equal parts. Let rest for 15–20 minutes. Roll each part into a round about 7–8 inches in diameter. Brush top generously with melted butter, then press onion slivers over the top.
5. Place loaf on a preheated baking stone or tiles in a hot (450–500°) oven for 12–15 minutes until puffed and lightly browned.

Makes 4 loaves

CHAPATTIS

Chapattis are an example of the most ancient kind of bread—flat, round, unleavened loaves baked not in an oven but on a griddle over a hot fire. To make these successfully use a heavy metal, preferably cast iron, griddle or flat pan that can take the sustained high heat of a gas or electric burner. Traditionally, *chapattis* are made only with flour and water; the added *ghee* or oil gives them more delicacy and flakiness. They are wonderful with rich curries.

2 cups whole wheat flour
2 cups white flour
1 teaspoon salt
2 tablespoons melted *ghee* or clarified butter or oil
about 1¼ cups warm water

1. In a large bowl combine flours and salt and mix until well blended. Make a well in the center and pour in the *ghee* or oil and the water. Mix the flour into the liquid, then knead thoroughly, at least 10 minutes by hand or somewhat less if you are using an electric dough hook. Dough should be very smooth and elastic and neither sticky nor crumbly. Wrap dough in a towel and let rest for at least 30 minutes or up to 2 hours.
2. Preheat griddle over high heat. Pinch off pieces of dough about the size of a small plum. Roll it into a ball in your palms, then flatten it and roll out on a floured board. Roll very thin into a flat circle about 6 inches in diameter.
3. Place circle on preheated griddle and cook for a few minutes, until bubbles appear on the surface. Flip the *chapatti* over, then press along the edges with a spatula. This will cause the middle to puff up a little. Cook *chapatti* on the second side for only about 20–30 seconds. Remove *chapatti* to a napkin-lined basket and keep covered until all the rounds are cooked. Serve warm.

Makes about 16 chapattis

TORTILLAS

If the truth be told, I have yet to master the art of making a truly fine tortilla. In Mexico, freshly made tortillas are thin, flaky, delicate. The traditional—and best—method of preparation, learned by women from early childhood, is to slap the dough between the palms of the hands. Many cooks use a tortilla press; I prefer the rolling pin.

2 cups *masa harina*
1 cup warm water

1. Mix *masa* with water until it forms a ball. If dough is too dry, add a few more tablespoons of water. Knead dough lightly, then let rest, covered, for about one hour.
2. Divide dough into 2-inch balls. Roll dough between plastic sandwich bags into 6-inch circles. (If using a tortilla press, place dough between 2 small plastic sandwich bags.)
3. Place circle of dough on a hot, ungreased griddle. When bubbles begin to form on the upper surface, turn the tortilla over. Cook on the second side for a few seconds until tortilla just begins to brown.
4. Remove cooked tortillas from griddle and keep wrapped in a napkin until serving.

Makes about 12 tortillas

CHALLAH

This rich golden-yellow honey and egg bread is traditional for the Jewish sabbath meal. It can be shaped into any form but the double braid is traditional. The deep yellow color comes from threads of saffron soaked in water; ground turmeric will produce the same result at a much lower cost.

⅛ teaspoon saffron threads or ⅛ teaspoon turmeric
⅓ cup hot water
⅔ cup hot water
1 tablespoon dry granulated yeast or 1 cake compressed yeast
¼ cup honey
⅓ cup vegetable oil
4 eggs (reserve 1 yolk)
2 teaspoons salt
4–5 cups white flour

Garnish: poppy seeds

1. Soak saffron threads in ⅓ cup warm water for 20 minutes (if using turmeric, dissolve in water and use immediately).
2. In a large bowl sprinkle yeast on ⅔ cup warm water; let stand for a few minutes. Mix in saffron (or tumeric), water, honey, oil, and eggs, and beat well. Add salt and 2 cups flour and beat until smooth.
3. Add in 2–3 cups additional flour to make a smooth elastic dough. Knead thoroughly. Cover with a towel and let rise in a warm place for about one hour or until doubled in bulk. Punch dough down and divide in half. Set one half aside and cover with towel.
4. Divide ball of dough into two parts, one about ⅓ of the dough, the other about ⅔ of the dough. Take the larger piece and divide into

three equal parts. Roll each part into a rope about 12 inches long. Braid the three ropes together, pinching them at the ends to seal.

5. Now take the smaller piece of dough and divide into three equal parts. Roll each part into a rope about 7–8 inches long. Braid the three smaller ropes together, pinching at the ends to seal. Place the smaller braid on top of the larger braid.

6. Repeat operation with second half of dough to form a second loaf. Place both loaves on an oiled baking sheet.

7. Beat reserved egg yolk with 2 teaspoons water. Brush both loaves thoroughly with egg mixture. Sprinkle with poppy seeds. Let loaves rise in a warm place for about 45–50 minutes.

8. Place loaves in a cold oven. Turn heat to 400°; bake for 25–30 minutes until deep golden brown. Remove to rack and cool.

Makes 2 loaves

JEWISH ONION BOARDS

1 tablespoon dry granulated yeast or 1 cake compressed yeast
1 cup very warm water
2 teaspoons sugar
2½–3½ cups white flour
1 teaspoon salt
about ¼ cup melted chicken fat
1 large onion, chopped (about 1 cup)

Garnish: paprika

1. Mix yeast, water, and sugar together and let stand for a few minutes. Add 2 cups flour and salt and beat until smooth.

2. Add enough additional flour to make a smooth elastic dough. Knead thoroughly. Cover with a towel and let rise in a warm place for about an hour or until doubled in bulk. Punch dough down and divide in half.

3. Brush two 9-inch round cake pans lightly with chicken fat. Place ½ of dough in each pan, flattening to the edges. Brush dough generously with remaining chicken fat, then sprinkle with chopped onions. Press onions into dough with finger tips. Sprinkle lightly with paprika.

4. Let loaves rise in a warm place for about 40–45 minutes. Place in a cold oven; turn heat to 450° and bake for 20–30 minutes until golden brown. Remove from pans and serve warm.

Makes 2 loaves

BEER RYE BREAD

The beer-rye tradition of eastern and northern Europe is used beautifully in a slightly sweet rye bread that is very good with butter, cheese, or cold cuts.

2 tablespoons dry granulated yeast or 2 cakes compressed yeast
½ cup warm water
1½ cups (1 bottle) dark beer
2 tablespoons butter or margerine
¼ cup molasses
2 teaspoons salt
2 tablespoons caraway seeds
3 cups white flour
3 cups rye flour

1. In a large bowl sprinkle yeast over warm water; let stand for a few minutes.
2. In a small pot combine beer, butter, molasses, salt, and caraway. Heat just until butter is melted. Cool until comfortably warm to the touch, then mix into yeast and water.
3. Add two cups of white flour and beat until smooth. Add in rye flour and knead; add more white flour as needed to form a smooth elastic dough. Knead thoroughly.
4. Cover with a towel and let rise in a warm place for about an hour or until doubled in bulk. Punch down; then form into two oblong loaves (or bake in two buttered rectangular bread tins). Let rise again for another hour or until doubled in bulk. Bake in a 350° oven for about one hour. If you want a shiny crust, combine one tablespoon molasses, one tablespoon soy sauce, and ¼ cup water; brush loaves lightly with mixture several times while baking.

Makes 2 loaves

VERMONT JOHNNYCAKE

Although never accepted as a bread grain in Europe, corn has been a valuable and traditional part of the American diet since earliest times. Many varieties of cornbread were developed, depending on the type of corn meal (white or yellow), the method of preparation (baked in the oven, cooked on a griddle, or fried in hot fat), and the type of sweetener. This version has been included to honor the publisher of this book and uses the traditional Vermont sweetener, maple syrup. It is a nice addition to the Thanksgiving table.

1 cup flour
1 cup yellow corn meal
3 teaspoons baking powder
½ teaspoon salt
3 eggs, beaten
¾ cup milk
½ cup maple syrup
½ cup melted butter or margarine

1. Combine all dry ingredients and mix thoroughly.
2. To beaten eggs, add milk, maple syrup, and melted butter, and mix well. Add liquid ingredients to dry ingredients and mix just well enough to moisten completely. No need to stir out all the lumps.
3. Pour mixture into a buttered 9-inch square baking pan (or buttered corn pone pan) and bake in a 375° oven about 30 minutes or until puffed and lightly browned. Serve warm with butter.

Makes 8 squares cornbread

 # DESSERTS

Because desserts are not a significant part of the daily diet in most cultures, unlike other foods they generally do not illustrate flavor principles. In many cultures, meals end with nothing more elaborate than some fresh fruit or a simple pudding, if that. Even in the Middle East and Europe, where there is a strong tradition of rich sweets and pastries, these tend to be eaten not at the conclusion of a meal but with afternoon coffee or tea.

I have included a section on desserts, not because they illustrate anything particularly important about ethnic cuisine, but because we like them and deem them an important part of our culinary tradition. Why this should be so is not clear; perhaps because we don't really need desserts, they become meaningful as art, as the elaboration of our most fanciful culinary whims. And there can be no doubt that they satisfy that most basic of cravings—for the sweet and the gooey. We can only agree with Shakespeare, who had something wise to say about almost everything:

The daintiest last, to make the end most sweet.

DESSERT RECIPES

FLAMING BANANAS

APRICOT MOUSSE

APRICOT SOUFFLÉ

APRICOT-ALMOND TORTE

PINEAPPLE-GINGER MOUSSE

LEMON MOUSSE

GREEK WALNUT PIE

ALMOND-GINGER ROLL

DULCE DE NUEZ

CHEESECAKE

HAZELNUT CHEESECAKE

MEXICAN CHOCOLATE ROLL

CHOCOLATE MINT PARFAITS

CHOCOLATE CHESTNUT CAKE

CHOCOLATE TORTE WITH CHESTNUT CREAM

CAESAR PIE

CHOCOLATE MOUSSE CAKE

MOCHA DACQUOISE

FROZEN COFFEE CHARLOTTE

RUM-RAISIN CAKE

ALSATIAN APPLE TART

WALNUT BUTTERCREAM CAKE

FRESH FRUIT TRIFLE

STRAWBERRY-RHUBARB SHERBET

FLAMING BANANAS

¼ cup butter, softened
½ cup dark brown sugar
½ cup orange juice
¼ cup lemon juice
6 firm ripe bananas, sliced
¼ cup dark rum, warmed
¼ cup Grand Marnier or other orange liqueur, warmed
1 quart vanilla ice cream

1. In a chafing dish or electric skillet cream butter and brown sugar together. Cook over low heat until smooth and syrupy.
2. Add orange and lemon juices and mix well. Add sliced bananas, warmed rum, and Grand Marnier and heat almost to simmering.
3. Ignite with a long match. While the bananas are still flaming, ladle them with sauce over individual servings of ice cream.

Serves 6

APRICOT MOUSSE

20 ladyfingers, split
8-ounce package dried apricots
¼ cup Grand Marnier or other orange liqueur or apricot brandy
2 8-ounce packages cream cheese, softened
1½ cups light brown sugar
4 eggs, separated
1½ teaspoons almond extract
¼ teaspoon salt
2 cups heavy cream, whipped

Garnish: fresh strawberries, marinated in Grand Marnier or apricot brandy, and drained

1. Dry split ladyfingers by placing on a cookie sheet in a preheated 200° oven 10–15 minutes. Cool.
2. Cook dried apricots in just enough water to cover just until soft. Purée apricots with water and Grand Marnier.
3. Beat cream cheese with one cup of sugar. Add egg yolks one at a time, beating well after each addition. Stir in apricot purée and almond extract and mix well.
4. Beat egg whites with salt and remaining ½ cup sugar until stiff.
5. Fold egg whites and whipped cream carefully into apricot–cream cheese mixture.
6. Line a deep 10-inch springform pan on bottom and sides with

ladyfingers, cut sides in. Carefully pour in apricot mixture. Cover and refrigerate at least 6 hours or overnight. Before serving, unmold and garnish with strawberries.

Serves 12–16

APRICOT SOUFFLÉ

1 cup dried apricots
⅓ cup medium dry sherry
2 tablespoons Cointreau or other orange liqueur
6 eggs, separated
¾ cup sugar
⅛ teaspoon salt
1 cup heavy cream, lightly whipped, flavored with a little sugar and brandy

1. Cook apricots in enough water to cover just until tender, about 5–6 minutes. Purée along with cooking water, sherry, and Cointreau until smooth.
2. In a large bowl beat egg yolks until thick and lemon-colored. Add apricot purée and sugar and mix well.
3. Beat egg whites with salt until stiff. Fold carefully into apricot mixture.
4. Butter and sugar a 2-quart soufflé dish or deep, straight-sided casserole. Pour apricot mixture carefully into soufflé dish and bake in a preheated 375° oven 30–40 minutes or until puffy and lightly browned. Serve immediately, with whipped cream.

Serves 4–6

APRICOT-ALMOND TORTE

Torte layers

6 eggs, separated
1 cup sugar
¾ cups sifted cake flour
½ teaspoon baking powder
½ cup toasted almonds, finely chopped
½ teasoon almond extract
¼ teaspoon salt

Filling

1 cup dried apricots
¼ cup sugar
2 tablespoons Grand Marnier or other orange liqueur
1 cup heavy cream

To make torte layers:

1. Beat the egg yolks until thick and foamy. Add the sugar gradually and beat until thick and pale.
2. Stir in the cake flour, baking powder, almonds, and almond extract and mix carefully until well blended. The batter will be very thick.
3. Beat the egg whites with the salt until stiff. Fold the beaten whites carefully into batter.
4. Divide batter equally between 2 buttered 9-inch round cake pans. Bake in a preheated 350° oven 20–30 minutes. Cool 10 minutes, then carefully remove cakes from pans.
5. Let cakes cool completely, then carefully cut each one in half horizontally with a sharp serrated knife, making 4 layers in all.

To make filling:

6. Put apricots in small saucepan with enough water to cover. Simmer gently until apricots are tender, about 5–6 minutes. Stir in sugar and Grand Marnier, then purée in blender until smooth. Cool.
7. Whip cream until stiff. Stir ¼ cup of the whipped cream into the apricot purée.

To assemble torte:

8. Place one torte layer on serving plate. Cover with ½ of the apricot purée. Place another torte layer on top and cover with ½ of the whipped cream. Repeat with third and fourth layers, covering the third with remaining purée and the fourth with remaining whipped cream. Chill several hours before serving.

Serves 8–10

PINEAPPLE-GINGER MOUSSE

1 envelope unflavored gelatin
¼ cup cold water
3 eggs, separated
¼ cup sugar
juice 1 lemon
grated rind 1 lemon
½ teaspoon ground ginger
1 cup crushed canned pineapple, in light syrup
¼ teaspoon salt
¼ cup light brown sugar
1 cup heavy cream, whipped
2 tablespoons crystallized ginger, finely chopped

1. Soften gelatin in cold water.
2. In top of double boiler combine egg yolks, sugar, lemon juice, lemon rind, ground ginger, pineapple (with liquid), and gelatin mixture. Cook over simmering water, stirring, about 10 minutes or until smooth and slightly thickened. Cool.
3. Beat egg whites with salt until foamy. Add brown sugar one tablespoon at a time and beat until stiff and glossy.
4. Carefully fold beaten egg whites and whipped cream into pineapple mixture, then gently fold in crystallized ginger.
5. Pour into serving bowl or individual dishes and chill several hours or overnight.

Serves 8–10

LEMON MOUSSE

1 envelope unflavored gelatin
2 tablespoons cold water
⅓ cup lemon juice
grated rind 1 lemon
4 eggs
¾ cup sugar
½ cup sour cream
1 cup heavy cream, whipped

Garnish: shredded coconut or candied citron

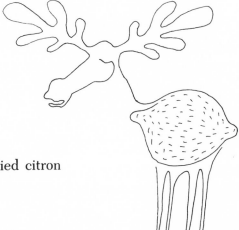

1. In small saucepan soften gelatin in cold water, then heat slowly until gelatin is dissolved. Remove from heat, cool slightly, then add lemon juice and lemon rind.
2. Beat eggs until light and frothy, then add sugar and beat until thick and lemon-colored.
3. Add gelatin mixture to eggs and mix well. Fold in sour cream, then whipped cream.
4. Spoon into parfait glasses and top with a little shredded coconut or candied citron. Chill several hours before serving.

Serves 6–8

GREEK WALNUT PIE

1 cup firmly packed dark brown sugar
1 teaspoon cinnamon
½ cup butter, softened
⅓ cup honey
3 eggs
¼ teaspoon salt
½ cup light cream
1¼ cups chopped walnuts
grated rind 1 lemon
2 unbaked 8- or 9-inch pie shells

Garnish: 1 cup heavy cream, whipped with 2 teaspoons sugar and ½ teaspoon cinnamon

1. In the top of a double boiler cream together brown sugar, cinnamon, and softened butter.
2. Place over hot water and stir in honey, eggs, salt, and light cream. Stir until well blended. Continue to cook over hot water 5 minutes, stirring constantly.
3. Remove from heat and stir in walnuts and lemon rind.
4. Pour mixture into pie shells and bake in a preheated 350° oven 35–40 minutes or until custard filling is set and lightly browned.
5. Cool pies on rack, then chill for several hours. Garnish with whipped cream before serving.

Makes 2 pies
Serves 12–16

ALMOND-GINGER ROLL

A good dessert to follow a heavy or highly spiced meal.

7 eggs, separated
6 tablespoons sugar
¼ teaspoon salt
¾ cup ground blanched almonds
1 teaspoon ground ginger
confectioners' sugar
1½ cups heavy cream
¼ teaspoon almond extract
2 teaspoons sugar
2 tablespoons crystallized ginger, finely chopped

1. Beat egg yolks until thick and lemon-colored. Add sugar, one tablespoon at a time, and beat until thick and pale.
2. Beat egg whites with salt until stiff. Mix a few spoonfuls of beaten egg whites into yolk mixture to lighten it, then carefully fold in rest of beaten whites. Carefully stir in almonds and ground ginger.
3. Butter a 17¼ × 11½ × 1–inch jelly roll pan, line with waxed paper, then butter the paper. Pour batter carefully into pan, spreading evenly to the edges.
4. Bake in a preheated 350° oven 15–17 minutes or until very lightly browned on top. Do not overbake. Remove from oven and cover immediately with a clean damp cloth. Cool completely.
5. Place 2 long sheets of waxed paper on a table, the long sides toward you and the front sheet overlapping the back sheet. Sift confectioners' sugar all over the paper. Unmold cooled cake onto sugared paper, then carefully peel off waxed paper.
6. Whip heavy cream with 2 teaspoons sugar and almond extract until stiff. Fold in crystallized ginger. Spread whipped cream evenly over cake to within ½ inch of edges.
7. Roll cake up carefully from the long side nearest you by lifting waxed paper underneath and guiding with your hands. Slide rolled cake onto serving plate. Chill before serving.

Serves 8–10

DULCE DE NUEZ

A traditional Mexican sweet to be served in very small quantities because it is very rich. The nuts should be fresh and of the best quality.

2 cups shelled pecans
2 cups (approximately) light cream

⅓ cup sugar
1 teaspoon cinnamon

1. Grind or chop the pecans, then pulverize in a blender with cream.
2. Add enough additional cream to make a thick, soft mixture, neither too pasty nor too runny.
3. Beat in sugar and cinnamon. The mixture should have the consistency of a thick mayonnaise. Chill 2 hours. It will thicken slightly when chilled.
4. Serve chilled in small cups or serving dishes.

Serves 6–8

CHEESECAKE

20 2½-inch square graham crackers
¼ cup butter, melted
1 teaspoon cinnamon
2 8-ounce packages cream cheese, softened
3 eggs
1 cup sugar
juice 1 lemon
grated rind 1 lemon
grated rind ½ orange
1 cup sour cream
3 tablespoons sugar
1 teaspoon vanilla extract

1. Crush or pulverize graham crackers. Mix crumbs with melted butter and cinnamon. Press evenly into bottom of 9-inch square cake pan or 9-inch round springform pan.
2. In a blender or food processor combine cream cheese, one cup sugar, eggs, lemon juice, and rinds. Blend until smooth. Pour mixture over crumbs in pan.
3. Bake in a preheated 350° oven approximately 40–50 minutes or until filling is firm and beginning to brown slightly. Remove cake from oven and increase oven heat to 500°.
4. Mix sour cream with 3 tablespoons sugar and vanilla and spread over hot cake. Bake 5 minutes.
5. Cool cake, then chill thoroughly before serving. Garnish with fresh fruit if desired.

Serves 10–12

HAZELNUT CHEESECAKE

This is but one of a number of possible flavor variations on cheesecake; it is delicious but quite extravagant, as hazelnut liqueur is rather expensive. The pear topping is optional, but it is very good and makes the whole thing very festive.

¾ cup toasted hazelnuts, finely chopped
10 graham crackers, rolled into fine crumbs
2 tablespoons melted butter
1 pound cream cheese
3 eggs
1 cup sugar
½ cup sour cream
⅓ cup hazelnut liqueur

1. Reserve ¼ cup chopped nuts for topping. Combine rest of nuts, graham cracker crumbs, and butter and mix well. Pat mixture into the bottom of a buttered 9-inch springform round pan.
2. In a blender or food processor combine cream cheese, eggs, sugar, sour cream, and liqueur. Blend until smooth. Pour over crumb layer.
3. If you are *not* making the pear topping, sprinkle reserved nuts in a border around the edge of the filling. Bake in a 350° oven for 50–60 minutes until middle of cake is set. Remove from oven and cool thoroughly.
4. After cake is cool, run a sharp knife around the edge, loosen the springform, and remove to serving platter. Chill. Serve as is or prepare the following pear topping.

3 cups water
½ cup sugar (which should include 3 tablespoons red cinnamon sugar—if not available, substitute a few drops of red food coloring)
2 tablespoons lemon juice
2 large or 3 small pears, ripe but firm
¼ cup melted apricot preserves

1. Combine water, sugar, and lemon juice and cook together for about 10 minutes.
2. Cut the pears into quarters, peel and core. Add pear pieces carefully to poaching liquid and cook for 5–7 minutes. Remove pears carefully from liquid with slotted spoon and cool.
3. Arrange poached pear quarters on top of the cooled cheesecake in a spoked circle design (tapered ends of pears pointed in to the center). Spread apricot preserves thinly over entire top of cake. Sprinkle reserved chopped nuts in a border around the edge. Chill.

Serves 8–10

MEXICAN CHOCOLATE ROLL

6 eggs, separated
½ cup sugar
1 cup semisweet chocolate bits
3 tablespoons strong coffee or rum
1¼ teaspoons cinnamon
½ teaspoon vanilla extract
⅛ teaspoon salt
confectioners' sugar
1½ cups heavy cream
2 tablespoons sugar
¼ cup toasted almonds, finely chopped

1. Beat the egg yolks until foamy. Beat in ½ cup sugar gradually and beat until thick and pale.
2. Melt chocolate with coffee until just smooth. Stir in one teaspoon cinnamon and vanilla. Cool slightly, then stir into the egg yolk mixture.
3. Beat egg whites with salt until stiff. Carefully fold beaten egg whites into chocolate mixture.
4. Butter a 17¼ × 11½ × 1–inch jelly roll pan. Line with waxed paper and butter the paper.
5. Pour batter carefully into pan, spreading it evenly to the edges. Bake in a preheated 350° oven 15 minutes. Remove from oven and cover immediately with a clean damp cloth. Let stand 15 minutes.
6. On a table place two 20-inch-long sheets of waxed paper, the long sides facing you and the front sheet overlapping the back sheet. Sift confectioners' sugar all over the paper. Unmold cooled cake onto sugared paper, then carefully peel off the waxed paper.
7. Whip cream with 2 tablespoons sugar and ¼ teaspoon cinnamon until thick. Spread whipped cream evenly over entire cake to within ½ inch of edges. Sprinkle chopped almonds evenly over whipped cream.
8. Carefully roll cake up from long side nearest you by lifting waxed paper underneath and guiding with your hands. Slide rolled cake onto serving plate. Chill several hours before serving.

Serves 8–10

CHOCOLATE-MINT PARFAITS

2 cups milk
2 tablespoons butter
½ cup sugar
2 tablespoons cornstarch
dash salt
2 eggs
3 ounces (3 squares) semisweet chocolate
1 ounce (1 square) unsweetened chocolate
1 teaspoon vanilla extract
½ teaspoon almond extract
1 cup heavy cream, whipped
⅓–½ cup crème de menthe

Garnish: ½ cup heavy cream, whipped

1. In a heavy saucepan, scald milk and butter over moderate heat.
2. In a small bowl combine sugar, cornstarch, and salt and mix well.
3. In another bowl beat eggs and set aside.
4. Pour about ¼ cup of the scalded milk into sugar mixture and mix well. Return this mixture to scalded milk in pot and cook over moderate heat, stirring constantly, until smooth and slightly thickened, about 2 minutes.
5. Gradually pour a small amount of the hot milk mixture into the beaten eggs, stirring constantly. Return this mixture to pot and cook, stirring constantly, about 2 minutes or until smooth and thickened.
6. Remove from heat and stir in chocolates and extracts. Stir until chocolate is completely melted and well blended.
7. Cover mixture with waxed paper and set aside to cool. When cool, carefully fold in whipped cream.
8. Fill a parfait glass about ⅓ full of the chocolate-cream mixture. Pour on one teaspoon crème de menthe. Fill up another ⅓ of the glass with chocolate mixture, then add another teaspoon crème de menthe. Repeat to fill glass.
9. Chill parfaits at least 6 hours or overnight. Garnish with a little whipped cream just before serving.

Serves 6–8

CHOCOLATE CHESTNUT CAKE

15–16-ounce can unsweetened chestnut purée
1 cup sugar
½ cup sweet butter, softened
½ teaspoon cinnamon
2 ounces (2 squares) unsweetened chocolate, melted
¼ cup rum

Garnish: slivered almonds and glacé cherries
       1 cup heavy cream, whipped

1. Combine chestnut purée with sugar, butter, cinnamon, melted chocolate, and rum and mix thoroughly. Pack into a lightly oiled or saran-lined 3 cup mold and chill at least 4 hours.
2. Just before serving, unmold cake and garnish with almonds and cherries. Serve in very small slices with whipped cream.

Serves 8

CHOCOLATE TORTE WITH CHESTNUT CREAM

Chocolate Torte Layers

12 eggs
1⅓ cups sugar
⅔ cup flour
12 ounces semisweet chocolate
⅓ cup strong coffee

1. Butter two 9-inch round springform pans. Line bottoms of pans with aluminum foil, then butter the foil.
2. Beat eggs until light and frothy. Gradually add in sugar and continue to beat until quite thick and pale (at least 10 minutes with an electric mixer).
3. Melt chocolate with coffee. Cool slightly.
4. When egg mixture is thick, stir in chocolate and mix well. *Sift* flour into mixture and stir until completely blended in.
5. Divide batter equally between the two prepared pans and bake in a 350° oven for 40–45 minutes. Cool completely, then remove from pans.

Chestnut Cream

1½ cups cooked or canned chestnuts, drained, or 1 cup canned
    unsweetened chestnut purée
¼ cup rum
⅓ cup sweet butter
⅔ cup light brown sugar
1 egg yolk
½ teaspoon vanilla

1. Purée chestnuts with rum in a blender or food processor until
   smooth, or mix prepared purée together with rum.
2. Cream butter and sugar together until light, then beat in egg yolk
   and vanilla and beat until smooth. Beat in chestnut purée until
   smooth.
3. Spread one chocolate layer with chestnut cream and place another
   layer on top of it. Frost sides and top of torte completely with cream.
   Garnish with shaved chocolate if desired. Refrigerate.

Serves 8–10

CAESAR PIE

Named for my brother who, since childhood, has adored the combination of chocolate and raisins.

½ cup sweet butter
1 cup sugar
3 eggs
¼ cup lemon juice
grated rind 1 lemon
½ cup dark raisins
2 ounces (2 squares) semisweet chocolate
½ teaspoon vanilla extract
½ cup walnuts, chopped
9-inch baked pie shell

Garnish: ½ cup heavy cream, whipped

1. In a heavy saucepan combine the butter, sugar, eggs, lemon juice,
   lemon rind, and raisins. Cook over low heat, stirring constantly, until
   butter is melted and all ingredients are well blended. Continue to
   cook, stirring constantly, until mixture is smooth and slightly
   thickened, about 8–10 minutes.

2. Remove from heat and stir in chocolate. Mix until chocolate is completely melted and blended in. Stir in vanilla and walnuts.
3. Cool mixture slightly, then pour into pie shell. Chill thoroughly. Serve in small slices garnished with whipped cream.

Serves 8

CHOCOLATE MOUSSE CAKE

This is always a great success. My youngest son says it's his "especial" favorite because it's "light, smooth, and not very rich." HA! That's why, he says, he's able to eat so much of it. If you are doing it a day ahead, don't garnish it with whipped cream until just before serving.

2 packages ladyfingers
12 ounces good quality semisweet chocolate
2 tablespoons strong coffee
6 eggs, separated
2 cups heavy cream
½ teaspoon vanilla
1 tablespoon sugar
⅛ teaspoon salt
1 tablespoon brown sugar

1. Use a 9- or 10-inch round springform pan at least 2–3 inches high. Line the bottom and sides of the pan with ladyfingers, cut sides in and up.
2. In a medium sized heavy pot, melt chocolate with coffee until smooth. Let cool slightly.
3. With a wire whisk beat egg yolks, one at a time, into chocolate mixture, beating well after each addition. Place egg whites in a bowl.
4. Beat cream with vanilla and one tablespoon sugar until stiff.
5. Add salt to egg whites and beat until foamy. Add brown sugar and beat until stiff.
6. Reserve ¼ of the whipped cream for garnish. Mix a few spoons of cream into chocolate mixture to lighten it; then carefully fold in beaten egg whites and whipped cream.
7. Spoon mousse carefully into pan lined with ladyfingers. Chill.
8. Unmold mousse right side up onto serving plate and garnish all around the edge with reserved whipped cream.

Serves 8–10

MOCHA DACQUOISE

Meringue Layers

6 egg whites
⅛ teaspoon salt
1½ cups sugar
1 cup ground blanched almonds, pecans or hazelnuts
½ cup fine zwieback crumbs
2 tablespoons unsweetened Dutch-process cocoa
2 tablespoons sifted flour

Mocha Filling

½ cup sweet butter, softened
1 cup confectioners' sugar
1 tablespoon instant coffee powder
4 egg yolks
2 tablespoons Kahlua or other coffee liqueur

Garnish: shaved chocolate curls

To make meringue layers:

1. Using an 8- or 9-inch round cake pan as a guide, cut 3 circles of aluminum foil 8 or 9 inches in diameter. Butter and flour the foil circles and place on a cookie sheet.
2. Beat egg whites with salt until foamy, then gradually add in ½ of the sugar and beat until stiff.
3. Gently fold in remaining sugar, nuts, crumbs, cocoa, and flour.
4. Spread ⅓ of the mixture on each of the foil circles, up to ½ inch from the edge. Bake in a preheated 250° oven 45 minutes. Cool layers, then remove from cookie sheets and carefully peel off aluminum foil. Handle layers gently, as they are very delicate.

To make filling:

5. Cream butter with confectioners' sugar and instant coffee.
6. Beat in egg yolks one at a time, beating well after each addition. Add coffee liqueur and mix thoroughly.
7. Spread ⅓ of the filling on each of the torte layers and stack up. Garnish top layer with chocolate curls. Chill before serving.

Serves 8–10

FROZEN COFFEE CHARLOTTE

This recipe may look complicated, but if you read it carefully you will see that it is simply a flavored custard and a flavored whipped cream blended together and frozen. The possibilities for flavor variations are almost endless. Since the dessert is frozen, it can be made well in advance.

10–12 macaroons
2 cups milk
2 tablespoons sweet butter
½ cup sugar
3 tablespoons cornstarch
⅛ teaspoon salt
3 tablespoons instant coffee powder
2 eggs
3 tablespoons Cognac
2 cups heavy cream
2 tablespoons sugar
2 teaspoons instant coffee powder
3 tablespoons butter, softened
⅓ cup firmly packed brown sugar
½ cup slivered blanched almonds
2 tablespoons Cognac

1. Place macaroons on a cookie sheet in a 250° oven for ½ hour. Cool, then crush into fine crumbs with a rolling pin or in a blender. Set aside.
2. In a heavy saucepan scald milk with 2 tablespoons butter. Set aside.
3. In a small bowl combine ½ cup sugar, cornstarch, salt, and 3 tablespoons instant coffee. Mix well and set aside.
4. In a small bowl beat eggs. Set aside.
5. Stir a small amount of the hot scalded milk into the sugar mixture, blend well and return to pot. Cook over low heat, stirring constantly, until mixture is smooth and thick.
6. Gradually add a small amount of hot milk mixture into beaten eggs, stirring constantly. Return this mixture to pot. Cook over low heat, stirring constantly, until thick and smooth. Remove from heat and stir in 3 tablespoons Cognac. Cool thoroughly.
7. Whip heavy cream with 2 tablespoons sugar and 2 teaspoons instant coffee until stiff. Fold carefully into cooled custard mixture.
8. Pat macaroon crumbs evenly into the bottom of a lightly buttered 9- or 10-inch deep springform pan. Pour coffee mixture over crumbs; place in freezer.

9. To make topping: in a small saucepan cream together butter and brown sugar. Cook over low heat, stirring, until smooth and syrupy. Remove from heat, stir in almonds and brandy, and cool.
10. When charlotte is frozen, spread almond mixture over the top and return to freezer.
11. Several hours before serving, unmold charlotte onto a serving plate and place in refrigerator (it should not be frozen solid when served.)

Serves 10–12

RUM-RAISIN CAKE

A rich moist cake that can be made several days ahead.

¾ cup butter, softened
1 cup sugar
½ cup firmly packed dark brown sugar
3 eggs
2½ cups sifted flour
1 teaspoon salt
1 teaspoon baking soda
1 cup sour milk*
1 cup raisins
grated rind 1 orange
grated rind 1 lemon
1 cup walnuts, chopped
3 tablespoons orange juice
3 tablespoons lemon juice
¼ cup dark rum

1. Cream butter, ½ cup sugar, and brown sugar together until fluffy. Beat in eggs one at a time, beating well after each addition.
2. Combine flour, salt, and baking soda and add alternately with sour milk to butter mixture.
3. Stir in raisins, rinds, and walnuts and mix thoroughly. Pour batter into a buttered 9- or 10-inch bundt pan. Bake in a preheated 350° oven one hour. Remove from oven and cool on rack 15–20 minutes.
4. Combine orange juice, lemon juice, and ½ cup sugar in a small saucepan. Cook, stirring occasionally, over moderate heat about 10 minutes until mixture is thick and syrupy. Remove from heat and stir in rum.

5. Unmold cake onto a rimmed serving plate. Using a thin skewer, poke holes all over top of cake. Slowly spoon rum mixture over top of cake. Keep spooning up excess sauce onto cake until all the liquid is absorbed.

Serves 10–12

*To make sour milk: place 2 tablespoons lemon juice or vinegar in a one cup measure. Pour in enough milk to make one cup. Do not stir. Let stand 10 minutes.

ALSATIAN APPLE TART

Instead of the traditional French pastry shell, this tart has a thin buttery cake layer. It is quite easy to do, looks impressive, and tastes very good.

½ cup (1 stick) sweet butter
½ cup sugar
3 eggs
½ teaspoon almond extract
1 cup flour
3 large good-tasting apples (Winesap or Granny Smith)
2 tablespoons sugar
½ teaspoon cinnamon
¼ cup apricot preserves, melted and sieved

1. Cream butter with sugar, add eggs one at a time, beating well after each addition. Add almond extract, stir in flour and mix until well blended.
2. Spread batter evenly in a buttered 11-inch fluted tart pan with a removable bottom.
3. Quarter apples, peel and core, and cut in uniform slices. Starting at the outside of the tart ring, arrange apples just touching each other in concentric rings to cover entire batter.
4. Combine sugar and cinnamon and sprinkle evenly over the apples.
5. Bake at 375° for 35–40 minutes. Remove from oven and let cool.
6. Remove tart from tart ring and place on serving dish. Glaze with the apricot preserves.

Serves 10–12

WALNUT BUTTERCREAM CAKE

6 eggs
1 cup light brown sugar
¾ cup flour
1½ cups walnuts, freshly ground
¼ cup (½ stick) sweet butter, melted
½ teaspoon vanilla

1. Beat eggs until light and frothy. Gradually add in sugar and beat until quite thick. When you think you have beaten it enough, beat it a little more.
2. *Sift* into flour mixture, and stir until well blended, then stir in walnuts, butter, and vanilla and mix gently but thoroughly.
3. Pour batter into a buttered 9-inch round springform pan and bake in a 350° oven for 35–40 minutes just until middle is set. Remove from oven, cool in pan for ½ hour. Run a sharp knife around the edge, then unmold the cake. Cool completely. Frost with the following buttercream:

¼ cup sweet butter
½ cup light brown sugar
1 egg yolk
½ teaspoon vanilla
½ cup walnuts, freshly ground

1. Cream butter and sugar until light, then beat in egg yolk and vanilla and beat until smooth. Stir in walnuts and mix thoroughly.

Serves 8

FRESH FRUIT TRIFLE

Most attractive if served in a clear glass bowl so the many layers of this appealing dessert can be seen.

2 cups ripe peaches, sliced
3 tablespoons peach or apricot liqueur
2 cups fresh blueberries
2 cups milk

2 tablespoons butter
½ cup sugar
3 tablespoons cornstarch
2 eggs
½ teaspoon each vanilla and almond extracts
1½ cups heavy cream
1 tablespoon sugar
½ cup raspberries (if not available, substitute sliced strawberries)
1 package (12) ladyfingers, split

1. Combine peaches and liqueur, mix well, and set aside.
2. Wash blueberries, drain thoroughly, and set aside.
3. In a medium saucepan scald milk with butter. Set aside.
4. In a small bowl combine sugar and cornstarch, mix well, and set aside.
5. In a small bowl beat eggs. Set aside.
6. Stir a small amount of the hot scalded milk into the sugar mixture, blend well and return to saucepan. Cook over low heat, stirring constantly, until mixture is smooth and thick.
7. Gradually beat a small amount of hot mixture into beaten eggs, then return to pot. Cook over low heat, stirring constantly, until thick and smooth. Remove from heat, stir in extracts, and cool.
8. Beat cream with one tablespoon sugar until stiff.
9. To assemble trifle: Line the bottom of a 2–2½ quart bowl with ½ of the ladyfingers, cut side up. Sprinkle the ladyfingers with ½ of the liquid from peaches.
10. Spread ½ of the cooled custard mixture over the ladyfingers. With a splotted spoon, place sliced peaches over the custard, reserving peach liquid.
11. Place rest of ladyfingers, cut side up, in a layer over the peaches. Sprinkle ladyfingers with reserved peach liquid.
12. Spread rest of custard over ladyfingers, then spread blueberries in a layer over the custard.
13. Spoon whipped cream in a layer over the blueberries. Garnish the whipped cream with raspberries.
14. Cover bowl with plastic wrap and chill several hours.

Serves 8–10

STRAWBERRY-RHUBARB SHERBET

2 pounds fresh rhubarb, cleaned and trimmed
½ cup water
1 cup sugar
1 pint fresh strawberries, hulled
2 tablespoons strawberry liqueur or Cassis (black currant liqueur)
¼ cup orange juice
1 tablespoon (1 envelope) unflavored gelatin
2 egg whites
⅛ teaspoon salt

1. Cut rhubarb in small chunks and place in a large pot with water. Cover and cook over low to moderate heat until rhubarb is tender, about 8–10 minutes. Stir in sugar and cook about 5 minutes. Stir in strawberries, remove from heat and set aside. Cool.
2. Combine liqueur and orange juice in a small pot. Sprinkle in gelatin and let stand a few minutes to soften. Heat mixture over low heat, stirring, until gelatin dissolves.
3. In a blender or food processor purée fruit mixture until smooth. Stir in gelatin mixture and mix thoroughly.
4. Place mixture in freezer for about one hour or until it begins to thicken and get slushy.
5. Beat egg whites with salt until stiff.
6. Remove fruit mixture from freezer and beat with a whisk or an electric mixture until it is smooth and a little fluffy. Fold in beaten egg whites gently but thoroughly. Return to freezer and freeze.
7. Allow sherbet to thaw slightly before serving; it should not be frozen solid.

Serves 6–8

FOREIGN INGREDIENTS

Included in this list are items that must be obtained from foreign specialty stores and that are not ordinarily available in most supermarkets.

ORIENTAL

Bamboo shoots: available canned. Rinse in cold water before using. Remainder can be kept covered in water in refrigerator for a few days.

Bean sprouts: crunchy sprout of the mung bean. If not available fresh, omit; the canned variety is useless because it is too soft to provide the proper texture.

Black beans: salted and fermented Chinese black beans used in preparing black bean sauce. Store in tightly covered jar in pantry.

Coriander leaf (cilantro): pungent fresh green herb that looks very similar to Italian flat parsley. Generally sold in a bunch with the roots attached. Store in plastic bag in vegetable compartment of refrigerator.

Dashi: Japanese soup stock made from kelp and bonito. Available in instant form in small packets; use one packet per one cup water unless packet instructs otherwise.

Dried mushrooms, tree ears, tiger lily buds (golden needles): varieties of dried fungi used for flavor and texture. Keep tightly wrapped in plastic on pantry shelf.

Duck sauce: a sweet-sour condimental or dipping sauce, generally made from peaches or apricots, vinegar, and sugar.

Egg roll skins or wrappers: available fresh by the pound in most Oriental groceries, they can also be frozen. Cut egg roll wrappers in quarters for won tons.

Fish sauce: salty fermented fish sauce used for seasoning and cooking. One Vietnamese variety (*nuoc mam*) based on anchovies will serve all your needs.

Five-spice powder: a blend of powdered aniseed, licorice, clove, ginger, and nutmeg.

Gingerroot: knobby brown rhizome of the ginger plant. It is an essential ingredient in Oriental and Indian cooking, and powdered ginger is not a satisfactory substitute. Buy a smooth round chunk, not dry or shriveled; store unwrapped in refrigerator and cut off slices as needed.

Hoisin sauce: a sweet bean sauce used in Chinese cooking and as a condiment. Stores indefinitely in the refrigerator.

Hot bean paste: a paste of fermented soy beans with hot chile pepper added, used frequently in Szechuan cooking. Store in refrigerator.

Hot sauce: a sweet-sour sauce with hot chile pepper added, or a sauce of garlic and hot chile pepper. Store in refrigerator.

Lemon grass: dried fragrant herb that looks like small wood shavings. Imparts a delicate lemony odor and flavor without any sourness. Keep tightly wrapped in plastic on the pantry shelf.

Litchi (lychee) nuts: small, round, white, distinctively flavored fruits available canned in sugar syrup. Expensive and good.

Mirin: Japanese sweet cooking wine.

Miso: a thick dark paste made of fermented soybeans. Used extensively in Japanese and northern Chinese cooking. Store in refrigerator.

Noodles: literally hundreds of varieties of Oriental noodles are available, made of rice flour, bean starch, and wheat flour. Have available cellophane noodles (thin translucent noodles made from bean starch, and pho noodles (thicker vermicelli-like noodles made from rice flour, used in Vietnamese soups). Fresh noodles are usually available by the pound in Chinese groceries.

Plum sauce: a sweet-sour sauce made of plums, vinegar, sugar, and garlic. Store in refrigerator.

Rice paper: large, thin, round sheets made from rice flour. Used for wrapping Vietnamese egg rolls. Must be dampened before using. Keep tightly wrapped in plastic.

Sake: dry Japanese rice wine, used extensively in Japanese cooking. Dry sherry is a reasonable alternative.

Rice vinegar: white vinegar made from rice; somewhat milder than most vinegars.

Sesame oil: a dark, flavorful oil made from crushed sesame seeds. An indispensable flavoring ingredient in Oriental cooking. Buy a good Chinese or Japanese variety, not the kind sold in health-food stores.

Snow peas: sweet edible pea pods. If not available fresh, omit.

Soy sauce (soya, shoyu): available in many varieties, you should have on hand one all-purpose Chinese or Japanese regular (thin, light) variety, and one dark (heavy, black) variety, which is thicker, sweeter and more heavily flavored than the regular. Buy Chinese or Japanese varieties, not the domestic supermarket kind.

Star anise: a star-shaped dried flour bud with a sweet anise flavor. Store in a tightly covered jar on the spice shelf.

Tofu (bean curd): white pressed cakes made from soybeans; very high in protein and a good meat substitute. Covered with water it can be stored for several days in the refrigerator.

Trasi (blachan): concentrated paste made from dried, salted shrimp. Tightly wrapped it will keep indefinitely in the refrigerator.

Szechuan pepper: brown peppercorns with a hot afterbite. Roast lightly, then grind in a pepper mill.

Water chestnuts: available canned. Rinse in cold water before using. Remainder can be stored covered with water in refrigerator for a few days.

INDIAN

Coconut: a dried unsweetened shredded variety for making coconut milk or cream. Store in the pantry.

Coriander leaf: see under *Oriental* list.

Curry powder: buy good quality in small amounts.

Ghee: clarified butter used extensively in cooking. Buy butter ghee, not vegetable ghee, and store in refrigerator.

Gingerroot: see under *Oriental* list.

Mustard oil: not essential, but does give a characteristic flavor to some regional curries. A small bottle will last a long time.

Spices: buy small amounts of the following ground spices: cumin, coriander, cardamom, fenugreek, ginger, turmeric, cloves. Buy small quantities of the following whole spices: cumin seed, fennel seed, black mustard seed, cloves, bay leaves, cardamom seeds, crushed dried hot red peppers.

MIDDLE EASTERN

Bulgur: parboiled cracked wheat, a basic grain food used much like rice. Comes in medium, fine, and coarse textures; a medium variety will serve most needs.

Falafel mix: a mixture of ground chick peas or fava beans and spices; mixed with water and egg it can be made into patties and fried, or used as a kind of flavored bread crumb. Store in the pantry.

Filo (phyllo) leaves: paper-thin pastry leaves used in strudel, baklava, and cheese pastries. Generally sold in one-pound packages, it can be frozen.

Grape leaves: if you can get fresh ones from a grape arbor, by all means do so. If not, buy them bottled in brine. After opening, store in refrigerator.

Pine (pignolia) nuts: small, sweet white nuts used in meat and dessert preparations. Store covered in the refrigerator.

Pomegranate syrup: ruby-red, sweet-sour syrup made from the juice of fresh pomegranates. Can be bought commercially prepared in Middle Eastern or Armenian groceries, or you can make your own (see p. 65).

Tahini: a thick paste made of ground sesame seeds; it is the basic vehicle for many sauces and dips. Can be purchased bottled or canned. Once opened, store in a covered jar in the refrigerator; bring to room temperature before using.

MEDITERRANEAN AND EUROPEAN

Olive oil: well worth experimenting with to find which variety you like best. I only use a robust Spanish or Greek variety, and if I want a milder taste, I cut it half and half with ordinary vegetable oil. You may prefer the flavor of the more delicate French or Italian types, but for some recipes the stronger varieties are advised. If you use enough of it, as I do, it is worth buying in a gallon container.

Wines and liqueurs: worth buying good quality; generally so little is used in cooking that the extra cost is not significant, and the difference in flavor is worth the expense. Useful to have on hand: a dry white wine, dry sherry, cream sherry, a sweet wine such as Marsala or Madeira, a good Cognac, and several sweet liqueurs such as Grand Marnier or Cointreau, Kahlua or Tia Maria, Hazelnut, Peach or Apricot. Well capped, these all store well.

MEXICAN

Chiles: except for the Southwest and parts of California, it is hard to find the large variety of chile peppers that provide such a wide range of flavors in Mexican cooking. Still, you should be able to find and have on hand (1) crushed dried red peppers, (2) canned green chiles (jalapeño and serrano), (3) whole dried red chiles, and, probably the most widely used of all, (4) dried *ancho* chiles, either whole or powdered. One tablespoon of the powdered is approximately equivalent to one large dried chile. Other dried chiles to try are the *pasilla* and the *poblano*. Fresh red and green chiles are frequently available in supermarkets; they should be tried (cautiously) to determine their flavor and hotness.

Achiote (annatto): a small, hard red seed used primarily as a coloring agent in both Mexican and Indian cooking. Try to buy it already ground, but if not available, buy the seeds and grind them yourself.

Masa harina: ground corn flour used in making tortillas. Made in this country by Quaker, it is available in 5 pound bags. Store like flour.

Adobo paste: small compressed squares of ground *achiote*, garlic, vinegar, and other spices.

COOKING EQUIPMENT

This is by no means a complete kitchen inventory, but simply a mention of some of the equipment most useful for the modern cook.

Absolute musts: a variety of sharp knives, a good heavy garlic press, a large slotted spoon, a variety of spatulas, a couple of wire whisks of different sizes, at least one cutting board, strainers, colanders, a nut chopper, a hand grater, a good electric mixer.

Blender: essential for puréeing liquids. Not so good for solids, where the food processor does a better job.

Dough mixer (electric): this may come as part of an electric mixer set or as part of a food processor. You should know the "feel" of kneading dough by hand, but the electric dough hook certainly does the job efficiently. Not essential, but it is a time-saver.

Food processor: one of the best pieces of equipment to come along in years. I'm not a gadgety person, but I think that the food processor is something the modern cook can hardly afford to be without. Unlike pasta machines, for example, whose function is limited and whose design has yet to be worked out satisfactorily, the food processor does a variety of tasks and does them well. Wonderful for puréeing solids; also good for grating, chopping, and slicing.

Meat grinder: either manual or electric.

Spice grinder: not absolutely essential, but very useful if you really want to get as close as you can to the authentic flavor of certain complex spice preparations. The flavor and aroma of freshly roasted ground cumin seed, for example, is quite a bit different from commercially prepared ground cumin. A small electric push-button coffee or spice grinder is worth having.

Wok: shallow, round-bottomed metal pan used in Chinese and other Oriental cooking. If not available, a large frying pan can be substituted, but the wok is easier to use for stir-frying. It should be placed directly over the heat (gas, electric, or charcoal), and not on a metal ring that lifts it above. The whole idea of the wok is to get a very high heat over as large a surface as possible, in order to cook the food very quickly.

GENERAL COOKING INFORMATION

1. Always, always, always read the recipe through a couple of times before starting. You'll avoid a lot of disasters if you know where you're going and the steps you have to go through to get there.
2. Eggs are always standard large size, unless otherwise specified.
3. Flour is unsifted all-purpose unless otherwise specified.
4. Oil, unless otherwise specified, is a bland light vegetable oil (soybean, corn, etc.).
5. Oven is always preheated unless otherwise specified.
6. Herbs are always better fresh than dried, but some are better than others. There is no substitute for fresh coriander leaf (cilantro), and it cannot be successfully frozen. Dried parsley is a disaster. Dried dillweed and dried basil are reasonably good and can certainly be used when fresh is not available. Fresh garlic is a must, though dried, granulated garlic is a useful product to have on hand.
7. Always buy small quantities of good quality herbs and spices. They tend to lose flavor with age and should be replenished frequently.
8. Freshly ground pepper does make a difference. Get a pepper mill and some peppercorns and see for yourself.
9. Homemade stock is always better than commercial products, but canned stock, bouillon cubes, and granulated bouillon are certainly a time and energy saver. Shop around for the best flavored varieties. These products are best used in preparations in which other seasonings and ingredients are used, thus masking the "commercial" flavor.

PRACTICAL METRIC CONVERSIONS

Volume (workable approximates)

Teaspoon, **tsp**; tablespoon, **T**; fluid ounce, **fl.oz**; pint, **pt**; quart, **qt**; gallon, **gal** (all non-metric forms = established U.S.A. and Canadian measures); milliliter, **ml**; cubic centimeter, **cc** (1 ml = 1 cc); liter, **l**.

¼ tsp = 1.25 ml

½ tsp = 2.5 ml

1 tsp = 5 ml

1 T (½ fl.oz) = 15 ml

2 T (1 fl.oz) = 30 ml

¼ cup (2 fl.oz) = 60 ml

⅓ cup (2.7 fl.oz)· = 80 ml

½ cup (4 fl.oz) = 120 ml

1 cup (8 fl.oz) = 240 ml/ 0.24 l.

1½ cups (12 fl.oz) = 360 ml/ 0.36 l.

2 cups (16 fl.oz/1 pt) = 470 ml/ 0.47 l.

4 cups (32 fl.oz/1 qt) = 950 ml/ 0.95 l.

2 qt = 1.90 l.

3 qt = 2.85 l.

4 qt (1 gal) = 3.8 l.

*   *   *

100 ml = 3.4 fl.oz

500 ml = 17 fl.oz

1 l. = 1.06 qt

1.5 l. = 1.59 qt

2 l. = 2.12 qt

5 l. = 1.30 gal

Weight/Mass (workable approximates)

Ounce avoirdupois, **oz.av**; gram, **g.**; pound, **lb**; kilogram (1,000 g.), **kg**.

½ oz.av = 14 g.

1 oz.av = 28 g.

4 oz.av (¼ lb) = 113 g.

8 oz.av (½ lb) = 226 g.

12 oz.av (¾ lb) = 340 g.

16 oz.av (1 lb) = 454 g./ 0.454 g

1½ lb = 680 g./0.680 kg

2 lb = 908 g./0.908 kg

5 lb = 2.27 kg

10 lb = 4.54 kg

*   *   *

100 g. = 3.5 oz.av

1,000 g./1 kg = 2.2 lb

2 kg = 4.4 lb

5 kg = 11.02 lb

10 kg = 22.04 lb

Temperature

Fahrenheit, **F.**; Celsius (Centigrade), **C.** (rounded to nearest digit).

F.	C.	F.	C.	F.	C.	F.	C.	F.	C.
0	−18	80	27	195	91	275	135	425	218
10	−12	100	38	205	96	300	149	450	232
20	−7	145	63	212	100	325	163	475	246
32	0	165	74	220	104	350	177	500	260
40	4	185	85	238	114	375	191	525	274
50	10	190	88	240	116	400	204	550	288

INDEX OF RECIPES BY FOOD CATEGORY

MEAT AND POULTRY

Beef

INDEX

263